BAN

MACMILLAN STUDIES IN MARKETING MANAGEMENT

General Editor: Professor Michael J. Baker
University of Strathclyde

This series is designed to fill the need for a compact treatment of major aspects of marketing management and practice based essentially upon European institutions and experience. This is not to suggest that experience and practice in other advanced economies will be ignored, but rather that the treatment will reflect European custom and attitudes as opposed to American, which have tended to dominate so much of the marketing literature.

Each volume is the work of an acknowledged authority on the subject and combines distillation of the best and most up-to-date research findings with a clear statement of their relevance to improved managerial practice. A concise style is followed throughout, and extensive use is made of summaries, checklists and references to related work. Thus each work may be viewed as both an introduction to and a reference work on its particular subject. Further, while each book is self-contained, the series as a whole comprises a handbook of marketing management.

The series is designed for both students and practitioners of marketing. Lecturers will find the treatment adequate as the foundation for in-depth study of each topic by more advanced students who have already pursued an introductory and broadly based course in marketing. Similarly, managers will find each book to be both a useful *aide-mémoire* and a reference source.

The titles so far published in the series are:

Michael J. Baker, (ed.), *Marketing: Theory and Practice,* 2nd edn
Michael J. Baker and Ronald McTavish, *Product Policy and Management*
J. R. Bureau, *Brand Management*
Gordon R. Foxall, *Consumer Choice*
Roy W. Hill and T. J. Hillier, *Organisational Buying Behaviour*
Frank Jefkins, *Public Relations for Marketing Management*, 2nd edn
F. Livesey, *Pricing*
James M. Livingstone, *International Marketing Management*
James M. Livingstone, *A Management Guide to Market Research*
Ronald McTavish and Angus Maitland, *Industrial Marketing*
Arthur Meidan, *Bank Marketing Management*

BANK MARKETING MANAGEMENT

ARTHUR MEIDAN

Senior Lecturer
Sheffield University

M
MACMILLAN

First published 1984 by
Higher and Further Education Division
MACMILLAN PUBLISHERS LTD
London and Basingstoke
Companies and representatives
throughout the world

Filmsetting by Vantage Photosetting Co. Ltd
Eastleigh and London

Printed in Hong Kong

British Library Cataloguing in Publication Data
Meidan, Arthur
Bank marketing management. —(Macmillan studies in marketing management)
1. Bank marketing
I. Title
332.1'068'8 HG 1616.M3
ISBN 0-333-36584-4
ISBN 0-333-36585-2 Pbk

To my mother

Contents

Foreword

Although there is a tendency to regard 'marketing' as a recent phenomenon, there can be little doubt that the function which it performs has existed ever since human beings first entered into exchange relationships as a means of improving their overall well-being and standard of living. In the case of barter the two parties are in direct contact with one another and it seems reasonable to assume that any exchange would be seen as acceptable to both in terms of their particular needs and wants at the time of the exchange. Certainly both parties would have the opportunity to state their requirements and any conditions attached to their mutual agreement.

With industrialisation and the development of international trade in the nineteenth and twentieth centuries the opportunity for producers to interact with consumers diminished significantly. Thus there can be little doubt that the 'rediscovery' of marketing is a direct consequence of the physical and psychological separation which had developed between manufacturers and end-users of products with a major emphasis being to re-establish contact between the parties.

I used the word 'manufacturer' in the preceding sentence advisedly, for until very recently few were prepared to acknowledge that providers of services might possibly have become distanced from the consumers of those services. After all, an intrinsic characteristic of a service is that production and consumption occur simultaneously, which must presume a high degree of contact between the supplier and the user. The appearance of this book is a timely reminder that this is no longer the case and that the application of marketing concepts and techniques is equally as relevant to service industries as it is to manufacturing industries. Nowhere is this more so than in the case of banking services.

In recent years one can detect many changes in service industries of the kind that prompted Theodore Levitt to write his famous article 'Marketing Myopia', which many now regard as the watershed which separates the present marketing orientation of industry from the production and sales orientations which preceded it. It is ironic that Levitt used a service industry – the US railroads – to show how an enormous, powerful and once-dominant industry could be reduced to a shadow of its former self within a few decades. According to Levitt, the cause of the railways failure was complacency – a belief that no one else could improve on the service they provided. In turn this developed out of a failure to define their business in terms of the benefits enjoyed by the consumer – transportation – rather than in terms of the hardware, the software and the systems needed to deliver the benefit, in short a failure to innovate and keep pace with the changing requirements of the customers.

Even the most casual observer of the banking scene in recent years cannot help but be aware of the immense changes which have occurred and continue to take place. Money is the classical undifferentiated product, and the only way which those dealing in the commodity can secure any competitive advantage is through the range and quality of the services they offer. To determine what these service needs are they must undertake market research, to cater for these needs they require a product development function, to promote the existence of their new products they need advertising, and to sell them they need good packaging, competitive prices and sales incentives. In sum, then, banks need a marketing approach to their business, and this book has been written especially to show how to develop and apply such an orientation.

Arthur Meidan is eminently well qualified to write what I am sure will be seen as a valuable contribution to the growing literature on bank marketing. With extensive knowledge of current thinking on the subject Dr Meidan also possesses two other distinct advantages. First, he has actively participated in management development programmes for bank managers, and so is more than familiar with the philosophical problems of persuading professional people that 'marketing' is not an anodyne designed to disguise what formerly was discarded as high pressure selling. By the same token he knows from personal experience just what topics are of interest to bank managers and how to present these clearly and succinctly. Second, Arthur Meidan has had the benefit of direct comment and criticism from senior practitioners and, being a marketing man, has incorporated this consumer feedback into his product design.

As Editor of the Macmillan Studies in Marketing Management series I am more than pleased with the result and commend it wholeheartedly.

MICHAEL J. BAKER

Chinese University of Hong Kong
December 1983

Acknowledgements

Many people have been influential in the successful completion of this book. It is with gratitude that these individuals are acknowledged here.

I am particularly indebted to Professor Michael J. Baker of the University of Strathclyde, Scotland, for reading the full preliminary draft of the manuscript and councelling me on how to better organise and alter certain parts and sections, as well as for writing the Foreword. Professor Baker has been instrumental in securing advice and helpful criticism from some of his bank marketing doctoral students (particularly Mr E. El Sahn), as well as from other experts in the field. For all of his extremely helpful assistance and support I am very grateful.

To Mr B. McKenna, the Secretary of the Institute of Bankers in Scotland, I offer my thanks for reading the whole manuscript and for offering very useful comments and advice that have substantially contributed to improving both the content and the format of this book.

The author is grateful to Mr B. J. Walter, the Director of Education and Training at Midland Bank, and his team of assistants in bank marketing who have assisted with thorough and useful professional inputs. The final version of this text is greatly improved because of their suggestions and comments.

Acknowledgements are extended to the editors of the following journals for their permission to use and reproduce material that originally appeared in my own articles in these journals: *International Journal of Bank Marketing, International Journal of Physical Distribution and Materials Management, Quarterly Review of Marketing.*

I am also indebted to my secretary, Rebecca Jackson, and to Mrs A. Rixham, who have both assisted with the typing of this manuscript.

Last, but not least, I must thank my wife and family for considerable patience, understanding and support.

Responsibility for any errors or omissions is mine.

ARTHUR MEIDAN

List of tables

List of figures

CHAPTER 1

The roles of marketing in bank management

Contents

Introduction

As the role of the financial services sectors – banking, insurance, building societies, hire purchase, franchising, consumer credit and general household financial services, etc. – continues to grow in the economies of most of the Western nations, pressures are mounting for a more effective marketing management of the financial services offered by the banks. This applies especially to the banking sector, as it represents probably the most important financial sector, not just in terms of turnover, profits and employment, but also in its paramount impact on the other spheres of the economy. For these reasons, in the last few years there has been a growing interest in applying marketing techniques and tools in the field of banking. This growing interest has generated a relatively large number of publications, mostly descriptive, mainly in the last four to five years. Along with this change in approach has come a change in the banks' services, training, attitudes and images, marketing strategies, and patterns of organisation and control as elaborated in this book.

Marketing is becoming increasingly necessary in today's banks' competitive environment. Intensified rivalry from other institutions has caused the banks to think seriously about how they can compete effectively. This has led them to pay increasing attention to marketing techniques. Obviously owing to the very nature of banking, it cannot be treated in exactly the same way as, for example, a manufacturing firm. It is important to recognise the two fundamentally different functions that bank marketing must perform. It must attract deposits on the one hand, and attract borrowers and users of services on the other. This double-sided nature of banking business brings marketing problems that are more complex than those that normally face commercial concerns. If one adds to this the very special place that banks hold in society and in monetary policy, one begins to see that a simple transfer of techniques and concepts from other areas of business is hardly likely to be appropriate. Faced with this situation there is a noticeable (and justifiable) tendency on the part of the major banks to move with caution.

The major characteristics of bank services

Bank marketing has been defined as 'that part of management activity which seems to direct the flow of banking services profitably to selected customers'.[1] The need for marketing in banks stems from intense competition, not just from other banks, but also financial corporations, insurance companies, building societies, etc. The banks service two markets, corporate and retail customers. Or in 'marketing language', banks serve industrial markets and ultimate consumer markets. These two markets can be subdivided into five main types, namely: the government/public sector, the private sector, the commercial sector, industries and lastly the international markets.

The main functions of a commercial bank are:

(a) *the safekeeping function*, whereby firms and individuals 'store' their funds with banks for safekeeping and for the interest they can earn on funds (often called 'deposit taking function'):
(b) *lending funds*; and
(c) *providing a variety of financial and related services* that are indirectly related to the previous two main banking functions (above). This would include transmission services.

The banking services have the following characteristics:[2]

(1) *Intangibility*. Banking services, except in particular instances, meet a general rather than a specific need. Particular benefits are not readily apparent and therefore banks are dependent on getting their message across to the public effectively and ensuring that their image and service are attractive.

Indeed, a service such as bank credit that cannot appeal to a buyer's sense of touch, taste, smell, sight or hearing, places a burden on the bank's marketing organisation. The credit a bank offers is represented by its acceptance of demand and time deposits, and by making loans. Since a bank is often selling an intangible or an idea, and not necessarily a physical product, it must tell the buyer what the service will do. It is not always able to illustrate, demonstrate or display the services in use. Therefore, since banks market intangible products, the concern with storage, transportation and inventory control are not relevant for the bank marketer. This is partially attributable to the absence of middlemen. As a result, it severely limits the alternatives available to the bank marketer and often necessitates the use of direct channels of distribution.

(2) *Inseparability.* Because of the simultaneous production and distribution of bank services, the main concern of the marketer is usually the creation of time and place utility, that is, have the services available at the right place and at the right time. This implies that direct sale is almost the only feasible channel of distribution. But as can be seen later, one way of overcoming the inseparability factor is the use of bank credit cards, whereby the service is transferable.

(3) *Highly individualised marketing system.* When selecting channels of distribution, the goods marketer will usually have a marketing system containing several established middlemen. More often than not, such systems are the most efficient. Unfortunately, this is not the case for the banker, who has few traditional channels of distribution. Hence, the banker is induced to locate branches of his outlets as conveniently as possible. In many bank transactions, a client relationship exists between the buyer and seller, as distinguished from a customer relationship. This would be especially true in the case of many corporate and trust accounts. Where such a close personal, professional client relationship must exist, direct channels may be the only feasible choice, as elaborated in Chapter 3 of this book.

(4) *Lack of special identity.* To the public, one bank's service is very much like another. The reason a particular bank or branch is used is often due to convenience. Each bank must find a way of establishing its identity and implanting this in the mind of the public. As the competing products are similar, the emphasis is on the 'package' rather than the product. The 'package' consists of branch location, staff, services, reputation, advertising and, from time to time, new services. As the major competitors offer similar services, the emphasis will be on the promotional aspects, rather than on the inherent uniqueness of a particular bank's service. This is one of the reasons why banks do very little positive selling but mainly rely on indirect methods.

Once a customer is with a bank he is unlikely to be easily persuaded to change. It is only when the customer or the corporate customer move to a new area, or if there is an exceptional degree of inefficiency or discourtesy, that this is likely to happen.

(5) *Wide range of products/services.* Banks have to offer a very wide range of products and services to meet a variety of financial and related needs from different customers in different areas. On the one hand it provides a special one-off management service for an industrial customer and on the other hand a retail service covering money receipt, storage, supply and transmission.

(6) *Geographical dispersion.* There has to be a branch network in any bank of size and scope, in order to provide benefits of convenience and to meet both national and local needs. Therefore all services or promotions must have an appeal and wide applications.

(7) *Growth must be balanced with risk.* When selling loans, the bank is buying risk. There has to be a well-controlled balance between expansion and prudence.

This rising importance of marketing in the banking sector is underlined by four major factors: (i) increased competition for customers, (ii) increased sophistication of those customers, (iii) increased technology, (iv) the increased cost of meeting customer needs profitably.

The bank management system

Most commercial banks have two types of objectives: (i) *flexible goals*, for example increasing (or decreasing) deposits of certain kinds, increasing (or decreasing) loans of certain type(s), directing customers to certain types of products/services, and (ii) *fixed objectives*, for example, profitability, high return on investment, achieving certain market share(s), and growth rates, development of certain bank image(s), spread of bank customers types in order to minimise risks and business fluctuations, etc.

A written statement of objectives is still exceptional in banking, but is becoming increasingly necessary. Bearing in mind the need to maintain good business and public relations, the general banking business objective is profits sufficiently high to protect depositors and shareholders. Depositors are of special importance since in the clearing banks they finance 90–95 per cent of the assets. The return on investment required by the chief executive will influence the operational managers' targets, as will planned growth and size. The latter may not necessarily yield economy, but can sometimes yield competitive advantage. Lastly comes an increased market share, not only because an increased share of a market often brings competitive advantages, but usually the objective is a larger share of selected customers' groups, and not of the total market.

The bank marketing function is one of the five *subsets* of management *controllable* variables (Figure 1.1). The bank management system is comprised of four major sets of variables: (i) bank objectives (already discussed), (ii) bank environment (or non-controllable) variables, (iii) the controllable (or management) variable sets, and finally (iv) bank's organ-

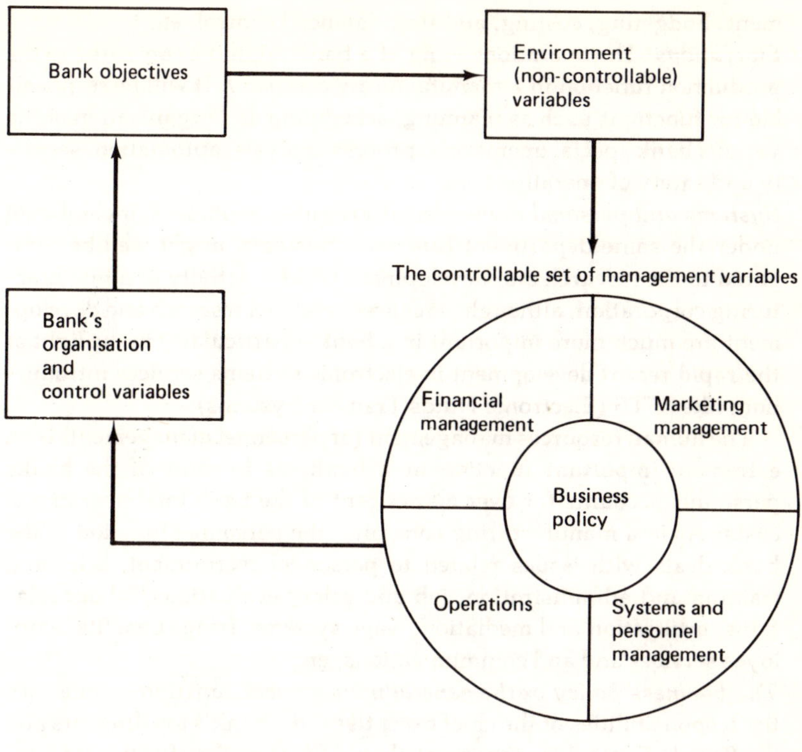

Figure 1.1 The bank management system

isation and control variables. The four sets (or facets) of variables are interrelated and operate together as a system (Figure 1.1).

Non-controllable variables are the factors that cannot be effectively controlled by the bank's management, but they affect the attainment of the bank's objectives and the way the bank has to make use of its various marketing tools and its organisation and control techniques. The non-controllable variables include foreign exchange regulation (determined by the government or the market forces), inflation, government economic policy, competition (from other commercial banks and financial firms, for example, credit firms, insurance companies, etc.), legal systems and regulations, political factors, and similar additional factors that might influence the bank management operations.

The controllable facet of variables in banking are those factors under the control of the bank that can be used to influence the bank's business activity. These factors are also called management tools and they can be split into five activity areas:

1. *financial management* (dealing with issues such as sources and costs of capital funds, management of bank's cash, tax and risk manage-

ment, budgeting, costing, auditing, financial control, etc.).

2. *Operations.* The operations wing of a bank might be compared to the production function in a manufacturing company. It will be responsible for functions such as planning, scheduling and organisation of the various bank special operations, process analysis, automation, security and safety of operations, etc.
3. *Systems and personal management* are either separated or combined under the same department/function. 'Systems' might well be compared to the research and development (R&D) activity in a manufacturing corporation, although, of course, systems research and development are much more important in a bank – particularly in the light of the rapid recent development in electronic systems services introduction, like EFTS (Electronic Funds Transfer Systems).

   The human resources management (or personnel management) is an extremely important function in a bank, as in most of the banks personnel accounts for over 60 per cent of the bank total operational costs. As in a manufacturing company, the personnel function in the bank deals with issues related to personnel recruitment, selection, training and administration, job and salary evaluations, labour relations, arbitration and mediation, wage systems, fringe benefits, employee services and and communications, etc.
4. *The business policy or the general management* function emphasises the responsibilities of the chief executives, the bank's top directors and the Board. General management should focus on the effective interaction of the three functional areas of management (mentioned above) with the marketing function, and in order to do so it deals with activities uniquely located at the top of the organisation, such as: establishing the bank's objectives, planning and business forecasting, establishing policy, directing and controlling, evaluating branches' and the bank's managerial and business performance.
5. *The bank marketing function* focuses its attention on the following activities:

   (a) customers' behaviour, attitudes and segmentation;
   (b) branch management, locations and distribution of banking services;
   (c) advertising, communication, promotions and publicity;
   (d) product/service development and introduction;
   (e) pricing of the bank's services;
   (f) defining marketing strategies, administering and controlling the marketing programme; and finally
   (g) marketing research that attempts to collect, investigate, analyse and interpret market developments, in each of the six aforementioned areas, in order maximally to contribute to the attainment of bank objectives in the light of the existent non-controllable factors,

and in consonance with the four other major functions of bank management (discusssed previously and portrayed in Figure 1.1).

The organisation and control variables are discussed in detail in Chapter 7.

The marketing concept

In the early 1960s marketing in the banking industry generally meant advertising and public relations. However, a number of interrelated forces in the business environment have contributed to the impetus of rapid change in banking. These include: lowered margins of profit, increased competition both within and outside the banking industry, demographic development (i.e. expanding population with increasing affluence), bank holding company movement, technology making new products possible, quest for new consumer markets, national and international expansion, crumbling barriers to branching, consumerism and social responsibility, etc.

The major competitors within the banking industry are:

(a) public and quasi-public sector: National Savings movement; trustee savings banks; national and local government authorities; Post Office Giro; and
(b) private sector: building societies; finance houses, discount market; inter-company market; stock exchange.

Competition takes several forms: (i) deposits, and (ii) the provision of financial and other services (e.g. leasing, factoring, finance broking, hire purchase, second mortgage lending, computer bureaux).

What is marketing for banks? According to the official definition of the American Marketing Association, marketing is 'the performance of business activities that direct the flow of goods and services from producer to consumer or user'.[3]

The concept of bank marketing has been defined by various bank marketers as that part of management activity that seeks to direct the flow of banking services profitably to selected customers. Marketing is a banking activity of relatively recent origin and this is not surprising since the marketing concept itself is, as opposed to the sales concept, also relatively new. Kotler defines the marketing concept as 'a management orientation that holds that the key task of the organisation is to determine the needs and wants of target markets and to adapt the organisation to delivering the desired satisfactions more effectively and efficiently than its competitors',[4] and while it is an exaggeration to suggest that the banks have totally encompassed the implications of this definition, it might be argued that the banking institutions now recognise the need for a more positive marketing approach and are moving towards the development of marketing in their organisations.

The seeds of the applications of the marketing concept to banking can be related to the American Banking Association Conference of 1958. In the USA the 1960s was the growth period of retail bank marketing.[5] In Europe, the development of the marketing concept in banking probably came later; Reekie[6] suggests that it was not until the 1970s that the conventions of a century or more were questioned and marketing for banks became a widely discussed topic in British banking circles. Reekie considers that even as late as the 1960s, the marketing concept was not considered relevant to the banking environment. There is no doubt that overall the last ten years have brought about remarkable changes in high street banking. A much greater interest in the development of the marketing approach implies a change of attitude among the banks; one of the aims of this book is to identify some of the significant instruments of change, while the major purpose is to analyse some of the ways in which marketing has developed in banking in relation to the various components of the marketing mix.

The marketing concept basically requires that all activities that have any relation with the customer should be entirely co-ordinated by the marketing element in the bank. In other words, that a way of thinking along marketing lines is permeated into all areas of banking so as to enable the establishment of a marketing-oriented operation.

R. Brien and J. Stafford in their article 'The Myth of Marketing in Banking' offer a twofold role for marketing in bank management.[7]. One is at the level of formulation of the marketing mix for the development of market segments which seem – according to market research – to hold the best opportunities for profitable exploitation. While the second is of a philosophical nature – that all bank activities should be so geared as to focus on the needs and wants of the customer – which is a reiteration of the total marketing concept of Wasem.[8]

The first act of a market-oriented bank is consequently to learn about the market it operates in. Unless the characteristics of the market are known the bank will be unable to provide the range of services necessary for different customer types. Segmentation of the market allows the bank to tailor its approach to the customers' requirements. Segmentation can be based on private individual behaviour that will be affected by social class, age, sex, income group, geographic location, etc. The more characteristics the market is segmented by, the more precise the managers' knowledge of the customer is. The manager needs to know how big the segment is in volume terms, in order to decide whether to continue to operate in the present market or to look elsewhere where profits may be higher. For example, would it be worthwhile branch managers' time soliciting deposits from small accounts and simultaneously offering cash-handling facilities and interest to do so, or would the bank be better off lending bigger loans, by attracting larger deposits from the short-term loan market? The manager will also need to know who his clients are and what they use the bank services for.

The marketing concept applies to a service industry like banking for the primary reasons that it applies to all businesses – that is, to serve the customer at a profit. If the bank adopts the marketing concept properly, it will be committed to the organisation as a whole rather than a department or/and a narrow interest.

Bank management is renowned for its caution and resists very strongly attempts to change 'traditional' approaches. To a bank manager marketing is a function and course of action to be judged by its contribution to the bank's objectives. It has already been outlined that sufficient co-ordination between banking and marketing executives should be enough to eliminate divergence of results.

The adoption of the marketing concept will recognise that bank customers are changing in terms of their wants, needs, desires, expectations and problems. Banks must define these in explicit terms and then evaluate their offering in customers' terms, that is, satisfying customers' needs at a profit to the bank.

The comparative development of marketing for banks

USA

One can put down the earlier marketing approach to banking in the USA to a number of factors. Perhaps the most important of these has been the greater restrictions on branch expansions, the nature of business and even the interest rates payable and chargeable. Historically this had led to a different attitude from the UK banking system. For the US banks have been unable to rely on branch expansion to increase their profits. This meant that in the USA banks *had to* sell their services to the customer. To do this they have used a marketing approach gaining feedback from the customers and staff on their product and service development. It is noticeable that most US banks keep their staff areas well stocked with advertisements and leaflets for the cross-selling of new service suggestions. After a screening process, any seemingly viable proposition will be tested by market research to establish whether the combination of expected demand and projected price justifies launching the service.

Research is of prime importance in the USA. Recently, certain banks are moving towards more detailed investigations into motivation, market segmentation by sex, age and income attitudes. This leads to more effective service designing, advertising and marketing. Bank computers are used for numerous marketing purposes, from detailing existing market shares to listing persons suited to new service offers. In the USA a good deal of computer-generated material is shared by the banks, and they pool together in external market surveys.[9]

Advertising is used to great effect in the USA. The spending of the US banks far exceeds that of the UK banks. The main areas they advertise in are the media, concentrating on television, radio and the newspapers. Commercial banks are now abandoning free gifts and moving to premium offers. Even these are less frequent now, following a premium war a few years back.

Staff participation in branch marketing is well developed and cross-selling is undertaken at every opportunity, especially when customers open new accounts. Owing to the greater competition in service, they make greater efforts to maintain high standards of service efficiency and competitiveness. They do this by paying greater attention to factors such as the actual bank premises. Here the public areas are spacious with an open-plan layout. The decorations are bright and modern, with paintings, plants and flowers. The furnishings are soft with fitted carpets. The bank staff generally sit at desks to one side of the public area and counter screens are now very rare. Alternative methods of security are used, such as circuit television and secutity guards. The rest of the public area is used for exhibitions of art. This creates extra traffic and hopefully new customers; for example, the branch opening of the Hibernia National Bank in New Orleans was linked with an exhibition of bronzes depicting the American West. Car-parking facilities are essential in the USA and are placed adjacent to, or in, the basement of the bank. The objectives are to produce a relaxing and comfortable atmosphere to do business in. Most US banks have recently moved towards universal tellers and the opening hours of banks are extremely flexible and match the locale in which the bank operates. In commuter areas the banks open at 7.00 a.m. and by means of shifts and part-time working, staggered starting and finishing times are achieved. Some banks open from 8.00 a.m. to 5.00 p.m., others 10.00 a.m. to 8.00 p.m., the variations are endless. Saturday opening is now common in surburban areas and Sunday banking is currently being introduced.

In time all banks will provide twenty-four hour banking. Cash dispensers are used and some are also available to credit card holders. The use of automatic tellers is particularly used in large cities. These machines can accept deposits and effect transfers between any of the customer's accounts – the amount being determined by the customer. Some four years ago the First National Bank of Seattle started off the 'In Touch Service' which meant that for $6.50 per month all your banking could be done over the telephone.

US banks are strongly committed to community service and feel it a duty to be involved in the life of the society on whose well-being their progress depends. Slum area communities are helped by donations and financial assistance, as well as expertise and involvement of the bank employees.

Owing to this new era in banking, the banks have sought sales and marketing talent to go with their new image. The San Francisco Wells Fargo Bank and the Continental of Illinois both use product management systems. The men who work in these systems have been attracted out of consumer marketing. Even the higher education system is responding. In 1972 the Bank Marketing Association started a school at the University of Colorado. Its students, mostly mature, study by correspondence or full-time. Summer classes are also available.

UK and Western Europe

Until the 1960s, UK banks acted merely as institutions where cash could be deposited or loans procured. The cheque book was the sole means of transacting business through an account. The appearance of the so-called 'personal loan' in the 1960s and the acquisition by a Scottish bank of a hire-purchase company signalled the beginning of a new era in banking. The large banks in the UK formed marketing departments only in the early 1970s. Their task was to 'sell' the ever-increasing number of customer services that are familiar today, such as safe deposit, credit and cheque cards, executorship services, and even insurance and travel. The diversification of the banks' activities and services has been an excellent marketing opportunity since the audience the services are aimed at is captive – that is, they are already customers of the bank.

The abolition by the government of credit control regulations and bank rate control in 1971 sharpened the competitiveness between banks, since they became free to set their own base rates on which to base the interest offered to depositors and charged on loans. The 'big four' UK banks (National Westminster, Barclays, Midland and Lloyds) declared total profits of £1,000 million for the financial year 1980/81. The presence of such large profits in the industry are attracting greater competition and marketing efforts than ever before and the need for a co-ordinated, well-planned marketing approch has become extremely important.

The situation in the UK is slightly different than in Europe owing to the different banking structure in this country. Also, the banks are far more concentrated as in Europe there are no legal holds on banks' expansion. It seems that a point of saturation has now been reached, which may lead to the closing-down of unproductive branches.

There is still a great deal of scope for growth in the UK, as 20 per cent of the population have no accounts (1982). The 20 per cent tend to be mainly manual workers.

To sum up, the reasons for the recent changes in marketing for banks in the UK are as follows:

1. Prior to 1971 the UK clearing banks were obliged, by convention and statute, to hold 30 per cent of total deposit liabilities. With the abandonment of both in that year, the ceiling on bank lending was removed thus opening the way for an increase in competition between the banks in the market for loans.
2. Also in 1971, the clearing banks ended the informal cartel agreements on interest rates to lenders and borrowers. They were now free to compete with one another on deposit, lending and overdraft rates.
3. There was a growing tendency for big business to bypass clearing banks in the lending and borrowing process. The result was the emergence of specialist bodies, both in the USA and Europe, geared to the specific task of matching lending and borrowing capacity. This development was a matter of concern to the clearers affecting, as it did, their profitability.
4. Also with some concern in the 1950s and 1960s the banks witnessed the huge expansion of hire-purchase lending by the finance houses. Partly this was at the expense of existing bank lending; however, it also disclosed a gap in traditional banking activities, in what was seen to be a growth area. The outcome was the acquisition by banks of existing finance houses and the setting up of their own hire-purchase subsidiaries.
5. As a consequence of the cartel arrangements previously referred to, the banks found themselves outmanouvred by the finance houses in offering sufficiently competitive interest rates to attract large-scale depositors with funds to lend for seven days and upwards. This business, and the increased lending capacity that went with it, was obtained by the finance houses.
6. Foreign banks, particularly from the USA, began to locate major branches in London to the detriment of the clearing banks. Their total deposits and number of banks rose as follows:

1957	80 foreign banks with £130 million
1965	100 foreign banks with £2,215 million
1970	150 foreign banks with £9,759 million
1976	200 foreign banks with £30,000 million
1982	400 foreign banks (approximate)

7. Other financial institutions were seen to be making preparations to enter a market that banks historically had always regarded as their reserve. For example, the Guardian Royal Exchange Insurance Group in 1971 widened its objectives to include 'all normal aspects of the business of banking'; around the same time the Abbey National Building Society began a planned increase in second mortgage busi-

ness and dropped a broad hint that in the future they would be interested in the general concept of lending money.

The recent debate in banking circles was how far should they go in pushing for new business and how much to improve existing services. Most UK bankers still want an air of respectability in banking, stressing big profits that will give the investors confidence, while more modern entrants in the industry want to move towards a more market-oriented approach. The British Trustee Savings Bank has shown an example of positive marketing and attracted lower-paid workers. The new talent points to money shops with a consumer-banking approach with attractive shop windows, and shop hours appealed to the unbanked.

The US invasion has been another driving force behind new development in retail banking in the UK and new vigour in the marketing of bank loans. This is at last percolating through to UK bankers, used to less aggressive climes. Many banking executives are visiting the US banks to see how they operate.

During 1975 the 'big four' banks were preoccupied trying to improve banks' images; Midland has tried extremely hard to put its image across to industry and the farmers in recent years. At present, the copy-content of its advertising is the Midland Bank Symbol as a cog in a machine. Stressing it will aid UK industry in the present recovery. Lloyds Bank has stressed successfully its symbol, the black horse, in its television advertising, hiring 'Black Beauty' to perform various action shots.

Beneath the surface, UK banking is in the same situation as European banking. Marketing has still some way to go before it becomes an essential part of UK banking. In areas of standards of service and opening hours, the UK banks have to follow the US lead, and already are doing so. Changes must be made, both on the surface and in the organisation beneath, if the US challenge is to be averted and the resources tapped of the 20 per cent unbanked.

The 'retail banking revolution'

As mentioned in this chapter, the possible application of the marketing concept in banking was mentioned for the first time some twenty-five years ago in the USA, at the American Banking Association (ABA) Conference in 1958. During this period and especially in the last fifteen years or so, banking throughout the Western world has seen a kind of revolution that is often called the 'retail banking revolution'.

This 'revolution' had several characteristics, as follows:[10]

1. A decline of the big business's use of banking directly. Instead, firms pooled their resources to lend and borrow, therefore bypassing the banks. This has generated the appearance of specialist bodies growing

up and geared to investments in the USA, Germany, France, the UK and throughout other countries in Western Europe.

2. A significant increase in the number of bank branches, that is, increase in the competition. For example, in the last twenty years the number of foreign banks (not branches) in London has more than quadrupled and naturally so has the value of transactions.
3. Intensifying rivalry of other financial institutions, for example, the finance houses during the 1950s and 1960s expanded their hire-purchase lending at the expense of the banks; insurance companies are more actively interested in financial operations, including money transmissions, etc. Germany's saving banks headed by the central Girozentralen Organisation have enjoyed spiral growth. Similar trends have occurred in Belgium, Holland and Italy. Even insurance companies are lately competing on the private savings market. For example, the Guardian Royal Exchange Group in England in 1971 decided to widen its objectives to include all normal aspects of the business of banking. There have also been parallel expansions in Sweden, Germany, France, Spain and the Benelux.
4. Loosening of legal restrictions, such as the abandonment of cartelisation in most of the EEC countries and loosening of the competitive restraints in the USA.

It has been suggested that the resistance to the marketing approach has been greater in the UK banking system than in the USA. One factor that may account for the slow development of marketing is the organisation of bank branches. In the USA banks the corporate market operates on a targeting basis whereby account managers might each be allocated thirty or so carefully identified accounts, so that they become experts in the businesses and industries in which they operate. This system is not operated in the UK and British banks know relatively little about their customers.

Another factor that aggravates the problem of slow marketing development is the question of product range. It is claimed that a branch may have 250 or more services that it can sell to the customer. Such a number is too high to be marketed effectively and it requires considerable branch staff time and enthusiasm; it has already been implied that the latter may be difficult to generate. Associated with this problem is the perception of the bank customer who traditionally sees the bank as a provider of loans, rather than a supplier of other services.

Thus a number of factors combine which to some extent help to explain the resistance in banking circles in the UK and Western Europe to the concept of bank marketing and its relatively slow development. The changes of attitudes towards the marketing approach in banking can thus be summarised in relation to factors associated with both the external and internal environments of the bank organisation (Table 1.1).

Table 1.1 External and internal factors affecting the change in attitudes towards bank marketing

External factors	*Internal factors*
Resistance to change to the marketing approach – approximately prior to 1958 in the USA and prior to 1970 in Western Europe	
1. Government's regulations and laws	1. Senior management's perception of the business role of banks
2. Cartelisation and anti-cartelisation regulations	2. Staff attitudes
	3. Organisation of bank branches
	4. Product range
Stimulus to change – post-1960 (USA)	
1. Relaxation of government controls	1. Changing attitudes of top management in the banks
2. End of bank agreements	2. Introduction (slowly) of staff with marketing expertise
3. Increasing competition from other financial institutions	
4. Growth of the marketing approach in other service activities	
5. Influence of trends in US banking (on the European banks)	

The elements of marketing

The marketing approach refers basically to four steps: (i) research to determine customers' financial requirements, (ii) design new services or innovate old ones according to the findings, (iii) market services to the customer for whom they were researched and designed (and this includes pricing, promotion and distribution) at a profit, and (iv) in doing so, satisfy the customers' financial needs. The objective of the marketing process is profitable sales of services that satisfy customers' financial requirements and needs. It puts the emphasis on customers' needs satisfaction, at a profit to the bank. Competing successfully means doing it on a profitable basis. A bank can do this by stressing profit growth, ahead of volume growth and by focusing on maintaining the margins by pricing for profits. The marketing approach to banking services is presented in a circular form in Figure 1.2. As can be seen, it starts and concludes with identifying and satisfying customers' needs. Stages 2 through 4 of this process is called the marketing mix and has a special

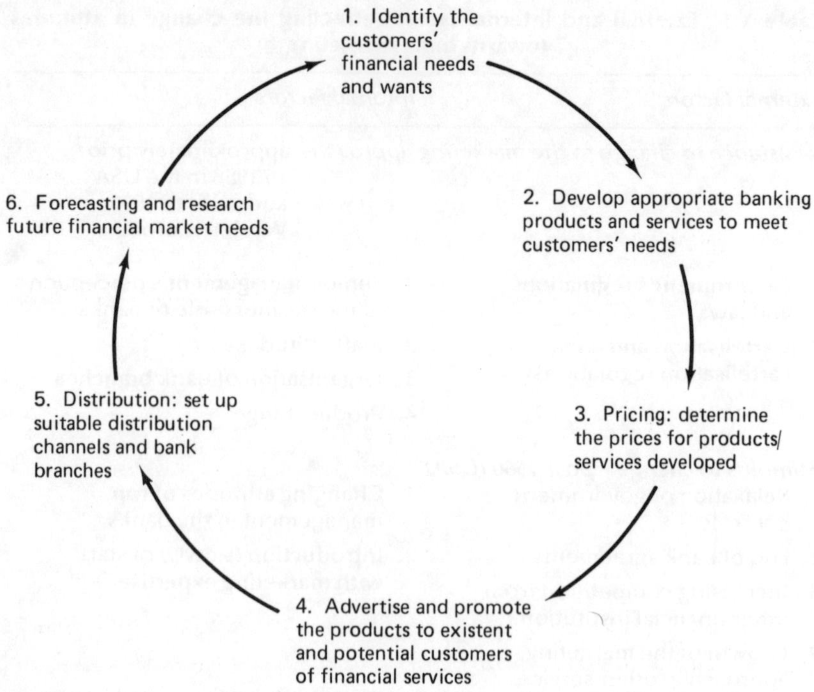

Figure 1.2 The marketing approach to banking service

importance in any marketing programme. A marketing mix is a term used to describe a blending of decisions about product services, place, promotion and price. It must also be remembered that these decisions act on each other, while they are being 'mixed' together; for example, a decision on price affects decision on promotion. Thus these decisions must be evaluated continually, if the total marketing programme is to succeed.

Banks must manage a collection of marketing mixes because they sell a collection of customer-satisfying services to diverse target markets. The five main categories of customers are: private, commercial, industrial, government/public, and international market. Furthermore, a bank must be doubly marketing-oriented. It must create marketing programmes designed to attract funds; it must then convert these funds into other customer-satisfying services from uses of credit and buying power and create marketing programmes to attract customers for these funds. Figure 1.3 depicts the banking's marketing task.

It should be noted that both of these tasks are crucial to the bank. As more than two-thirds of banks' funds come from private deposits, and out of these more than 50 per cent are loans to the customers, while users of banks' fund and services account for 70 per cent of banks' profits.[11]

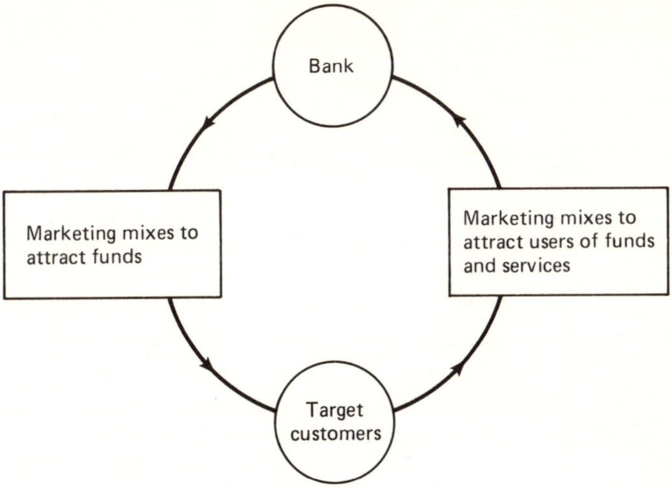

Figure 1.3 Banking's dual marketing task

The overall marketing programme of the bank, as Figure 1.3 suggests, may involve a large number of marketing strategies and mixes. As mentioned previously, and discussed later in this book, the marketing strategy includes: (i) a very clear definition of target customers, (ii) the development of a marketing mix to satisfy the customers at a profit to the bank, (iii) planning for each of the 'source' markets and each of the 'use' markets (well-conceived marketing strategies must be planned and executed if the bank is to make the most of its marketing opportunities), and (iv) organisation and administration. All these elements of the marketing strategy, together with (the roles of) marketing research and their relationships with the bank's management objectives, are presented in Figure 1.4, suggesting the overall bank marketing management system.

The development of an 'appropriate' market mix implies the recognition of a target market. It might be suggested that the traditional market for the banks has been corporate institutions and salaried white-collar workers. This market has evolved for historical reasons rather than through positive action by the banks themselves. With a movement towards the marketing concept, the banks appear to have begun to analyse market opportunities and to develop new target markets through market segmentation. While attempting to develop their traditional segments the banks seek to add new segments to their spheres of operation.

Target marketing implies segmentation of the market. The market segmentation that has been carried out by the banks appears to have been in relation to consumer demographic and socio-psychological characterisation. Thus, for example, student and wage-earner segments have been recognised. Once market segmentation has been carried out, the bank

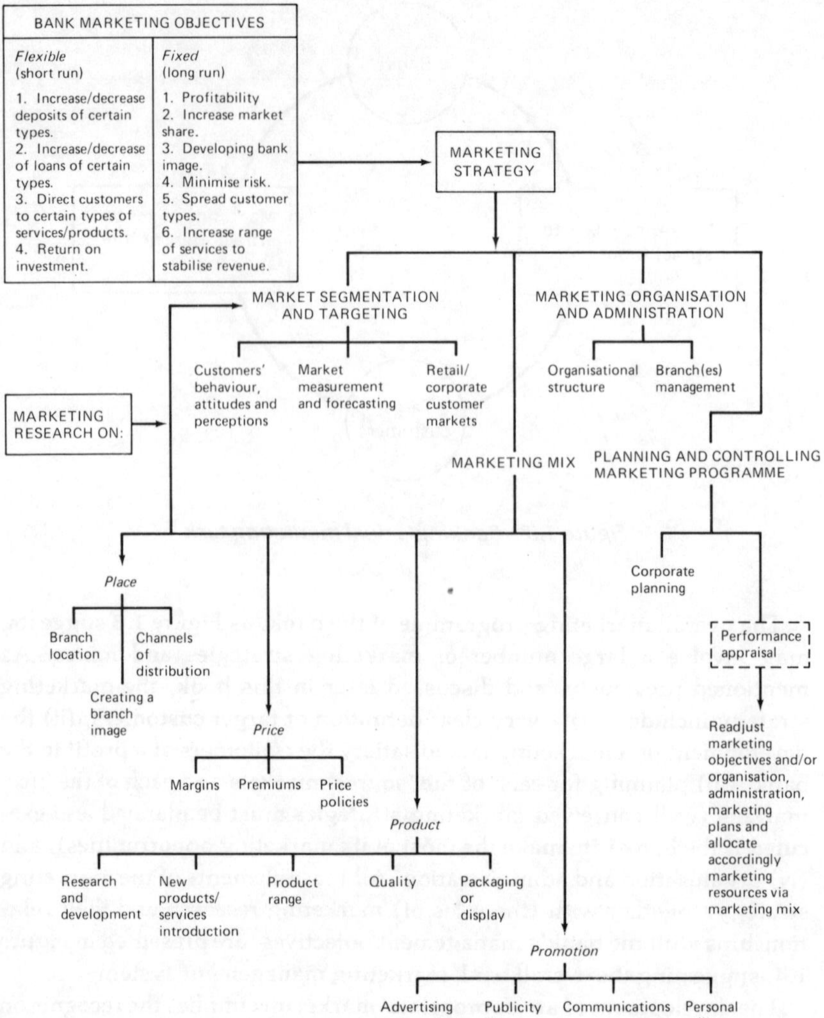

Figure 1.4 The bank marketing management system

should ideally decide on its broad strategy in terms of undifferentiated, concentrated or differentiated marketing approaches. Although these approaches have been highly developed in the product field, in banking the general approach appears to be through differentiated marketing where the organisation is operating in a number of segments of the market, each with its appropriate marketing mix. Whether this approach is the result of systematic planning or historical evolution is open to question. It would appear that the banking system has only fairly recently recognised the possibility of market segmentation and is gradually identifying new segments of market potential. The extent to which there is a different marketing mix for each segment is difficult to ascertain, but certainly some aspects of the mix, particularly promotion, are geared to particular target markets.

Product, price, place and promotion represent the four main elements of the marketing mix. Once the characteristics of the market are known through market segmentation, the bank can then ideally develop a market strategy. Once the firm has decided on its marketing expenditure level, it has to allocate this in relation to the four elements of the marketing mix. The ways in which the banks have developed the various elements are examined in three chapters in this book. Chapter 3 deals with distribution and branches' location, Chapter 4 studies advertising and communications, while product development and pricing by banks are discussed in Chapter 5.

There is also the question of bank organisation, and administration, and the planning and control of marketing programmes, to be considered as indicated in Figure 1.4.

By bank marketing organisation we mean the way marketing people within the bank work together in order to achieve the bank's goals and objectives. In its organisation a bank must find the degree of specialisation, departmentalisation and hierarchy that structures its management into a co-ordinated and effective group or team. Organisation is not an end in itself but a means to an end. There are various forms of bank marketing organisations and these are discussed in detail in Chapter 7.

Organisation and control problems in bank marketing are to some extent interacted, because the form of bank marketing organisation affects the degree of control. The basis of control are the objectives, as portrayed earlier in this chapter (Figure 1.1). Control is the process of checking to determine whether or not progress is being made towards the objectives and the goals of the bank.

There are two widely held views about the meaning of the word 'control'. One view concentrates on the people who manage, and the other is control viewed as part of all activities. Considered in this way, control is the essence of management and it involves the following four steps:

(a) establishment of performance standards;
(b) measurement and feedback of performance results;
(c) evaluation of actual performance against standards; and
(d) taking action as indicated by the evaluation.

Control should relate to performance (in terms of profits, market shares of loans, deposits, usage of bank credit cards, bank's services usage, etc.) by groups/segments of customers (on the retail, corporate and international markets), by branches and/or by main services, as elaborated in more detail in Chapter 7.

The environment for bank marketing is constantly changing and this is caused by rising standards of living and changing competitive situations. Although these changes are felt slowly, they must be anticipated as early as possible to cope with the challenges of ever-changing marketing conditions.

In fact, with the recession biting deeper and existing markets not expanding, marketing has a very important role to play in helping the banks remain in a profitable situation. Since change is the key event, the bank, through marketing management, must be able to meet any changes in the markets it serves by changing itself with respect to long-run objectives, and adapt these and its own resources to meet the changes that have taken place externally.

CHAPTER 2

Customer behaviour and market segmentation

Contents

Introduction

The initial studies of bank customer behaviour started with the banks' interest in the services they offered, and the customers' attitudes, beliefs and perceptions about those services. The questions employed in the market research tests asked six basic questions, namely: who is the customer; what does the market buy; when does the market buy; who is involved in the buying; why does the customer buy; how does the market buy? The information gained has been used to improve the design of services, relationships and bank communications. The studies highlighted the importance of factors such as the bank's image and identified the existence of market segments. Much of the current research efforts concentrate on segmenting the market into customer groups with different needs, buying styles and responses to promotions. Strategies are then developed to appeal to the identified segments.

Market segmentation was one of the first aspects of marketing to be employed in banking. Traditionally segmentation tended to be based on demographic and geographic lines. It was soon realised that greater depth in segmentation can be achieved by an additional psychographic dimension based on consumer behaviour, as elaborated later in this chapter. The techniques in segmenting bank customers themselves had advanced. They have advanced from investigations on single products or services like savings accounts, credit cards and cash dispensers, to investigations on packages of products. Investigations on packages of products are more appropriate now because most bank services are offered in packages – seldom is a single service offered on its own.

The major uses of the findings from these investigations are in allocating promotional effort and advertising expenditure at the operational level. At the planning level these results can be used to design product/services packages and other marketing-mix elements to suit segments of the market. As will be seen in this chapter, through these segmentation processes the investigator is able to obtain an insight into the reasons for using a certain service or a package of services and also to identify customers' perception of that service or package.

Consumer behaviour and attitudes

Traditionally bankers used a purely financial analysis to analyse their customers or clients, particularly in the provision of loans, extension of overdraft, credit and cheque facilities. Arguably this analysis presents only half the story, as the results presented can only be accepted at face value. Behind these financial analyses there are the behavioural characteristics of the customer. To understand the financial analysis fully, we need to look into the customers' attitudes and behaviour characteristics. To ignore such factors in analysing a customer is tantamount to ignoring all psychological differences between individuals that result from such important characteristics as social class membership, attitudes, needs, motives, etc.

A recent investigation[1] has indicated that behavioural characteristics are vital to understanding the customer. These behavioural characteristics are basically influenced by three sets of factors[2] as follows:

1. *External factors* arising from influential persons and reference groups. There are two types of reference groups: membership and non-

membership. Membership groups are various groups to which the individual belongs. These include occupation, age, social class, geographic, and so on. Non-membership groups are reference groups that the individual admires or aspires to belong to.

2. *Internal factors* arise from internal attributes of an individual. These have been identified as motives, attitudes, learned behaviour and perception. They differ from individual to individual owing to a person's cultural background, upbringing, education, location, etc.
3. *The consumer process.* This is a series of stages through which a customer goes when contemplating the purchase of a bank's service. When a customer is satisfied with his present situation he is said to be in a cognitive balance or homeostatic position. When he is aware of other more desirable conditions than he is presently experiencing, he is said to be in a cognitive imbalance position.

Factors and influences on bank customers

The major factors influencing the bank customers are divided into external, internal and the consumer process, as presented in Figure 2.1 and mentioned in the previous section. We will consider each of these in turn. There are a number of external factors. These can be divided into (i) cultural, and (ii) social factors. The major cultural factors are the social class and the influence of culture, as elaborated below.

(1) *Culture.* There are a number of examples of national banks based on cultural lines. Treating bank services as a homogeneous product for

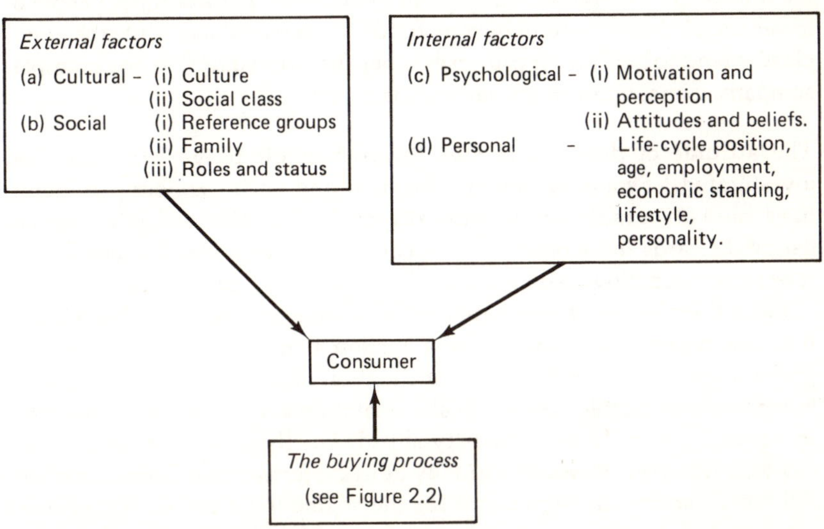

Figure 2.1 The main factors influencing bank customers' behaviour

one moment, we find culture especially important away from the country of origin. For example, in countries with large numbers of expatriates or immigrant populations, banks from the country of origin have established operations to cater for the needs of their own people. These needs are overwhelmingly influenced by cultural considerations. The UK is a good example. No less than 250 small bank branches exist, some just to cater for needs based on this ethnic factor. This issue is an emotive one, for it is natural for overseas Americans to want to bank with Chase Manhattan or First National City Bank, or for overseas Asians to be associated with their own respective national banks. Beside the obvious influence of culture, there is also the fact that some services can only be provided by their own national banks, like the remittance of funds to and from their country of origin. And it is not unreasonable to expect that a Pakistani in Britain would feel more comfortable in requesting a loan from a Pakistani bank than from, say, a UK bank. Such is the strength of cultural influence that for some banks distinct segments of a market can be located where they have an advantage. Some of these segments can be quite substantial and profitable too. In countries with large immigrant populations some overseas banks even have branches in major cities where there is a concentration of their own emigrant workers, and not just in the capital city.

(2) *Social class influence.* As may be expected, consumer behaviour towards banking is very much a function of social class. The demand for bank services by the different classes differs more in the intensity of usage by the various classes than in the classes themselves, since banking nowadays is no more a privilege of the upper classes. But it must be mentioned that there are still lines of distinction. For example, people of lower social classes tend to borrow funds for personal use while the upper classes tend to borrow for purposes other than consumption, for example, company loans, home improvement loans, etc.

The attitude of different classes towards credit usage has also been investigated.[3] People of higher education and socio-economic standing have more favourable attitudes towards credit than others and they tend to use credit cards more often. This is contrary to the belief that people of a lower status employ credit extensively to buy now and pay later.

From the point of view of tapping the savings market it has been found that the higher the social class a person belongs to, the greater the probability of him/her having an inclination to save. And even where the lower socio-economic classes do save, savings tend to be non-investment in nature, primarily as a security shield. For those who do invest their savings, however, it would normally be in the form of something tangible. All these aspects are significant for the segmentation of banks' savings markets and this can be generalised into the following conclusions:

1. Different social classes exist and they constitute the bases for market segmentation. Special strategies (with particular marketing mixes) could be developed and employed to tap the potential of a particular segment.
2. Vast psychological differences exist between the classes, and in attempting to reach the segments advertising can be tailored to the goals and aspirations of that group.
3. Income may not be the most important factor in determining economic behaviour. For banking operations this is especially important since income and financial analyses have been the key tools in all banking activities.

The *social* factors are reference groups, family and roles and status.

(1) *Reference groups.* The most significant factor under this category of influences is the consumer's need to relate to others. This need is manifested during the purchasing process in the evaluation stage (see Figure 2.2) and its importance will be outlined later. Some research findings[4] on the effects of the 'need to relate' may be outlined as follows:

1. When information supplied to the consumer agrees with the information he receives from his reference group, the attitude towards the product (in this case service) will be more favourable.
2. Accordingly, where information presented to customers is contrary to information from the reference group, an unfavourable attitude is formed.
3. Where there is uncertainty as to the reference group's requirements, and the information received is contrary, the uncertainty towards the product/service is increasing.
4. The customer's cognition is increased when information received reinforces the information provided by his reference group.

These conclusions point to the fact that the reference group is used as a basis to evaluate the information presented by the bank. Information for the reference group always carries more weight in the consumer's mind than information provided by the bank. This means that advertising by the banks has to be based on knowledge of the reference group(s) of the consumers in that particular segment. Therefore, the bank marketing staff should (i) know the consumers' reference groups for every segment, (ii) incorporate this to enhance advertising appeal, and (iii) know that different reference groups exist for different segments and consequently one single bank message cannot appeal to all the customers.

Where the reference groups are social class and values, for example, even the attitude towards the product differs. Middle-class customers are more concerned with financial advantages and disadvantages of a loan, while the lower socio-economic classes are more concerned with their security aspect of undertaking a loan. This difference arises from their frame of reference.

(2) *Family.* The second factor that affects bank customer behaviour is family influence. For some, in addition to behaving according to the norm of their reference groups, their purchasing decisions are to some extent dependent on family and friends. This is especially so in the student market. Research[5] carried out points to the fact that for students opening accounts for the first time, parent influences rank second only to branch location, and the nearer the student is to home when opening an account, the more probable that custom is given to the parents' banks. Also, the younger the customer the more probable his purchasing decision is influenced by his parents. The banks realise the importance of this influence although there is very little that is within their control. However, various attempts to secure the younger market have been made. The availability of services for the young, encouragement offered by the banks to promote the 'savings habit' in younger children constitute efforts to capture this market of the young. Parents are encouraged to bring their children in to the bank and start accounts from a very young age in the hope that banks retain youngsters' loyalty and continued patronage in the future.

Another significant influence is that of friends. As we would expect, new student accounts are often decided on the advice given by friends and relatives. Whether the student has opened an account before university, on arrival, or already has one, advice from friends scores highly on all three possibilities in influencing their decision. This may be exploited by banks in the same way as some mail-order firms do. Instead of offering book tokens to attract new accounts (which has been found to be an insignificant inducement anyway), banks could give benefit to a student who recommends the patronage of another.

Perhaps it is important to note that bank services are a special commodity in the sense that advertising very often has little impact on consumer behaviour. Whether this is the result of poor advertising strategy is hard to say but beyond doubt the opinions and advice of other people are trusted more than the advertised message. This means that banking will be particularly susceptible to existing customers. Perhaps this is why banks pay more attention to image building – friendliness, listening to problems, etc. – than to service features.

(3) *Roles and status.* The last component among the external factors is the role and status of the consumer. In this instance role and status is more useful when related to the age and life-cycle concepts. For example, when the consumer is a child his major source of influence is parental. When independent and unmarried his decision is partly based on socio-economic factors and partly on psychological factors. On finding a partner his role changes and so does his purchase decision, perhaps switching banks for easier future planning or some other reason. On marriage the usual

practice is for husband and wife to patronise the same bank, usually with the decision resting with the husband.[6] Husbands select the principal bank for the family in two-thirds of the cases, but for convenience-oriented customers there was more joint consultation. Wives dominate the decision in the case of service-oriented customers.

Later in life, the parents in turn exercise their influence over their dependants. We can see from this that distinct stages can be isolated in the life-cycle process, and particular causal factors isolated. This means that on the basis of changing roles, consumer behaviour changes through the life-cycle and thus the purchase decision alters. Banks can isolate these particular segments and adopt a special mix to appeal to the different behavioural phases.

Internal factors

This refers to the thought process within the consumer, that is, the psychological influences on the one hand, and the personal characteristics of each consumer – such as lifestyle, personality, occupation, etc. – on the other. Between the two sets of influences there is no doubt that the psychological set exerts more force and for this reason this will be discussed in more detail.

Psychological influences. Under psychological influences we have motivation and perception, and attitudes and beliefs.

(1) *Motivation and perception.* To understand consumer thought it is necessary to know what the public perceives of banks. Consumers know banks as public organisations, necessary institutions to the economy, but are not well aware of their other functions, except those that directly involve the consumer. The consumers gather that banks are profit-making institutions, not always holding the consumer's interest at heart, and sometimes are even mistrustful of banks. People have often regarded banks and bankers as 'cold', 'aloof', and 'for the rich'. Such conclusions have prompted the banking industry to be more aware of how it is seen and steps have been taken through advertising to change the overall image. Even physical arrangements on the banking floor affect the perception of the public. Interior decoration and counter positions, booths and lighting, have all been changed to create an atmosphere of friendliness and warmth. People also develop new perceptions even to new services. Cash machines take on a new significance as the human element is removed from transactions. People are more afraid of depositing cash into a machine instead of into a 'safe' pair of hands. The effects of symbolism are very real indeed. Some years ago a Barclays advertisement portrayed a car being repossessed by a finance company with the message that Barclays would be kinder in such circumstances. Research later indicated that the public perceived and interpreted the advertisement as Barclays repossessing the car.

(2) *Attitudes and beliefs.* Various researchers have placed emphasis on banks, services and facilities. Some of the variables found significant were: (i) drive-in facilities, (ii) satisfaction with loan policies, (iii) hours of opening, (iv) convenience of location, (v) efficiency and accuracy of statements, (vi) appearance, friendliness and professionalism.

Attitudinal variables are featured in research because it has been found that a direct relationship exists between usage and attitude. Regression and statistical correlation analyses have been employed and some of the findings were that users of drive-in facilities, credit cards and loans generally have less favourable views towards parking facilities and more to drive-in services. Non-users of drive-in facilities and users of instalment loans and credit cards have a favourable attitude to loan policies and business hours, but unfavourable attitudes towards drive-in facilities.

Attitudes towards bank packages were also investigated[7] and significant consumer preferences were identified. Three product packages were offered in the research and respondents asked a series of questions to determine preference. Only 8 per cent of respondents were satisfied with traditional banking services offered, while 59 per cent wanted to switch to one of the other packages, whose services included free checking with a minimum balance, safe deposit boxes, traveller's cheques, financial advice and counselling, notary facilities, life insurance offers and credit cards. Five product attribute variables were additionally identified as determinant factors in the choice process. Ease of budgeting, ease of understanding of combined statements, ease of obtaining instalment loans, convenience of using the service and security were listed. For segmentation purposes, the study offers some general conclusions as follows:

1. Most people are dissatisfied with the traditional services offered by the banks and would readily switch to some other service or package of services when given the chance.
2. Banks can design services and products to suit the two underlying dimensions that consumers demand convenience and security. A third dimension has been recently added, that of service.

Personal factors. These include life-cycle position, age, employment status, economic situation, lifestyle and personality. We have already referred to the influence of some of these variables on consumer behaviour but socio-economic standing needs particular elaboration.

Socio-economic variables have been used as common segmentation variables, especially occupation, education and income.

Socio-economic standing is really a subset of variables contributing to social class behaviour and common segmentation variables used are occupation and employment status, the level of education and income. Other variables among this group, but not commonly featured in banking research, are length of residence, number of banks, type of accounts and time held.[8] It appears that those customers exhibiting high mobility are good clients for banks to the extent that they frequently require more major durable purchases and household fittings. Banks can therefore appeal to them via safe deposit facilities and instalment loans whose payment mode matches the mobility of the consumers.

Some households deal with more than one bank at a time and this measures their acceptance of banking as an integral part of life and their susceptibility to banking offers. Length of time in holding an account is often used as a measure of loyalty to banks. The socio-economic variables used reveal the behaviour and characteristics of a particular segment denoted by the use of one or more of the bank's services.

The consumer process

This is arguably the most critical part of understanding consumer behaviour in banking. Several advantages are gained via a thorough understanding of the buying process:

1. On understanding behaviour, prediction is easier and therfore buyers' reactions can be anticipated.
2. Bank communications become more effective, because they will be on issues that matter to the consumer. For example, not all the customers are interested in financial details and therefore these should not always be communicated.
3. Future bank users' needs may be identified.
4. Services and needs are brought closer to the introduction time.
5. The 'marketing concept' in banking (presented in Chapter 1) is implemented.

As Figure 2.2 shows, the process by which the consumer makes a decision to purchase a product may be divided into stages. At different stages the consumer requires different information and banks can, via advertising and promotional means, provide the information that is consonant with the client's stage, as presented in Table 2.1.

We have already examined some of the influences that affect the consumer at the information search stages, where psychological and social factors play. By tuning the bank's message and services to the identified needs of the consumers, the bank can move its position from the consumer's consideration stage to the choice stage. To see how and why the customers choose one bank rather than another, or prefer one service to another, we need to reduce consumers' criterion to one or two only. In doing so, we arrive at distinct needs and therefore distinctive market segments.

After having made the decision to patronise a particular bank, it is also advantageous to understand consumers' post-purchase feelings. This is

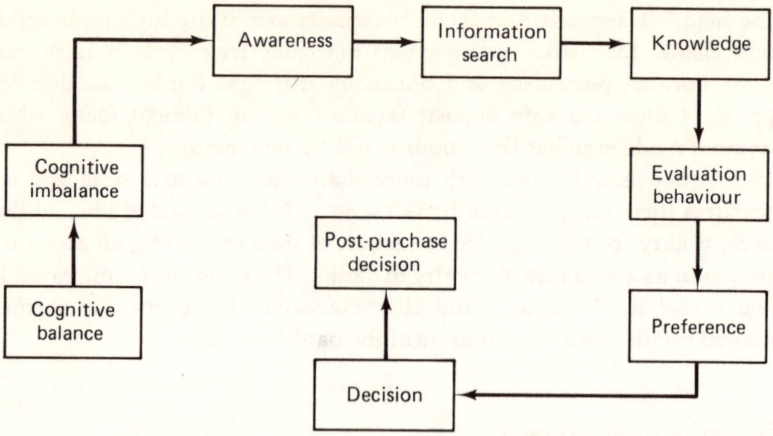

Figure 2.2 The consumer process

important because competition is getting more intense and banks must, after having achieved the patronage of customers, retain that patronage. It is very important for instance to capture the student market and retain it after students' graduation for it is then that banks profit from student patronage. The promotional exercise towards winning students is strategically minded.

The post-client process is basically dealing with the case of bank loyalty. There are several factors both physical and psychological that

Table 2.1 Stages in bank customers' decision process

Stage	*Information required*	*Means by which banks can inform*
Cognitive balance	Comparative position information	Promotion, personal communications
Cognitive imbalance	Demonstrative information	Advertising, word of mouth
Awareness	Alertive information	Advertising
Information search	Relevant information	Advertising, promotions
Knowledge	Detailed information	Brochures, personal communications
Evaluation behaviour	Comparative information	Advertising, word of mouth
Preference	Comparative information	Advertising
Decision	Contractual information	Personal communication
Post-purchase	Continual information	Advertising in mass media

were found to be of importance.[9] Behavioural characteristics can also be found in these factors. The factors are:

1. *Branch coverage and customer mobility.* Branch coverage has no effect on bank loyalty, provided that the customer in non-mobile. Mobility affects loyalty with the degree of effect depending on branch coverage. The higher the branch coverage, the more mobile customers will remain loyal to that bank.
2. *Time.* The longer the elapsed time period between two different life styles – like student and working wives – the lower the likelihood that the customer will remain loyal. Unidentified influences – working as time passes – cause decay in loyalty.
3. *Prior patronage.* There is a higher probability that a customer will remain loyal to the bank if he has a history of patronage with it during the period immediately after graduation.
4. *Loans.* A customer having a loan outstanding with the bank tends to increase the probability of his continued patronage.
5. *Sex.* Males (in the USA) have a higher probability of remaining loyal to banks than females. This may be due to some of the females getting married and switching to their husbands' banks.

In general, a university branch was shown to increase sharply a bank's share of accounts and to provide significant carry-over business after graduation. Continuity in patronising a bank was higher for a respondent with a history of patronage at the bank, a loan, and among males. It was lower among mobile customers, particularly if the bank has low branch coverage.

Therefore, for effectiveness, we must find out at which stage on the consumer process the customer is at, before presenting him with the desired information. For example, it will be premature to present a customer with detailed information of a loan contract when he is still trying to find out more about different loan schemes, or is still evaluating the different loan schemes available to him.

Types of market segmentation

Segmentation involves identifying customer groups that are fairly homogeneous in themselves, but which are different from other customer types. Its purpose is to determine differences between customers that are of relevance to the marketing decision-maker. Obviously, the man in the street requiring a relatively small personal loan to buy a television, for example, will require a different approach to that of, say, a business firm wishing to invest a large sum in capital equipment. Still further segmentation is possible: private individual behaviour will be affected by social class, age, sex, income group, geographical location, etc., as elaborated earlier in this chapter. The more characteristics the market is segmented by, the more precise is the bank manager's knowledge of his customer.

Current trends in banking are towards increased emphasis on retail, as opposed to wholesale, banking. This move towards retail banking has taken place at the same time as the growth of more sophisticated financial management in many companies, and it is tending to conclude that they have found less need for bank services under present circumstances, and that the banks, in order to maintain their business, are being forced more and more into the retail end of the market. The explanation could, however, be different. The banks may simply be wanting to get as big a share of this retail market as possible, through fear of being left behind by competing banks or by other financial institutions who are also interested in this sector.

An illustration of the way in which the market can be subdivided is given by a survey carried out by Barclays Bank, which preselected a number of segments that it considered important in devising a marketing strategy.[10] These segments included the following: (i) the middle classes, (ii) the younger generation, a segment particularly receptive to innovation, (iii) students, (iv) the sedentary population, (v) businessmen, (vi) farmers. The market segment involving youth and students is of increasing interest for Europe's major deposit banks.

Many banks have for years designed their promotional and marketing efforts to aim at only the very broad mass markets. Their philosophy has been to utilise a 'shotgun' or 'blanket' approach in the hope that something in their advertising message would strike a responsive cord with someone. In most instances banks were not sure who that someone might be. The term mass market suggests a homogeneity of needs on the part of the consumer. Recently, however, banks have become increasingly aware of the possible improvements in productivity and resulting economies to scale by using market segmentation when appealing to new customers or promoting banking services to present customers. The segmentation is not limited just to divisions, such as user or non-user, and those who can or cannot afford, or even the extensive demographic classifications, but can also encompass practical, emotional and intellectual lines. In order to gain a full appreciation of the way in which market segmentation can benefit banking, it is first necessary to understand the concept itself. Marketing segmentation has been defined as a means of guiding marketing strategy by distinguishing customer groups and needs. Market segmentation is the subdividing of a market into distinct subsets of customers, where any subset may conceivably be selected as a market target to be reached with a distinct marketing mix. In essence the key to market segmentation is to take the so-called mass market, with a heterogeneous set of needs and, via creative research efforts, divide it up into smaller parts of segments, each reflecting a homogeneous set of needs, thus giving the marketer some direction in shaping his product offerings. The major benefit that will accrue to the bank is that it may be able to promote more effectively to each of the smaller relatively homogeneous markets than could be done to the larger heterogeneous market.

There are three conditions that must be met for effective segmentation. First, the characteristics of a segment must be indentifiable and measurable. Second, it should be accessible in that it must be possible to reach a segment effectively with proper marketing strategies. Third, a segment must have the potential to generate profit. A fourth criterion for market segmentation that may be added is that each segment should react uniquely to different marketing efforts. The reason who different market segments exist, and the need to treat them separately, stems from one of the most fundamental aspects of marketing – the consumer buying process, presented in Figure 2.2.

The process itself is simple in concept. First the person experiences a need he wants to satisfy. This 'need arousal' can be due to the lifestyle of the individual, or as a result of the promotional activity of a bank. Once the person is aware of this need, he then sets about determining the alternative ways by which it can be satisfied. He does this by evaluating each alternative against the other alternatives, using his own criterion as individually perceived and weighted by him, and selecting the alternative that best meets his requirements. A typical example in the case of banking would be the person who is dissatisfied with the service he gets from his present bank and wishes to find a bank that gives better service. He would obtain information about each of the banks available to him and, using that information (e.g. the rate of interest, cost of bank services, branch location, etc.) he will evaluate each bank against the others. He will then go to that bank which has the 'most favourable' overall image according to his own criteria, and deposit his money there.

The relevance of the purchase process to market segmentation is based on the important relationship that exists between the image of a bank (which can be conceptualised as the 'bank's personality'), as perceived by the market, and the fact that one of the components of this relationship can vary between customers.

Another major alternative technique to identify homogenic sub-groups of customers is typology.[11] The two approaches are fundamentally different. In the segmentation process we take an explained variable (e.g. bank credit card usage) and starting with the total bank market population we progressively divide this population into classes and sub-classes, trying to define them so that the explained variable differs as little as possible among a class or a sub-class, and is as different as possible from one class to the other or from one sub-class to the other. The explained variable can be either a measurement for the acceptance degree towards a more or less defined product (e.g. bank credit card penetration), or a behavioural variable (e.g. light, medium and heavy card usage). The segmentation is then carried out on the basis of explanatory variables that can be socio-economic, behaviour or personality characteristics.

The typology technique starts from the individuals and studies their profiles according to a *whole set* of characteristics identified through market reseatch; it progressively groups these individuals according to the similarities between these profiles; we start from nuclei that progressively enlarge to become groups (or clusters) hence the concept clustering. The clustered preferences can be thought of as natural market segments. If we consider consumer segmentation by preferences, then we can define three patterns of segmentation: homogeneous, diffused and clustered preferences.[12]

If the problem is to know the market situation in order to be able to offer certain services, we must use a typology; if the issue is to promote a well-defined service, we must carry out a segmentation study.

Any of a large number of bases, the following can be used to segment the bank market: social class (including geographic and demographic segmentation), psychographic and behaviouristic (or consumer perception) segmentation. Some major bases for segmentation in banking are presented in Table 2.2.

Social classes segmentation

Bankers traditionally use purely financial analysis to analyse their customers and, initially, segmentation in banking was basically along demographic lines. Categories such as age, sex, education, income, family size and religion were used. Such terms as 'housewives', 'consumers', 'men', 'women', 'buyers', 'investers' and 'savers' were used casually. However, it was soon realised that this form of segmentation was very general and was often used as a matter of convenience.

There are basically two approaches to the so-called segmentation by social class: geographic and demographic segmentation:

1. *Geographic segmentation* examines potential differences in the relative attractiveness of different marketing mixes by geographical location of the consumers' home, or of a firm's plant facilities and offices. The banks could obtain differential advantages by programming different marketing offerings for customers living in the centre of the city, as compared to those living in the suburbs.
2. *Demographic segmentation* occurs when the marketer determines that customers respond differently to marketing offerings on the basis of their age, sex, size of immediate family, income level, occupation, formal education, religion, race, or stage in the family life cycle.

Table 2.2 Some major bases for segmentation in banking

Base of segmentation	*Breakdown*
Geographic	
Regional	
(i) Cities	London, New York, San Francisco
(ii) Provinces	States (in the USA, Canada, etc.), departments (in France), counties, boroughs, etc. (in other countries).
Size	Under 5,000, 5,000–20,000, 20,000–40,000 customers, etc.
Density	Urban, suburban, rural.
Demographic	
Age	Under 15, 15–18, 18–21, 21–35, 35–50, 50–65, 65 and over.
Sex	Male, female
Family size	1–2, 3–4, 5–6, 7 and over.
Life-cycle stage	Single young, single married, full nest 1, 2, 3, empty nest, solitary survivors.
Income	Under \$8,000, \$8,000–\$14,000, \$14,000–\$20,000, \$20,000–\$35,000, \$35,000–\$50,000, \$50,000+, etc.
Occupation	Professional, technical, clerical, sales, craftsman, housewives, farmers, shopkeepers, pensioners, students, unemployed.
Education	College, university, professional, vocational, technical.
Nationality	Australian, British, Canadian, Asian, etc.
Social class	Lower-lower, upper-lower, lower-middle, upper-middle, lower-upper, upper-upper.
Behaviouristic	
Benefits sought	Convenience, service, security.
User status	Non-user, potential, first-timers, regulars, ex-users.
Loyalty	None, medium, strong.
User rate	Light, medium, heavy.
Marketing factor sensitivity	Charges, reliability, service, friendliness, etc.

Demographics are a popular basis for segmentation, since they often have a strong and significant relationship to banks' sales, and are easier to recognise and measure than most other variables.

It can be said that people of different social classes perceive issues and problems differently. That is particularly so in people's attitudes towards 'save–spending' situations, as portrayed in Figure 2.3.

In other words, research findings imply that the lower socio-economic groups exhibit a characteristic of 'impulse following' which involves free spending, that is, buy now, pay later. On the other hand, the higher socio-economic groups are characterised by 'impulse renunciation', that is, by renouncing a variety of their satisfactions or gratifications. This leads to the connotation of 'deferred gratification' which refers to the postponement of satisfactions where the higher socio-economic groups feel that they should save money and postpone purchase.

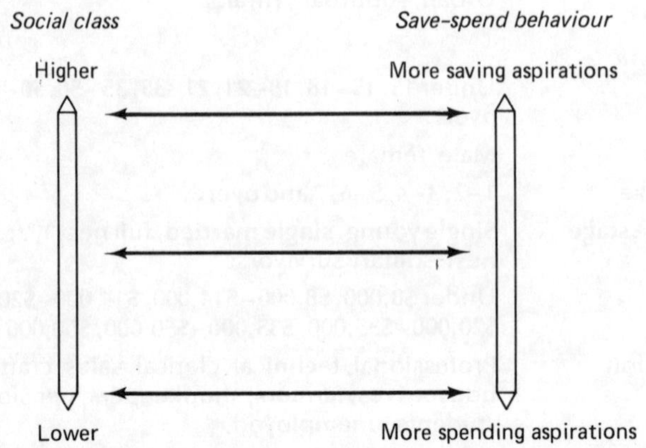

Figure 2.3 Save–spend behaviour and social class

By taking a stage further, Berry[13] has categorised the various social classes according to their perceptual attitudes towards their financial outlook, viz.:

(a) the 'sophisticated investor' segment – upper class, upper-middle
(b) the 'time consuming' segment – upper-middle class, middle class;
(c) the 'caution-first' segment – lower-middle class, lower class;
(d) the 'rainy day' segment – lower-middle class, lower class.

In addition, it looks like non-investments saving appeals more to the lower-status group. The lower-status groups tend to go for something tangible like savings accounts, which they can point at and display. They tend to take less risks and prefer something that can be readily changed into cash. On the other hand, the higher the status a person has the more likely it is that his savings will take the form of investments. These persons tend to take more risks, involve themselves in longer-term commitments and possibly look for a higher return, in less tangible savings such as bonds and debentures, stocks and other long-term investments. The major differences between bank customers of different social classes is summarised in Table 2.3.

Table 2.3 Some major differences between bank customers of different social classes

Higher class/status	*Lower class/status*
1. Pointed to the future	1. Pointed to the present and past.
2. His viewpoint embraces a long expanse of time.	2. Lives and thinks in the short expanse of time.
3. More urban identification	3. More rural in identification.
4. Stresses rationality	4. Non-rational essentially.
5. Has a well-structured sense of the universe.	5. Vague and unclear structuring of the world.
6. Horizons vastly extended or not limited	6. Horizons sharply defined and limited.
7. Greater sense of choice making	7. Limited sense of choice making
8. Self-confident, willing to take	8. Very much concerned with security and insecurity.
9. Immaterial and abstract in his thinking	9. Concrete and perceptive in his thinking.
10. Sees himself tied to national happenings.	10. Work revolves around his family and body.

Segmentation by life cycle

Haas and Berry[14] advocate the classification of customers in households according to their stages in the life cycle. There is ample evidence, according to them, that the banking needs and expectations of households will vary according to their stages in the life cycle. For example, although young married couples with no children have the same size household as older couples whose children no longer live at home, the financial service needs of two segments that a bank marketer should identify would tend to differ in certain respects.

The life-cycle segments are as follows:

(a) the bachelor stage – young single people;
(b) newly married couples – young, no children;
(c) the full nest I – young married couples with dependent children;
(d) the full nest II – older married couples with dependent children;

(e) the empty nest – older married couples with no children living with them;
(f) the solitary survivors – older single people.

The crucial element should be that the customer is being sold a co-ordinated system of services designed for his life cycle circumstances so that his financial services needs, latent or otherwise, can best be met. This form of systems selling is an opportunity for the full-service banking concept to realise its full potential.

Psychographic segmentation

Psychographic segmentation utilises consumer lifestyle and personality differences to determine variance in buyer demands. For example, the banks market differently to swingers, (young, unmarried, active, fun-loving, party-going people, seeking up-to-date goods and fast-paced hedonistic living), than to 'plain Joes' (older, married, home-centred, family-centred people seeking ordinary, unfrilled goods that do their job). A bank might discover that independent, relatively aggressive entrepreneurs respond more effectively to a personal selling approach characterised by passive, unstructured advice-giving, whereas the more dependent, less aggressive middle management of branch offices of large corporations respond better to a more structured, authoritative sales presentation.

The uses of psychographic segmentation are for:

1. *Predicting behaviour.* By identifying a customer segment and understanding why its members are interested in making a bank-related decision, we can estimate the probability that they will react in a certain way, or at least predict several possible reactions.
2. *Client interaction.* The process of psychographic segmentation allows more effective communication between a customer and bank personnel. A more meaningful dialogue, with more information, will flow either way.
3. *Anticipation of future market needs.* With valuable information flowing in from customers, it will provide a better opportunity to analyse future customers' requirements. It will also help provide a basis for determining future bank objectives.
4. *Relevance of practice.* By understanding the behavioural patterns of customers, services can be tailored to meet the changing customers' needs and demands. The idea is to meet as many as possible of the needs of a target market.

Customers react to bank characteristics and services in-keeping with their various identities as 'types' of people, and in terms of what the characteristics and services signify to them.[14] The bank becomes a symbol and the bank's actions become symbolic occurrences with which the customer can identify. For example, Lloyds Bank uses the Black Horse, the Midland Bank uses the 'Listening Friend' and Barclays uses the Eagle. Words like 'big' and 'friendly' have also been used to signify the bank's image to appeal to customer attitudes.

Behaviouristic segmentation and consumer perceptions

Behaviouristic segmentation can be best discussed in terms of volume and benefit segmentation:

(1) *Volume segmentation* relates to the best set of geographic, demographic and psychographic variables that should be used in segmenting the market. Banks distinguish between heavy, medium, light and non-users of its services. Then they attempt to determine the demographic, geographic, or psychographic differences between these groups. The bank marketer is usually interested in more effective programming of marketing strategies to the heavy user, since these represent the biggest contribution to revenue. He may also be interested in how to more effectively programme marketing appeals to the light and medium user, either to increase their demand or to convince enough customers of the superiority of the bank's services in order that they become a profitable segment. The bank marketer may also desire to analyse the non-user segment in order to determine whether or not it can be converted to a profitable user segment and, if so, what specific marketing programmes will be needed.

(2) Another useful segmentation variable is *benefit segmentation.* The assumption underlying benefit segmentation is that the priority listing and relative importance of the principal benefits sought by consumers is the best predictor of consumer behaviour. Benefit segmentation attempts to get customers to list, in order of importance, the primary benefits they are searching for in the bank's services. Each segment of the market is identified by the benefits it is seeking, and these identifiable segments are cross-classified as to geographic location, demographic and psychographic characteristics, and product/services preferences.

Since the market is generally heterogeneous in what it expects from the banking community, the behaviouristic approach inherently groups together people with similar perceptions or attitudes towards the banking community. Robertson and Bellenger[16] have identified seven factors of consumer perceptions with regard to a list of bank features: (i) ego-enhancement, (ii) location convenience, (iii) pricing, (iv) integrity, (v) expertise, (vi) philosophy, and (vii) time convenience, and they are profiled in terms of demographics, financial attitudes, banking habits and media habits. Robertson and Bellenger have subjectively determined that convenience is of primary importance to some USA market segments like the older, blue collar and lower-level white-collar residents, in addition to those new-to-the-area residents. The upper-level white-collar residents look for quality and personal service and as such integrity and ego-enhancement factors are important to them. In order to satisfy customers' 'ego-enhancement', banks should show more interest and respect to their customers and attempt to become more personal and friendly. 'Pricing' means mainly 'good' loan rates, low service charges and liberal loan policies. Integrity stands for safe, reliable, honest and trustworthy bank services. Bank expertise means the level of banks' management capability and knowledge. There are various banks' philosophies – seen through customers' eyes; for example, aggressive v. traditional banks. As far as 'time convenience' factor is concerned, banks' customers prefer a twenty-four hours service.

Other consumer segments

This section focuses on segments that have already been briefly mentioned by that deserve special attention.

(1) *Women* With the liberation of women and equal opportunities, women are increasingly featured and taking an active role in the economy. Bearing in mind that they form something like 50 per cent of the population, they demand very special attention on the very basis of substantiality. For the banking sector, the new independent role of women means a new market segment, whether they are single, married or unmarried mothers.

Previously, banks have largely neglected this market and have even been accused of treating women as second-class citizens in terms of service received from banks. This has arisen from the traditional view that assumed a woman's place is in the home. Lately the banks have come to terms with the new situation and have adopted special measures to tap the women's market. Primarily they have recognised that an increasing number of women are attaining management positions through better education opportunities, and as such are capable of exerting commercial influence. In addition, the financial independence of women means that banks can assume a special role in maintaining independence and security. Hence the female segment offers opportunities for satisfying demand for financial advice, loans services, investments, mortgages, etc. The 'education needs' of women were also recognised.[17] By offering specially tailored seminars for women in business many US banks aimed to gain the partonage of this segment, and by increasing their usage of bank facilities, banks hope that a new channel of communication may be established. The State National Bank of Maryland has gone further. They converted a branch and devoted it specially to the needs of women, providing services such as: advice on rights of women and how to start businesses. Seminars on business opportunities, marketing, budgeting, law, credit and cash flow are offered. The results were startling: the rate of new accounts opening has trebled, two-thirds of new business is provided by women and half of personal loans were made to women. Most first-time women loan customers come to the branch. In the UK there are a number of banks that operate ladies' staffed branches to serve women customers, for example, The Royal Bank of Scotland.

(2) *Students*. Various references have been made to this segment in this chapter. Here the picture as a whole is presented in an attempt to integrate the information available. This segment is recognised by banks for its future potential, and measures aimed to cater especially for students are based on the philosophy that students will retain their loyalty (after graduation) unless they have a major reason to do otherwise. Survey results[18] suggest that three segments in the market were revealed for first-year UK students. These are: (i) those students who had a bank account prior to entering university, (ii) those who opened a bank account in the summer before coming to university, and (iii) those who opened an account on arrival at university. Bannister's *et al.* study indicates that in deciding which bank to join only a few inducements really mattered to first-year students. In general, they were found to be convenience of location, parents' use of the same bank, the advice of friends or relatives, and the presence of an automatic cash dispenser. Most other inducements, like book tokens, tend to have little or no bearing on the first-year student's choice of bank.

The student market in the UK is one of the first clearly identified and most highly developed segments. Barclays was the first to aim its marketing effort directly at students, offering a variety of incentives and concessionary rates on small loans and overdrafts. Students of today are considered the successful businessmen of the future. The earlier the banks get them, the better their chance of keeping them later on.

The other banks quickly realised the importance of this market and today there is a welter of different incentive schemes. No one makes any money from students, as student accounts are the banking industry's version of a 'loss-leader'. But competition for student accounts is intense, and free banking is the norm.

(3) Another segment that was exploited by Lloyds (UK) during the spring of 1980 was the *young married couples* setting up a first home. It presented this segment with (in addition to the normal banking services) incentives in the form of gift vouchers worth over £300 in the form of cash discounts ranging from 10 per cent to 15 per cent on a wide variety of leading branded household goods. Offers included £10 off a Hoover dishwasher, £20 off a Toshiba colour television or a Sony stereo system, £100 off a Wrighton fitted kitchen, etc.

(4) *Ethnic minorities segments.* Certain ethnic minorities segments like, for example, the black segment in the USA,[19] are of interest as they possess some unique characteristics that require unique marketing strategies. Researchers have pointed out that the per capita income of American blacks, for example, is considerably higher than the per capita income of the population of Asia, Latin America and Africa combined, and slightly higher than the per capita income of a citizen in Western Europe. Over 40 per cent of all black families in the USA own homes, and 75 per cent of those homes have television. Their ownership of automobiles amounts to thirty times more than the citizens of the Soviet Union.

The essence of the above observation is the core marketing environment of certain ethnic minorities has potential. It is expected that these segments will continue to be more attractive. While segmenting the market by way of economic and demographic factors may prove beneficial for the present, other variables should also be examined. Consider, for example, a place strategy. This would need to take account of the fact that the majority of ethnic minorities reside within a certain geographical area and their businesses are mostly operated within the community. Their need for banking services would be best served by making these services easily and conveniently accessible to them. Therefore, in order to receive business from these segments, more branches need to be opened where they are located. This could bring banking facilities physically closer to both industrial users and consumers of this segment and product offerings of the branch could be adapted to the particular needs of the segment.

Segmentation of retail v. corporate markets

The bank market can be broadly divided into retail (or mass market) and corporate (or individual market). The current trend is towards the retail market but the importance of small businesses in the corporate segment should not be ignored. Hence the corporate market can be further categorised into large companies and small companies, but specialised services are essential in the case of multinational corporations, for example.

Where the retail market is concerned, segmentation can be achieved through various approaches such as segmentation by social class, life cycle and consumer perception, as discussed earlier in this chapter. Social class segmentation is generally useful in designing the distribution of credit card services. The life-cycle approach considers a package form in distributing the bank services; it also is useful in supplementing the social-class approach in deciding credit-card usage.

Whatever the underlying reasons for the increasing trend towards the retail market, many banks failed to take advantage of the great opportunities inherent in the corporate sector in their attempts to storm the retail sector. The Bolton Committee on Small Firms discovered that: '92 per cent of the firms surveyed did not attempt to obtain finance through financial institutions other than their local commercial bank. This was because small companies held financial institutions in great suspicion and the only institution which escaped this suspicion was the local branch of a commercial bank.'[20]

Banks will lose a lot of the custom of these small companies as they grow larger, which incidentally is being experienced in the North American market. As these firms grow, increased sophistication in financial management brings the ability to retain earnings for growth to manage short-term funds profitably. Also, suspicion of other financial institutions, for example, those offering leasing and factoring services, disappears. The banks at this stage appear as only one of many sources of funds and also the need to keep funds in current and deposit accounts is considerably diminished. Unless the banks can themselves offer services that are relevant to the financial needs of smaller companies as they grow, their position is likely to be eroded.

In the corporate market scene it is also important to segregate the large companies into giant international corporations and those that are not. These multinational corporations call for highly specialised services like freight payments, export financing, etc. from the banks concerned. Indeed, the importance of the international divisions in banking has increased, and so has the need for qualified, international operations. It is also pertinent that some medium-sized customers may join the ranks of the multinationals and in order to avoid sooner or later being cut off from the growing multinational market, the bank marketer must find means to retain them.

Hence the bank marketer in deciding his distribution channels should recognise that one can segment the corporate markets into: (i) large companies, (ii) small (and growing) companies, and (iii) multinational corporations. This is shown in Figure 2.4.

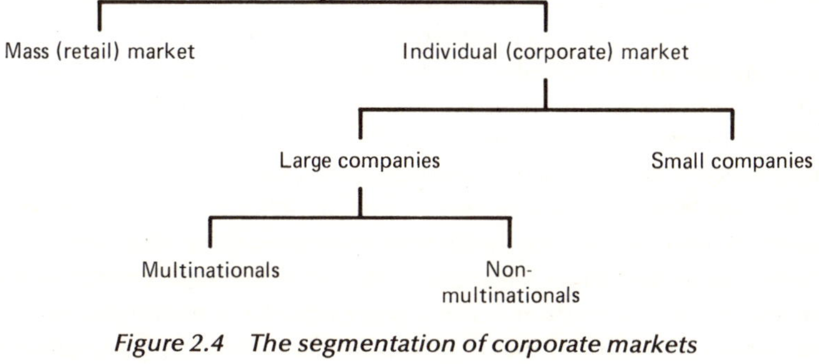

Figure 2.4 The segmentation of corporate markets

Implications of segmentation for effecting banking

Early segmentation studies on banking services have focused upon consumer behaviour for a single product or service. Some of the segments investigated were on savings accounts,[21] bank credit cards,[22] and cash dispensing machines[23] as single services. However, one of the characteristics of bank services is that they are offered in packages. It was then realised that segmentation studies concerned with packages of services were needed. When it is possible to determine that a homogeneous market exists for a range of products or services, marketing-mix variables can be adjusted to exploit this market.

Multivariate statistical techniques, like canonical correlation, provide a means of identifying patterns of use of bank services that can be associated with certain respondent characteristics. This technique can be used to the extent that users of multiple services can be identified by common characteristics. Marketing effectiveness can be increased and marketing costs can be reduced by targeting a range of services to a single market segment.[24]

Two basic sets of variables are used in this form of segmentation. One is the dependent, or usage criterion set. This consists of various bank services like safe deposit boxes, trusts services, loans, drive-in windows, certificates of deposits or Treasury Bills, automatic tellers, cheques, overdrafts, bank credit cards, cheque cards, etc. The second set it the independent or predictor set. It consists of dimensions of segmentation that are demographic, socio-economic, attitudinal and behavioural variables. Any segmentation of the market is based on the predictor set of variables. To each of the segments that result from such analysis that exhibit a cluster of variables from the predictor set, can be applied a marketing mix that consists of several variables from the criterion set. The demographic variables include age, sex, marital status, etc. Socio-economic variables include occupation, education, income, geographic mobility, number of banks with which the household deals, kinds of bank accounts used by the household, length status of accounts, etc. Attitudinal and behavioural variables include attitudes towards various attributes of the various services. This attitudinal and behavioural variables are basically those factors derived from a psychographic analysis. Understanding consumer behaviour in the fashion described in earlier sections will help us to make more use of these variables in segmentation. In the extreme, segmentation can be based on attitudinal variables alone with all other variables to be taken as dependent variables.

An interesting study was carried out in 1973 for the German Federal Bank[25] to establish the real needs of its customers. The initial object of the study was to determine the social structure of the bank's customers and the image that their customers and customers of competitive banks had of the banks. In addition, the investigation also considered the customers' judgement of the range of services the banks had to offer, the effectiveness of various advertising and other sales promoting measures, the customers' will to save and other habits, and a typological description of the customers.

The importance of a good image for a bank can be considered by an observation of the bank image as seen by customers who have seriously considered changing their account, in comparison with customers who have not considered such a change. Findings indicate [26] that satisfied customers are more positively minded than those who are critical of what their banks have to offer them, and who already have one foot in the door of the next bank. However, the published results cover up the fact that various image components play very different parts in bank loyalty. By being able to interact meaningfully with a client, the banks are in a better position to interpret future client requirements. Used as such, the client can be a source of valuable information and used to anticipate future market needs. The bank's services should, therefore, become even more tailored to the client's needs. A by-product of segmentation is that it encourages bank managers to think more about the customer, developing a balance between the manager's understanding of his financial services and the clients'.

A great insight becomes possible when segmentation is explored as the banks can consider the needs of specific groups,[27] such as professional and career women, new householders,[28] ethnic groups,[29] investors,[30] savers for specific goals, etc., and conceive strategies to attract those groups.

An obvious advantage of the application of the knowledge of consumer behaviour is that we will be in a very much better position to predict the behaviour of potential customers. We can identify the given client segment and understand the reason why the segment is interested in making a bank-related decision. Equipped with this knowledge we can estimate the probability of a client reacting in a certain way and consequently we can act in the most effective way to attract him to our bank.

CHAPTER 3

Branch location and distribution

Contents

Introduction

Branch location and distribution are an important but much overlooked area of bank marketing. In marketing, distribution is the means through which a seller makes his product available to the buyer. In the marketing of consumer or industrial goods, this is achieved through the use of various middlemen who comprise what is known as a channel of distribution. Since this is not possible with a service such as banking, a channel of distribution for banking should be considered in a somewhat different manner. A good definition of distribution in banking is any means of increasing the availability and/or convenience of a service that increases its use or the revenue from its use.

All the banking groups have a similar aim to be the all-purpose bank for their private and corporate customers. In considering branch locations and distribution means, banks are concerned not just with the two very large groups of customers (private v. corporate customers) but also with the major dimensions of their activities:[1]

(a) offering a very large variety of financial services; and
(b) competing for 'savings' (deposits) and 'chequeing', (i.e. current) accounts.

With the increase in inflation all over the world, the second type of activity in particular – that of getting in additional deposits and current accounts – has gained in importance and is today the main focus of most banks' marketing activities.

In distributing bank services, the bank marketer is faced with the problem of encountering a huge market that he should duly serve. Indeed, in recent years many banks, having already grown and diversified through acquisition, now face the necessity to develop profitable services for mass business.[2] For the bank marketer, the familiar distinction between 'standard' products and 'single orders' offers a useful concept. This concept can invariably aid the marketer to distinguish the two broad categories of markets in which he should serve, viz.:

1. *Mass (retail) market.* Standard products, relatively inflexible in performance and cost, can be offered to this market. It spells out the requirements of geographical decentralisation, standardised services, heavy advertising and promotion, attractive services and, above all, cost-effective processes.
2. *Individual (corporate) market.* This market constitutes single orders of sufficient size or importance that can be profitably singled out for individual treatment. It requires individualised services and counselling like comprehensive financial advice, the availability of research services and contact brokerage to the cushner, negotiated terms, etc.

It is important for the bank marketer to make the market target distinctions early – preferably at the product development stage – and carry it right through to the front office, both in the commercial and financial areas. To develop and distribute a service without a clear concept of the market can be a formula for disaster.

Means of distributing bank services

The channels of distribution for banks' services should be thought of as any means used to increase the availability and/or convenience of the services that help to maintain existing bank users or increase their use among existing or new customers.[3] In order to envisage such a criterion, the bank marketer must facilitate the right product for the right people at the right price and at the right place. Indeed, once the characteristics of the total banking market have been identified via market research and there is an appreciation of the problem areas, then the marketing mix can be tailored to exploit the selected customers' segments of the market in the most profitable manner.

Kotler[4] defines the marketing mix as 'the set of controllable variables and their levels that the firm uses to influence the target market'. Traditionally these variables have been defined as the four P's – product, price, place and promotion. Thus the organisation identifies its target market and then attempts to define the appropriate marketing mix to reach that market. The organisation can therefore control these variables but it is operating within a broader marketing environment where there are numerous uncontrollable variables, such as economic factors, technological change, and political and governmental attitudes, which may affect the scope and operation of the marketing-mix variables.

Thus if there is a change in the marketing environment then it might be desirable to change the marketing mix. This may, however, be difficult since the bank has to operate within a particular time span in developing its marketing mix; thus planning for new branch locations has to be done well in advance of the branch actually opening and an advertising campaign has to be planned well before it comes into operation.

The elements of the marketing mix lend themselves to further subdivision in relation to banking. In a sense the place element of the marketing mix is elementary – branches must be located where there are customers. The attraction of the urban area is obvious, as it is here where the customers are located. Centres of industry, commerce and population are the obvious locations. Less conventional locations include 'banks on wheels' at agricultural shows, leisure exhibitions and trade fairs. Some banks already have branches in factories and it is anticipated that this type of development will gather pace as the banks begin to tackle those segments of the population that make relatively little use of the clearing banks' services.

Channels of distribution

In distributing financial services, banks employ a number of channels: bank branches, credit cards, banking by mail, in-shop branches and in-touch services. These are shown in Figure 3.1.

(1) *Bank branches.* This is the most important channel of distribution and in certain instances some bankers regard the location of bank branches to be synonymous with distribution. Since branches are relatively fixed in location, they must be conveniently situated. As such, it is important to define a branch's trading area as that geographical region in

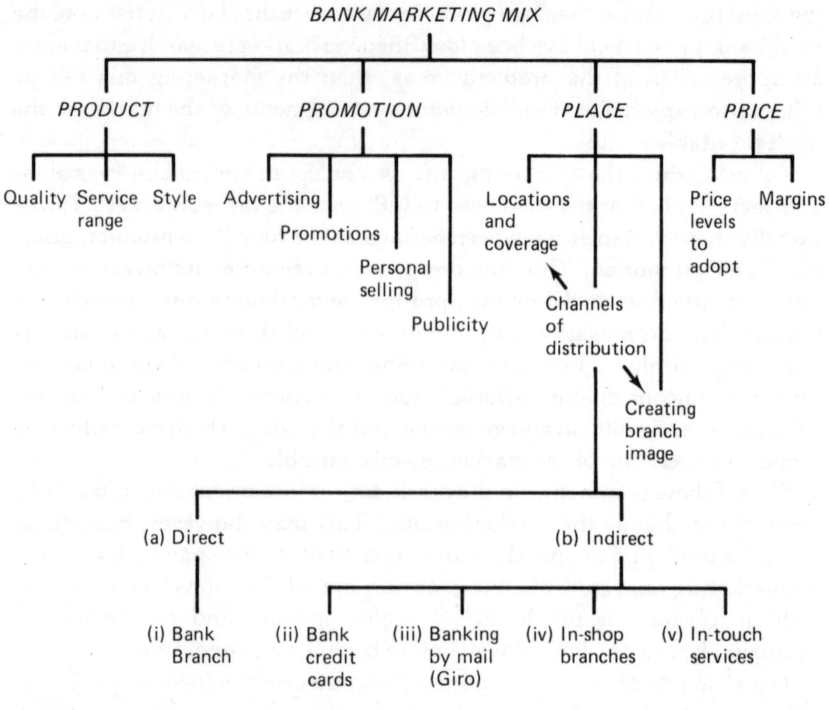

Figure 3.1 The elements of marketing mix and distribution channels in banking

which it can conveniently serve potential customers and from which the largest portion of business will be generated.[5]

(2) *Bank credit cards.* This is a means through which a bank offers its credit services to the users. Bank credit cards have enabled banks to overcome the factor of inseparability, by offering credit to customers far outside their immediate trading area. It has also prompted the increasing use of the bank's services by existing customers, as well as establishing contacts with a wide variety of traders and persons who may not otherwise use the services provided.

(3) *Banking by mail* (Giro). By using the facilities provided by the Post Office (who acts as the middleman), this method increases the availability and convenience of the bank's service, as well as possibly expanding the geographic area within which it can operate.

(4) *In-shop branches.* The use of shops as bank agents as employed by the Co-operative Bank in Britain is another means of effectively distributing bank services.[6] Through its sheer geographical spread of shop agencies (4,000 shops in 1974) and some forty-five operating branches, the ease of obtaining encashment outside normal banking hours, and the

much more relaxed attitude towards the management of customers' accounts, have given the bank a sizeable share of the banking market. Recently, Sainsbury's became the first British grocery store chain to install cash dispensers backed by 'big four' clearing banks, National Westminster, Barclays, Lloyds and Midland. Sainsbury's will primarily be offering an automated banking service; however, on some of the machines customers will also be able to call up bank statements. Other banks are currently considering opening branches in other leading chain stores such as Debenhams, Woolworths, Sears & Roebuck, etc.

(5) *In-touch financial services.* Another innovative means of distributing bank services has been pioneered in the USA through the application of computers. Computerised facilities have been used in supermarkets to record each transaction with the respective customer's account with the bank. More recently, the Seattle-First National Bank has promoted the In-Touch home financial service.[7] It can give a customer access to a talking computer from his home touch-tone phone. By calling up the bank computer, the customer can instruct the computer to perform financial services such as:

(a) paying bills by transferring funds from his/her bank account to that of a creditor;
(b) keeping his/her family book by reporting the expenses with a bi-weekly budget analysis broken down into several categories (food, housing, clothing, etc.);
(c) computing income tax data;
(d) storing household records like insurance policies, credit cards' numbers and drivers' licences and vehicle registration numbers.

Locating bank branches

Location decisions are extremely important as they involve the expenditure of considerable resources on a long time scale. The Bannister[8] study reveals that university students regard location convenience as being very important when choosing their bank. Among students who had not opened bank accounts before entering Sheffield University, the banks offering the best location in terms of convenience for the halls and for the university itself scored heavily over those that did not offer such advantages.

Three possible classes of objectives may be postulated for the building of bank location models: academic, social or commercial. Academic purposes will be served by building models that improve our conceptualisation or generalisation, that is, which explain the spatial distribution of banking outlets in terms that fit in with the theories of economics or social science, or that advance the building of a unified theory of marketing. Social purposes will be served to the extent that the models allow any government influence or regulations or direct operations to be based on a better understanding of the effect on banks. Examples of involvement of government/statutory bodies in matters relevant to bank location are the Post Office Giro, National Savings, income tax on building society interest, minimum lending rate, the Bank of America Green Paper on competition and credit control, Bank of England and other national banks' influence at the time of the 'Fringe Banks' crises, etc. Another social aspect in which the various government(s) are involved is the protection of consumer interests. In general, this will be achieved by the improvement of understanding just mentioned, coupled with the banks' achievement of commercial objectives – resulting in efficiency in service.

Commercial reasons are the most cogent motivators for the building of bank location models and these are important in two areas: (i) location decisions, (ii) performance monitoring and business development. Regarding (i), a recent study reports 'a good site can have twenty times the potential of a poor site'.[9] Costs and other factors besides potential are also relevant, but the benefits of a good prediction of performance are clear.

Thus, a good model of branch potentials is invaluable in 'targeting' the performance expected, as a basis for evaluation and control. Nevertheless, the prime motivation is likely to be the obvious one of deciding when and where to open or close branches. There are four major sets of models: economic, spatial, bivariate and regression models, as elaborated below.

Economic models

Early models by economic geographers to the *general* problem of location of enterprises were restricted by the lack of computational facilities to solve complex equations, hence the need for gross oversimplification in the model. Thus Losch[10] postulated: 'a broad homogeneous area with uniform transport features in all directions and with an even scatter of industrial raw materials in sufficient quantity for production'. Even so he was unable to solve the series of simultaneous equations that he produced. However, he offered some useful concepts, for example, that *different products* yield *different* (hexagonal) *market areas*, and that the overlapping vertices of these different hexagons form ideal 'production sites' for cities. Losch produced a formula for the distance between competing monopolists to give a theoretical value for the radius of the inscribed circle of the hexagonal market area. Isard[11] produced a more general theory and founded the discipline of regional analysis. His analysis was macro, and not directly applicable to individual firms.

A more recent macro model of the banking industry is given by Ali and Greenbaum[12] which attempts to contribute to the systematic explanation of the size-distribution of banks, their location, the spatial distribution of prices and profits, from the macroeconomic view.

Among the first economic models for locating bank branches, we have the 'Gravitation Theory'. Modern retail gravitation models are the direct results of approximately a century of empirical study that attempted to quantify social and economic interaction of all kinds. These theories drew analogies between the Newtonian idea of 'gravitational attraction' between bodies, and social or economic attractions. Reilly was the first retail trade theorist to use this approach: 'It is readily acceptable that the amount of outside trade which a city enjoys in any surrounding town is a direct function of the population of that city and an inverse function of the distance of the city from that town'.[13] In other words, consumers in another town are attracted by the size of the town and deterred by the distance to be travelled and this approach can be – in principle – applied to banks' branches' location problem, as well. Reilly's general law is:

$$\frac{Ba}{Bb}=\frac{(Pa/Pb)^N}{(Db/Da)^n}$$

Where

Ba = the business which city A draws from town T
Bb = the business which city B draws from town T
Pa = the population of city A
Pb = the population of city B
Da = distance from A to T
Db = distance from B to T
N, n = exponents to be derived empirically

If the model is being applied to bank locations, where cities A and B become established bank branches and town T becomes the proposed new branch, then the calculations of the indifference points can be made for the proposed new branch paired with each of 'reasonably near' established branches and indifference points calculated. This gives a number of points on the boundary of the proposed new site 'trading area' and a basis for beginning calculations of the potential of that area. Whether or not the 'indifference points' can be calculated exactly and precisely how these should be joined to indicate the 'market area' of the proposed bank seem to me less important than the following two basic problems: (i) no allowance has been made for *convenience of access* as distinct from distance. A good road, bus-route or railway, or a mountain ridge can play havoc with all the assumptions of this model; (ii) the application to locating a new branch would ignore the loyalty of the population to branches at which they currently bank and this loyalty is known to be considerable. It seems that these points are valid objections to any method based solely on the 'retail gravitation' approach. They are also the main objections to many of the models discussed below.

Spatial techniques

A number of models have been reported that use a two-step procedure of (i) predicting gross area potential, and then (ii) predicting market share within that potential. To a large extent, these approaches are particularly suitable to US banks, which tend to be local banks, expanding by 'branching' where state laws permit this.[14] This situation does not favour the approach taken, for example, by the Yorkshire Bank[15] in England, of using the banks' existing branches as a representative sample for the nation and then predicting results in a smaller area on the basis of that sample. In the USA banks' existing branches are quite likely to be *unrepresentative* of the area into which expansion is proposed. There is, therefore, a sound logic in taking a national sweep for areas worthy of detailed investigation and then having a much more detailed look at 'promising' areas. These techniques for finding 'promising' areas are, of course, similar to the 'engineering' approach to estimating deposit potential discussed by Soenen.[16] In his major work Soenen uses the Davidson Survey (1969) to show that 89 per cent of respondents banked at the office nearest their home or work. Convenience in terms of location was found to be the single most important reason for selecting a branch. In deciding the best location three major stages are involved:

(a) defining the trading area;
(b) gathering the raw data within the area and translating the data into actual potential;
(c) calculation of ROI and the final decision-making.

Only after each of these three stages had been investigated in considerable depth would it be possible to determine the optimum location (Table 3.1). This approach presented in Table 3.1 indicates the stages of the decision-making process that should finally produce an indication of whether or not a new branch should be set up. In reality, in many countries, including the USA, only a few banks have employed in the past such a procedure, and the present bank branch network is largely the result of the historical growth process and 'trial and error'. Some banks, notably the Co-operative Bank, have been handicapped in their growth by their lack of branch coverage as compared with the major banks.*

*This may perhaps explain why smaller banks may be prepared to show more initiative in some other elements of the marketing mix. Thus, for example, the Co-operative Bank did initiate 'free' current account banking services.

Table 3.1 The decision-making process for setting up a new bank branch

Stage(s) and objectives	*Methods/techniques that can be employed*
1. *DEFINE TRADING AREA* of the proposed bank branch. This is the geographic region in which the bank can conveniently serve potential customers.	(i) *Locate in an existing shopping centre.* Since banking might be regarded in the same category as convenience shopping then it is likely to be attracted to similar locations. (ii) *Method of limiting factors.* Try to identify and map the factors that might put spatial limits on the service area of the proposed branch, e.g. natural barriers (rivers), manmade barriers (motorway), alternative retail locations which include bank facilities, appropriate socio-economic factors. (iii) *Gravity models.* Reilly's law of retail gravitation is the best known of such models; it basically suggests that the area of influence of one town is a function of distance and population in relation to other surrounding towns. It may be possible to use this idea in relation to a proposed bank site relative to existing bank sites. However, the method may not prove too accurate. (iv) *Analogue techniques.* Various methods have been suggested but they attempt to define the potential use of a new location in an area.
2. *ESTIMATE THE CHANCES OF BRANCH SUCCESS THROUGH DEPOSIT POTENTIAL*	(i) *Statistical methods.* Use of regression analysis. (ii) *Summary of relative method.* The basic idea is to obtain the family or per capita deposit volume for an area in which the bank is to be sited and to subjectively calculate the likely deposit in the proposed branch trading area. (iii) *Analysis of market by type of deposit.* Several deposit categories can be used (e.g. individual, commercial, industrial, and public accounts), and there is an attempt to calculate this for a proposed trading area in each of the categories.
3. *CALCULATE THE RETURN ON INVESTMENT*	(i) *ROI or net present value.* After obtaining an estimate of expected deposits and loans, year by year, these can be compared with expected costs of operation. Alternatively, a particular return on investment may be required within a particular time span.

Bivariate methods

A number of models treat market share as dependent upon either distance or time and upon an assessment of the local competition.

John Devaney[17] describes a model that is used by Wilbur Smith & Associates, a retail bank locations consulting firm. The model is different from those previously described in that it uses a network approach. Nodes of potential are located and the major streets network is used to link the nodes together. Competitive branches are also assigned to nodes. The travel time between adjacent nodes is measured and recorded. A computer algorithm is used to find the minimum travel time between all consumer nodes and all bank locations.

Devaney's market share determination uses a distance (travel time) decay curve that shows the result of differing travel times upon the market share to be expected by a new banking office. This approach is unclear on the exact procedure for allocating share of market, and does not state the method of handling (or taking into consideration) the influence of competition. This is presumably handled by using a more severe distance decay function for a new location in a severely competitive environment. The approach, however, has the advantage of considering travel times rather than merely distances.

Using a fairly similar approach, John D. Nystuen[18] developed a method of forecasting market share for financial services. His method uses a distance decay function similar to Devaney's but performs a Bayesian modification of the market shares to make sure that they add up to 1.00. The method involves the following stages:

1. Obtaining a representative sample (several hundred random home addresses) of customers of a particular branch.
2. Plotting these addresses on a map and recording the distance from the branch to each home address.
3. Fitting a smooth curve to the data indicating probability of banking at the given branch as a function of distance.
4. Using that curve for each population node, census tract, enumeration district, or other geographic unit, calculating the probability of banking at each institution in the relevant market area.

A sophisticated method of branch site share of market analysis was reported to have been developed by Wadsworth and Gagnon[19] of the Wilmington Trust Company. The method is logically consistent in allocating market share – the allocated market shares sum to unity and uses a subjective evaluation of a 'competitive factor' weighting that factor by the inverse of the consumer's travel time to the branch in question.

Elements considered and included in the evaluation of the subjective 'competitive factor' are: (i) the services offered, (ii) the quality and quantity of personnel, (iii) the surrounding environment in which the office is located, (iv) the accessibility to and from the branch, (v) the physical facilities of the branch (size, appearance, drive-up, 24-hour machines, for example), (vi) parking facilities, (vii) visibility, and (viii) all other factors deemed appropriate.

Subjective weighting to the components of the factor are weighted and the assumption is that this factor can be multiplied by the inverse of travel time.

Multiple regression techniques

Multiple regression analysis can be used in bank marketing to estimate the linear relationship between a *dependent* variable and two or more *independent* (or *exogenous*) variables. The general form of the multiple regression model is: $Y = a + b_1x_1 + b_2x_2 + b_3x_3 + , \ldots, b_nx_n$, where the dependent variable is the parameter, Y, for example, annual volume of new savings deposits, which it is desired to forecast and the x values are the independent variables presumed to have some direct or indirect causal link with the dependent variable. Examples of independent variables in bank marketing are the 'per cent renter' – or proportion of households living in rented accommodation (as distinct from owner-occupied), 'retail square footage' (as a proxy for the volume of retail trade),[20] income data, for example, percentage of population over 65, or percentage of population age 45–65, which are believed to be related to 'disposable income' and 'banking habits'.[21] Standard computer programs are readily available and not difficult to use. Examples are IBM's 'Stepwise Multiple Regression Program', and SPSS's 'REGRESSION'.[22]

The objective of selecting a (new) bank site via the employment of regression analysis may be complicated in two ways:

1. The choice of criteria on which to judge a new site is not simple. Banks provide a wide variety of services that may be affected in various ways by the site location. Also, the relative profitability of the different services depends on external economic factors such as the level of interest rates. Ideally, therefore, a multiple regression analysis for the purposes of site location would yield a number of equations, relating relevant criteria to the independent variables.
2. The choice of independent variables could be complicated if this choice interacted with considerations of bank design or operating procedures – for example, drive-in windows, whether particular customers held savings accounts, whether they had a checking account at the same bank, and the banks' opening hours. These were obviously of little direct relevance to the site location problem.

A different approach in attempting to identify the best bank site location from *the customer's point of view* was undertaken in the USA,[23] and was

Table 3.2 The major quantitative methods for optimising bank branch location

Methods	*Based on:*	*Advantages*	*Limitations*	*References*
1. *Retail gravitation*	Reilly's general law and gravitational attraction theory $\frac{Ba}{Bb}=\frac{(Pa/Pb)^N}{(Db/Da)^n}$ (for index, see text)	1. Fairly simple. 2. Takes into consideration neighbouring established branches.	1. No allowance made for convenience of access as distinct from distance. 2. Ignores customers' loyalty to branches.	(13), (5)
2. *Spatial models*	Two-step procedure: 1. Predicting gross area potential. 2. Predicting market share; this is achieved in three stages: (i) defining trade area; (ii) translating data into actual potential; (iii) calculation of ROI (see Table 3.2).	1. Enable to find 'promising' areas subject to a thorough investigation. 2. Suitable particularly where local expansion by 'branching' is permitted by law.	1. A long, multi-stages decision process. 2. Unsuited for national branching decisions.	(14), (5), (9)

3. *Network technique* (bivariate models)	1. A computer alogarithm is employed to find the minimum time between all consumer nodes of potential and all bank locations. 2. Market share is determined via the use of a distance decay curve.	1. Considers travel time rather than distances.	1. Unclear on the exact procedure for allocating share of the market. 2. Does not state how the competition influence can be handled.	(17)
4. *Regression analysis*	$Y = a + b_1x_1 + b_2x_2 + , \ldots b_nx_n$ where Y is the dependent variable, e.g. annual volume of new saving deposits that the new branch will generate and $x_{1,2,\ldots,n}$ are the independent variables presumed to have a causal link with the dependent variable (e.g. branch floor area, income per capita, age of potential customers, etc.). Regression analysis is based on the method of least squares (22).	1. Provides an explicit way of showing the effects of changes. 2. Standard computer programs readily available and not difficult to use.	1. Degrees of freedom problem (i.e. the need of a large number of observations and equations to be employed). 2. The multi-collinearity (or joint correlation) problem. 3. Criteria for assessing a new branch is *not* simple. 4. The value of 'predictive', independent variables as predictors.	(21), (22), (13)

based on a survey of customers and banks at Farmington, Michigan. The study suggests that the question of what determines an individual consumer's choice of bank is subtly different from what parameters should a bank seek to satisfy in choosing a site, since many consumer-choice factors are not determined by the site location at all – for example, provision of both savings and checking accounts, opening hours, drive-in windows, etc. However, the analysis was also run using only the data relevant to bank location, and served to confirm the general impression in the literature that distance is a controlling variable in bank choice.

To sum up, in deciding on branch locations the banks need to be aware of the dynamic nature of the environment as against the static nature of quantitative models for site location, and to relate the distribution aspect of their marketing mix to the other aspects (product, promotion, price) and with the overall marketing plan. Models will be refined, modified, or even replaced as the user's understanding of the nature of the markets and the workings of various techniques improve. However, the problem of branch location will remain, and an understanding of the models currently available is the only basis for the proper selection and/or development of improved techniques for optimal bank branch location. The various methods are compared in Table 3.2.

New technology and branching

The impact of EFTS (Electronic Funds Transfer Systems) technology has had a profound effect on banks branching strategy. Consumer understanding of the use of automated telling machines (ATMs) is quite advanced in Western Europe as well as in the USA, owing to their earlier introduction and to the widespread existence for several years of pre-authorised payroll deposit and payments systems. Customer usage of ATMs has reached a point now at which there is little question of their cost-effectiveness. Up until now, ATMs have been used inside or outside branches to absorb additional customer demand during peak hours or outside regular bank opening hours – thereby facilitating savings in bank operating costs. There is, however, no reason why ATMs should not be established in satellite or remote away-from-branch locations in the future and indeed several banks have already installed ATMs in commercial complexes and shopping centres.

The number of branches relative to population served is not likely to expand in the near future. The principal motives for branch expansion – competition on the basis of location and satisfying consumer needs for convenience – are likely to be increasingly catered for by the establishment of automated teller machines. While the number of traditional branches may remain relatively constant, the frequency of status changes rather than closures, may increase as an expanding service-mix is tailored to the needs of each branch's customer base.

Automatic cash dispensers are one of the latest variations of the 'place' marketing factor. They increase the convenience factor as well as saving valuable staff time. The Bannister study[24] cites this as being one of the few inducements that swayed British university students when choosing their bank.

Consumer sophistication coupled with the development of Electronic Funds Transfer Systems may further change the basis on which branch location decisions should be made. The banks currently offer various 'free' services by mutual arrangement,* for example, 'Giro' for paying bills, and cash-drawing facilities are available to any account-holder of a participating bank, at any branch of a participating bank – not necessarily his own. Barclays Bank has recently withdrawn from the scheme on the grounds that it was attracting a disproportionate burden of cash withdrawals for other banks – without a balancing number of its own clients using the facilities of their rivals. This could well reflect their choice of city-centre sites and the consumer using the situation to his own advantage. If this speculation is correct, it tends to nullify the benefits to the bank of choosing a site convenient to its potential customers, and to weaken the link between the consumer and 'his/her' branch. The development of cash dispensers, automatic telling machines, and bank lobbies (unmanned collection of machines – rather like having a set of drink dispensers and food-vending machines instead of a canteen) will tend to weaken that link further. However, the consumer's tendency to regard a particular branch of a particular bank as 'his/hers' seems to be at the foundation of much of the marketing strategy behind site selection. To an extent, current accounts and in particular cash transmission seem to be 'loss leaders' to attract customers to other services. But the other services (e.g. insurance, loans, travel) are shopping goods for which the customer is likely to adopt an extended problem-solving approach that may decrease or nullify the initial advantage of the branch contact – especially if the customer rarely comes into the bank – by using a cash dispenser, cheque book and credit card for his most frequent needs.

Creating the branch image

An important aspect of branching strategy is the image projected by each branch. A uniform image for each branch is desirable on two counts. It advertises nationally the bank in question and second, it provides

* Recently all banks have started to charge other banks' customers.

psychological reassurance to the customer that no matter which branch he enters he is moving into an environment with which he is familiar from his home branch.

Branches should also be designed to have a uniformity of appeal. A design that is some sort of highest common multiple of attractiveness for each and every segment must be sought. Since a bank wants to attract most market segments, some architectural theme must be adopted that is attractive and not repellent to any major target segment.

Internal layout is likely to be an area where the banks will put more emphasis. Already the development of separate pay-in and withdrawal counters in banks shows some awareness of the possibilities. In the larger banks as part of the marketing effort we may see well-labelled counters specialising in other bank services as well. As well as being more effective than the largely ignored brochures, this may well save the time of the more senior staff.

In any city the point of maximum accessibility to the greatest number of customers is the central business district and this explains why the city centre is an area of concentrated retail and commercial activity. The main bank branches are *traditionally* located in this area. Even within this relatively small area there is competition for particular sites that afford maximum accessibility. Commercial enterprises that can offer the highest rents concentrate in this zone and the banks usually exist here alongside the large multiple stores. What is a 'good' location for one bank is likely to be highly suitable for another and there is often a tendency for banks to cluster, with a corner 'high street' site being quite common. This type of site offers convenience for the customer and some evidence suggests that this is an important element in bank selection by potential customers. This type of site also provides the bank with an opportunity to project an 'image' (by, for example, the architectural style of the building) and a presence to the maximum number of people. Other branches may be established at locations that serve particular segments or groups of segments; Reekie[25] quotes the example of one Scottish bank that has a branch in a large electronics factory while banks often have branches on a college campus or in particular suburbs. In the USA the development of large, planned suburban shopping centres has provided a suitable potential location for banks. Stahel[26] suggests that while these types of sites have advantages such as ease of market entry, parking facilities for customers and regional publicity, they also have some potential disadvantages in terms of loss and identity, lack of control over the human setting, and burdens of non-essential costs. However, the development of large suburban shopping centres has been severely restricted in the UK so that such sites for bank branches are not common.

The bank site may thus be a significant factor in attracting new accounts but it also serves to promote the bank. The well-chosen site helps to advertise the bank and the adoption of a corporate symbol may aid this process. Externally the type of building can help to project an image of the bank and it has been suggested that uniformity of design is advantageous.[27] The interior design of the bank can be utilised to create a particular psychological environment for the customer. Some years ago many banks changed their interior designs to a more open plan with fewer security grids. This was presumably to engender the feeling of 'friendliness' towards customers – to make the bank appear as a less 'offical' organisation. In recent years security problems appear to have resulted in the return of security grills.

For bank institutions location is thus a very significant element of the marketing mix with convenience to customers being particularly important. However, it is not difficult for one bank to 'imitate' (locate in close proximity) another at a site that appears to be particularly profitable or strategic.

Projecting the image of an institution with as wide a range of services as a bank is a complex process. The following principles are essential to the formulation of a cohesive marketing strategy:[28]

1. A bank's image is an important non-material asset that should be managed so that it supports and keeps in step with the developing strategy.
2. A distinction must be made between the 'identity' of the bank that is permanent, and its image, which may evolve over the course of time, for example, it may become necessary to increase security in the banking hall in such a way that it makes the image of the bank appear to be austere and unfriendly. This will not, however, affect the bank's identity as a financial institution. It is important that bank management makes this discrimination so that the bank's image retains flexibility within a changing market environment.
3. Managing the bank's image should be the province of a specialised group but this group must have the support and co-operation of all levels of management.
4. Branch personnel constitute a vital link in accurately projecting the bank's image as perceived by the marketing department. If the branches are not convinced that the strategy is correct, even the most carefully devised plan will flounder. It is, therefore, important that personnel are kept informed about what is being proposed and then trained to implement any specific projects. Obviously this is a problem of internal communications within the organisation.

Banks throughout the world are eager to increase the profitability of their branch networks and one means of doing this by extending the range of products and services offered. Thus the all-purpose bank, a sort of supermarket of financial services, is emerging. This causes problems, of course, in creating an image for such a diverse institution as it is not representative to seize on only one aspect or service of the business and then promote the bank on that particular basis to the exclusion of all others. Presenting a visual impression of the image of the bank is the job of the designer. Here a new style of heraldry seems to be developing with more or less abstract logotypes being used to convey an image of the bank to the man-in-the-street.

CHAPTER 4

Advertising and communications

Contents

Advertising is non-personal communication directed at target audiences through various media in order to present and promote products, services and ideas, the cost of which is borne by an identified sponsor or sponsors. Advertising in banking alerts a potential user that a service or product will help him to reach an objective, for example, somewhere to keep his money safely or borrowing to buy a new house.[1] The basic definition of 'communication' is to succeed in conveying one's meaning to others, but within the context of marketing this can be done in a variety of ways, using a variety of media. We will use communications in the marketing sense, that is, as a means of persuasion that results either in some desired action – such as buying a particular product or service – or in a change of attitude or behaviour that is likely to lead eventually to the desired action. The main techniques used for communications are personal selling, promotion and publicity (public relations), all of which will be dealt with separately.

The changes that have taken place in bank advertising from the post-war period to the present day are dramatic. In the past advertising, if done at all, was on a small scale and banks adopted an unprofessional approach. For two principal reasons, however, the banks were forced to stand up and fight for their customers through aggressive advertising and communications:

1. Competition from abroad and from other financial institutions such as the building societies and Post Office Giro meant that the banks could no longer enjoy their near to monopolistic position.
2. The birth of the computer age that opened up a whole new dimension of banking, offering a new range of services to the customer.

Unable to compete on the basis of price and interest rates and deciding, unlike their US counterparts, not to compete on the basis of opening hours, the European and UK banks concentrated on competition via service differentiation, and so a new wave of bank advertising opportunities arose.

The roles of advertising

When they first entered the world of advertising, the banks came up against two basic problems:

(a) banks had a somewhat poor image and most people could not distinguish one bank from another;
(b) the various services available to the public were largely known quantities.

In order to meet these problems the advertising policies of the various banks have evolved through three main stages. In the initial stage the campaigns were based on the bank's name, emphasising strength in order to convey a guarantee of security. In the second phase the advertising tended to be geared towards announcements of new or important services. The basic gimmick was the distinguishing of one bank from the others, by the offer either of exclusive services or of services claimed to be exclusive.

Having passed through these two stages, the banks then began to realise that most of their advertising copy was concerned only with money, and that the image they had been putting across was of a powerful, omnipotent bank that offered a number of goodies. As a result, the bank's image remained highly conventional.[2] Hence the banks have now reached the stage where they have tried to humanise themselves by creating an image designed to spark confidence in the customer and kindle his desire to drop in and pay a call on his banker.[3] This endeavour is essential for three reasons:

(a) what banks have to offer is abstract;
(b) they all offer similar products;
(c) a bank is far more than a mere sales outlet; it is a hub of encounters from which the customer expects to obtain not only advice, but also security and comprehension.

If we take a look at the banks' advertising campaigns going on at the moment, we find these can be divided into two types. First, there is a wide range of specific advertising dealing with the specialist services that banks provide. This advertising is informative and factual, almost always in the press and aimed very largely at a banked audience. 'The bank manager, friend or foe?' is a good example from Barclays.

To the extent that this kind of advertising is designed to help local branches extend the range of services they offer to existing customers, it is obviously useful, but as a method of attracting new business its value is questionable. By far the major part of all 'normal' bank advertising (with the exception of Williams & Glyn's) appears at present to be deployed against the unbanked prospect, or attracting new segments. There are, however, two distinct kinds of unbanked prospect. The first is someone who, it can be assumed, will inevitably open a bank account sooner or later, so that it is chiefly a question of making sure he opens it with your bank when the time comes. Students are a good example, and Barclays and National Westminster have produced two very different approaches to this particular segment. The second kind of unbanked prospect is the C2, high weekly wage earner, born and bred in a cash lifestyle. All the banks (except Williams & Glyn's) seem to believe that they would like this type of person's money flowing through a current account with them.

Only three banks are spending heavily and continuously on television advertising: Lloyds, the Midland and the Trustee Savings Banks (TSB). Lloyds have concentrated their advertising on the 'Black Horse' idea and have managed to come up with a television advertisement that contrives to give the bank an aura of friendliness and accessibility without losing its dignity – a quality that it consciously, and perhaps rightly, values more than do some of the other banks. This campaign has vastly increased the brand-recognition of Lloyds and significantly lowered the age of the new customer acquisition profile, and to that extent is obviously successful. None of the current advertisements, however, appear to be pointed directly at the cash lifestyle prospect. This may well be because the banks believe that the problem is one that cannot be solved by advertising because it involves, for example, the conversion of the weekly wage packet to the monthly cheque. Their advertising, therefore, tends to be basically aimed at making it easier to open an account, rather than at making it desirable to open one at all.

Barclays, having studied the cash lifestyle customer closely, has virtually decided that he is not for them. Barclays also seem to have discovered that their abrasive, rational, *verbal* style of communication is not really suited to television and have now moved out of it altogether.

Williams & Glyn's having fewer branches and a higher proportion of corporate customers, has decided to ignore the unbanked prospect altogether, let alone the cash lifestyle prospect, and concentrate on attracting the small businessman. In 1979 Williams & Glyn's decided to use a sort of 'Mark Telford', BBC persona 'Mr Wagstaff' to convey the idea that the bank is not the stuffy mausoleum that some people may think. Its advertisements featured Mr Wagstaff helping out with his customers' problems. As the small businessman is potentially a personal account holder as well, the copy in some instances was written to link the services offered by the bank to both.

The advertising of the Midland Bank is, in some ways, the most interesting of all. With its trendy, winning-team commercial they make a real attempt to reach the young unbanked prospect, with the cash lifestyle upbringing on his own ground. Overall, certainly the expenditure on advertising is now considerable. In 1976 the 'big four' and the Trustee Savings Bank spent £2.6 million on this form of promotion.[4] This growth of activity in advertising results from the development of the marketing concept in banking, the recruitment of marketers to middle management, and the recognition of the increasing banking potential of the unbanked wage earner. However, it should be noted that not all the major banks spend heavily on advertising; it has been suggested[5] that the highest spenders are Lloyds, the Midland, and the Trustee Savings Bank, while Barclays appears to have decided that it is a less important element in the communications mix.

The principal mission of advertising is to help move the consumer to a bank. Its basic role is to inform, while at the same time it is intended to persuade; it alerts a potential user that a service or product will help him reach an objective. What, when and how to advertise, however, should be determined only *after* the bank's objectives, as well as customers' needs, have been determined via market research.

The types of advertising that a bank may adopt will depend upon its short- and long-term objectives. For example, a bank that is attempting to achieve a long-term build-up of its name will be particularly interested in institutional advertising. On the other hand, a bank that is more interested in building up a brand name would adopt a policy of brand advertising. Whether a bank's objective is to create an institutional or brand name image for itself, it will also be involved in a certain amount of classified advertising, that is, providing information about a special sale, service or event.

Thus the two major types of advertising that would be appropriate in the banking industry are: (i) institutional advertising, (ii) brand advertising. Irrespective of which of the two is adopted, the same considerations underlie each choice.

These considerations are as follows:

1. *Budget.* In bank marketing, as much as in any other industry, it is not simply a question of getting a message across, nor even of getting a message across in a way that stimulates action; it is necessary to relate the cost of the communication to the benefit accruing to the organisation as a result.
2. *The target audience.* In order to persuade people to buy a product or service, or at least let them know it is available, the banker needs to know the type of individual, family group, or large organisation that would be interested in buying it. He also needs to decide who will be responsible (or at least contribute to) for making the purchasing decisions.
3. *The message.* Having identified the target audience, the message content must be such that it will produce the desired response from the target audience. The most common formulation of the message content in banking is rational appeal: appeals directed to the rational self-interest of the target audience. They attempt to show that the product or service will yield the expected functional benefits.

The persuasive effect of a communication is affected not only by its content but also by the manner in which it is structured. This includes the process of designing an effective marketing message with a very precise understanding, agreed between the originator and the professional communicator, on the specific news or claims to be conveyed and the general impression about the bank and its services that the message should reinforce. The message must be kept clear and simple.

Care must also be taken in deciding whether the message structure should be conclusion drawing – that is, should the communicator draw a definite conclusion for the audience or leave it to them, or whether a certain amount of ambiguity should be left so that the audience can draw its own conclusion. The order in which arguments are presented is also crucial and in deciding upon the final structure of the message it must also be remembered that in order to maintain the attention of the target audience the message must feature the words or pictures of something that will be of interest to that audience.

The remaining task in message development is to choose the most effective symbols to implement the message content and structure. Of course, the choice of format is limited according to what media are chosen.

Non-personal channels of communication are media that carry influence without involving direct contact. The most appropriate channel will depend on the size of the advertising budget and the size and nature of the target audience. Whatever approach is chosen, the bank can be sure that the customer will be less interested in buying the product than the bank will be in selling it.

Figure 4.1 Advertising and communication mix in banking

The major issues and types of advertising and communications in banking are presented in Figure 4.1.

Institutional advertising

Institutional advertising generates the long-term build-up of a bank's name. This can be broken down into two aspects:

(a) promotion of the banking image as a whole;
(b) promotion of the products to be offered by the bank, but major emphasis is placed on the bank's name.

In other words, by using institutional advertising the bank is seeking, through its marketing communications, to build an impression upon the customer of the bank and also to impress the customer who wants the best range of financial services.

Barclays Bank seems to favour the 'umbrella' approach of using the bank name to identify some of its main consumer products, for example: Barclaycard, Barclayloan and Barclaybank.

The reason why institutional advertising has been so important is because of the increasing effort to break down the old impression that banks are impersonal institutions with no interst in their customers as people. Few customers have much understanding of the finance industry. There is a deep in-built suspicion of financial institutions based on confusion and a deep-seated mistrust of money institutions that has not been helped by the generally secretive and often patronising nature of many banking practices. Since services offered by banks are abstract, and they all offer similar products, customers expect to obtain from banks not only advice but also security and comprehension of their financial problems. It is consequently important that before the customer ever sets foot inside the bank he has a positive image of the selected bank branch. Projecting the 'image' of an institution with as wide a range of services as a bank is a complex process. It is a problematic area, however, as with such an extensive range of products and services it is difficult to create a single uniform image. An institutional advertising approach as a means of bank image projection has become particularly relevant owing to the increase in competition between banks and from other financial institutions. Banks are now attempting to attract 20 per cent of the unbanked segment of the market, the majority of which are from the lower socio-economic groups.

Bank advertising has been until lately uncreative. This lack of creativity may have been due to a convention among bankers that a bank's image through its advertising must be conservative, straight arrow, soft sell, or no real sell at all. There was a feeling that a creative approach would 'degrade' the bank, its officers, personnel and maybe even its customers. There was a fear that potential customers may feel that such a bank would be frivolous and unreliable in looking after money.

In recent years, however, this philosophy has been proved incorrect since creative advertising need not be bad or destructive, but rather it can be contemporary. Realisation by the banker that the public changes its interests and attitudes is helpful for the acceptance of contemporary creative advertising. A creative approach is one effective way of being different and outstanding from the rest, and yet not losing dignity or the trust/faith factor that is an essential and almost implicit factor in banking.

Such creativity can take the following forms:

1. Establishing a modern logo, or signature, or symbol (e.g. the 'Black Horse' for Lloyds).
2. Establishing a spokesman, human or otherwise, for the bank. The TSB in particular have favoured this approach of communicating their services through either famous television actors whose characters are such that they generate a feeling of trust, belief and friendliness, or through ordinary people with whom the audience can identify. On the other hand, the Ulster Bank (a subsidiary of National Westminster) uses its logo to create a friendly cartoon character that appears on television.
3. Using a catch-phrase or motto that is believable, yet not cliché-ridden.

Institutional advertising is thus an integral part of any bank's advertising and communicative planning. The approaches that have been discussed serve to attract the attention of the target customers and to create an image that is honest, friendly and welcoming.

Another form of institutional advertising – the 'umbrella' approach – that is, of using the parent name to identify some of the bank's consumer products, will be discussed under the heading 'brand advertising' below.

Brand advertising

Brand advertising is advertising of services and is similar to the 'umbrella' approach. It aims to the recognition of the bank's name but it is also advertising the bank's different services; the one reinforces the other. Brand advertising follows closely in the footsteps of institutional advertising. Having attracted the attention of the customer, or at least having created an awareness, it is then necessary to hold the customer's interest by offering something that will appeal and will be of benefit to him. These individual campaigns must be compatible in tone and presentation with the image the bank has created, so that they reinforce one another.

The problems in brand advertising are to whom to advertise and how to advertise. The bank serves a mass of people: every age, ethnic and cultural group is represented. The 'product difference' is a tool much sought after by communicators. This entails finding a difference in one bank's savings scheme from every other bank's saving scheme. Or if it is not actually very different, trying to find a means of making it look legitimately different and exploiting it. It is fairly easy to create a superficial visual difference and particularly if the scheme is presented as a package complete with brand name, brochures, and integrated sales promotion. But to be different only in superficial respects will not be very successful when there is a serious decision to be made by the customer. The problem is to find a product difference that is both genuine and important enough to the reader for it matter to him. One approach combines the concepts of consumer benefit, reason why, and product difference into one concept: the *Unique Selling Proposition* (USP). The essence of this approach is that the communicator should find a central theme that describes an important benefit to the user or purchaser of the product that can be found only in this one service. This approach has been particularly favoured by banks in the past two years, as they have realised that the almost impossible task of advertising is to encourage people to open an account. If, however, the bank cannot achieve this combination, or it is not available, the recourse taken is to be first to fasten on to a claim that others could also well advance and by constant reiteration identify it with that particular bank or product. This latter means of identifying a product with a particular bank is very important in the banking industry which has such an intense level of competition that almost any initiative that is taken – unless it is immediately exploited to the full – will be matched by a competitor.

Who is the target audience? Whereas institutional advertising can be aimed at the whole population, the advertising pf particular products has to be much more selective because it has to show the consumer will benefit from the service. A 65-year-old pensioner is not going to be interested in a scheme that promises to organise a student grant. Traditionally, the limited amount of bank advertising that was undertaken attempted to cater for those who were already banked, has a sound financial background and, more importantly, had plenty of money to spend. The result was the practice of 'tomb-stone' advertising which recorded the name, address and capital resources of the institution in question, but nothing else. Today, however, greater competition in the retail market has meant increasing market segmentation with the banks aiming at specific target markets. One of the most clearly identified and most highly developed segments is the student market. Barclays was the first to aim its marketing effort directly at students, advertising a variety of incentives and free banking services.

Message content

Obviously the content must relate to the audience that the bank is trying to attract. Creativity is an extremely important aspect of advertising, although bank managers tend to be reserved about its value. An advertisement portraying Barbara Woodhouse is unlikely to appeal to the student market whereas 'Spandau Ballet' are unlikely to appeal to those in their sixties and over.

The message itself should be short and clear – too many people fall into the trap of ruining a good advertisement by adding additional information. A simple, clear message can be remembered – a long and complicated one cannot. For most people, whether as individuals or as managers of business, finance is often a difficult and complicated subject. The banker can easily forget that what is simple to him may be incomprehensible to his customers. Technical language needs to be translated into simpler terms when the banker seeks to communicate with his customers. It is also important, however, to find a level of simplicity that does not appear to be condescending.

The time for which a particular advertisement should run depends on the media used and the amount of repetition in any particular period. Repetition plays an essential part in getting all but the most dramatic messages to the target audience. To avoid losing the attention of those who are listening, a useful feature is to present the message in different ways through different media. The communicator of the advertisement often feels that within a few days/weeks the advertisement is becoming boring, so he stops it or changes it too soon. If this happens, the advertisement has been a waste of time, money and effort. It is only by repetition that some sort of impression will be made on audiences.

Advertising channels

The media that a bank chooses for advertising will depend upon its budget. A bank will choose the most cost-effective vehicle for carrying the message to a target customer segment. Depending on the budget and the size and nature of a bank's target audience, there is a considerable range of media to choose from, each with its own characteristics.

The TSB's advertising distinguishing feature is 'cosiness' and it exploits the fact that it is oriented towards the cash life style market already, with savings accounts, so that they can make a start by converting established savers into current account customers. (The cash lifestyle market refers mainly to those members of the working class who receive their wages in weekly cash rather than monthly cheques.) Much of the TSB's advertising is above-the-line, television and radio advertising.

Basically there are two types of advertising suitable to banks: 'above-the-line' media and 'below-the-line' advertising.

Above-the-line advertising

This consists of channels of communication such as television, radio, newspapers, posters, magazines, cinema, etc.

(1) *Television* is probably one of the most popular means of advertising[6] although it is the most expensive. It is the medium of the masses and combines the attention-getting attributes of sound, picture, colour and movement so it offers the opportunity to show a financial product or service and demonstrate it in actual use. It has also repeatedly proved its capacity to stimulate a quick response. Recent research indicates that as education and income levels decrease, television watching increases. The disadvantages of this medium, however, apart from the cost, are that it cannot easily sustain a long or complicated message and it tends to be unselective in the audience it reaches. This latter disadvantage means that many banks in isolated or geographically specific and confined markets may find that a good deal of their coverage is wasted with this advertising channel.

Over the past ten years a combination of the impact of television and the creative media skills of the advertising industry has increased the public's awareness of the range of financial services offered by banks. The advertising budgets of clearing banks have increased almost sevenfold in the last ten years, with nearly half of this being spent on television in 1980, according to Media Expenditure Analysis Ltd, 'Ten Year Trends' (Table 4.1).

What is interesting is the growing percentage of the overall advertising budget being allocated to television. In 1971 the banks spent 4 per cent of their budgets on television but this has substantially increased over the

Table 4.1 Clearing bank advertising expenditure between 1971 and 1980

Year	*Total advert-ising (000's)*	*TV £000s*	*TV %*
1971 (Index: 100)	2,615	105	4.0
1975 (Index: 216)	5,650	2,447	43.3
1980 (Index: 683)	17,859	8,649	48.4

decade to account for twelve times this share.

(2) *Radio* is as unselective as television in its audience, and cinema going is a habit that is rapidly declining. For the bank with a geographically restricted catchment area, posters, local radio or the local press may be the most economical.

(3) *Posters* tend to deliver a message repeatedly since they do not change places, but the message reaches virtually the same people over and over again. As we have said, however, repetition is good in advertising and posters force the wording of the message to be brief. As Lawson and Netherton[7] point out, the atmosphere accociated with poster sites is generated from the immediate physical environment. Poster sites at major international airports or busy railway terminuses and junctions may have an air of movement, work, time and pressure, while those in the City or West End will have a similar air of business and well-being.

(4) *Newspapers*, on the other hand, particularly the financial pages, are more selective. Each newspaper has its own readership and each has different editorial characteristics that can be expected to have some influence on the readers' attitudes. The disadvantage of newspapers, however, is that often only black and white presentation is available, and therefore it is difficult to create a dramatic effect – or to stand out – from the other competitors offering similar financial services. Advertising banking services in specialist magazines has a very limited scope – the readership is narrow and the cost can be disproportionate to the number of readers reached.

(5) *Direct mail*. While television is widely used for institutional advertising, that is, for promoting the bank's image, direct mail is coming into its own as a useful target-oriented tool for banks, particularly for advertising specific services. Direct mail is an inexpensive personal approach to selling, particularly for financial service institutions who must in any case communicate regularly with their customers to inform them of a new service or one that is particularly relevant to their particular individual

requirements. It offers banks a chance to be creative beyond the limitations of other media. Through census figures and other demographic breakdowns the opportunity is available to pinpoint exactly those people who the bank want to inform and eventually sell to on a one-to-one basis. As a means of reaching *new* customers, however, direct mail can be relatively costly, unless the communication is sufficiently persuasive and the mailing list sufficiently reliable to produce a good response rate.

Below-the-line advertising

This type of advertising forms a major part of the bank's activities and comprises leaflets, pamphlets, explanatory guides and manuals that can be used to support the selling activity of a particular service. It is difficult to draw a definite distinction between advertising and promotion in this area, but the banks place heavy reliance on such activities presuming that when customers come into their bank they will look at the numerous pamphlets offering different services and take away those that may interest them. At the point of sale these communications are useful information tools and reminders, but only in so far as they back up personal selling.

Below-the-line advertising has the advantage of being cheap and very easy to produce, but it has severe limitations in that it must be used discreetly; it does not attract new customers, but merely offers existing customers more services and it depends largely on personal selling for its effectiveness.

The choice of advertising channels for any particular bank will depend largely on its marketing strategy, its target audience and primarily upon its budget. Whatever the combination chosen, all advertising should be well planned and co-ordinated otherwise its value will be greatly diminished. It was a lack of planning and a lack of understanding of the art of advertising in the past that led many bank managers to maintain a conservative approach and suspicious attitude to its value. Of course, in spite of planning, extraneous factors can intervene and cause the shelving of advertising campaigns. For example, a government notice of a rise in interest rates caused one bank's newly created advertising campaign to be shelved recently.

The effect of advertising and communications on banks' employees

In spite of the increased attention given to advertising in general, little attention has been given to the impact of advertising on banks' employees. Advertising can have two effects on employees:

(1) *Indirect effect* that depends largely upon the contact between the bank's employees and the person exposed to the bank's advertising campaign. The problem in the banking industry revolves around the co-ordination of a vast number of branches belonging to each of the main clearing banks and the growing range of facilities offered. The Midland, for example, operates 2,500 branches employing some 27,000 staff. How is it possible to train and motivate an army of clerical and executive staff? The tendency has been for the banks to follow the trend for greater specialisation at the branch level.

Due to the nature of the banking sector, banks must deal with customers on a personal basis. Customer expectations are particularly important in shaping the nature of the close customer-employee interaction, common in such service companies. The employee therefore must be of service to the customer and the bank in two respects:

1. In helping to arrange and look after the customer's financial affairs and therby furthering the bank's sales. (An in-depth knowledge of the range of facilities offered is essential and so too is a knowledge of the advertising employed by the bank. If a customer comes into a bank asking for the service that has just been offered and the employee has not seen the advertisement then the result might be the loss of a potential sale.)
2. In encouraging the customer to come into the bank in the first place, by appearing friendly and welcoming and thus promoting the bank's image.

(2) *Direct effect*. A bank's advertising and communications may also cause direct effects on employees. Direct employee effects are those that result from employees seeing or hearing an advertisement for their employer which presents information that the employee may relate to their own work experience in the bank.

These effects arise when advertisements: (i) create an expectation as to how the employee will behave towards customers, (ii) convey an impression about how the employer treats employees, (iii) makes claims about product quality or employee performance. If any of the claims are inconsistent with operating procedures and internal structure, then again negative effects will be generated in employees. They will be put under stress by trying to meet customer expectations that have been raised to an impossible level and will feel the bank is being untruthful in its communications programmes that will lead to dissatisfaction and cynicism. Even a campaign initiated to raise employee morale will fail if the bank does not understand and appreciate how its employees are affected by advertising.

As bank employees are the bank to the customers they serve, it is essential that the advertising claims made by the bank are realistic. Advertisements should therefore be announced internally before they are launched and the employees consulted. If use is made of advertising campaigns to launch new services, care should be taken that all areas that will be affected by the advertising have had time to prepare for their introduction. During and after the advertising campaign employees should again be consulted as a constant source of feedback, as they represent a direct link with the customer.

If, however, advertising and communications are carefully handled, taking employee considerations into account, they can play a vital part in boosting morale and sales effort. Employees are proud to work for a bank that offers good services and backs up its claims by maintaining high standards through an efficient internal structure and through genuine concern for customers and employees. By supporting its staff the bank can in turn rely on the staff supporting the bank's advertising campaigns.

Advertising and communications can produce negative and positive effects on employees and the importance of staff attitudes should be constantly to the fore when considering the type of campaign to launch. In the banking industry where the product and services are largely dependent on the staff, it must be remembered that the staff have the power to make or break the bank.

Promotions

The term promotions is used to refer to the use of persuasive information which, in conjunction with other elements of the marketing mix, relates to the target market. The bank has to decide how information about the organisation and its services will be disseminated. Four elements of the marketing communications mix are generally recognised:[8]

1. *Advertising* – paid non-personal presentation and promotion of goods and services by an identified sponsor, for example, television bank advertising.
2. *Personal selling* – verbal presentation of persuasive information to potential customers. In the banks this is generally confined to the branch manager and his staff.
3. *Publicity* – non-personal stimulation of demand through news that is not paid for by sponsor. In banking, newspaper reports give various types of information about the banks.
4. *Sales promotions* – short-term incentive to encourage use of a service. In banking these include the use of book tokens, pictorial cheque books and the provision of special services for groups. Sales promotions, or promotions in short, are discussed in this section.

Sales promotions can be defined as short-term incentives to encourage the purchase or sale of a product or service. The sales promotions have two distinctive qualities:

1. *'Bargain' chance.* Many sales promotion tools have an attention-getting quality that can break through habits of buyer inertia towards a particular product or service, telling the buyers of a chance that will not be available again to purchase something special. The disadvantage of promotions, however, is that although they appeal to a wide range of buyers many of those buyers tend to be less loyal to any particular brand in the long run.
2. *Product demeaning.* If promotions are used too frequently and carelessly the potential buyer may be led to wonder whether the bank's service is reliable or reasonably priced.

Thus given these conflicting ideas on the benefits of sales promotions, a bank's decision must be based upon the relevance and usefulness of promotional campaigns and their cost-effectiveness. Ultimately, however, it does appear that sales promotion is most effective where used in conjunction with advertising.

Bankers identify a number of objectives sought in using promotions. The primary ones are:

(a) to attract new customer current and deposit accounts;
(b) to increase the level of deposits in deposit accounts thereby increasing the bank's share of savings pounds;
(c) to lower the cost of acquiring new deposits by seeking to avoid direct price competition with other financial institutions.

Secondary objectives, some of which overlap with the primary ones, include: (i) reaching specific market segments for current accounts and deposit accounts, for example the female market, (ii) modifying the bank's image, (iii) obtaining deposits when needed by the bank for its loan operations.

An aspect of banking sales promotions that is not particularly well developed in the UK is that of 'give-aways' (or premiums). One area, however, where such inducements have featured largely in some campaigns has been the student market. The value of the inducement has been relatively small – around £3 or £4, and limited to book tokens or half-price rail cards. Bannister's study[9] reveals that book tokens had little impact and falls well behind location, advice of parents, friends, relatives and the availability of automatic cash dispensers when determining students' preferences. However, Lloyds in 1979 gave an option of either a book token or a half-price rail card. Normally they give away around 28,000 tokens but in 1979 they gave away 42,000 tokens and half-price cards.[10] This gave them 29 per cent of the student banking market and, no doubt, the other banks food for thought.

To be successful, promotions must relate to a real customer need and they must be large enough to act as an incentive to use the service. Although spending on promotion was relatively low in the USA as compared with that on advertising, there does appear to be more initiative shown in this field. It has been suggested that in the USA incentives range from a Mercedes 450 S.L. for the depositor of $150,000 to 'free' carpeting with a $1,200 home improvement loan.[11] There may well be scope for development in this form of promotion in the banking system in the UK. However, the cost-effectiveness of increasing promotional activity is probably unknown in this country but could warrant some market research by the banks. In the USA McConnell[12] reports that since 1945 more than one in four banks have tried premium promotions and only 5 per cent were dissatisfied with its results. Although it was felt necessary to enter a number of caveats – in relation to the North American experience in banking promotions – recent research indicates the followng:

1. New demand deposits opened by bank customers receiving a premium perform as well for the bank during the six months following their opening as those deposits not attracted by such a premium.
2. New time deposits opened during premium programmes, although showing significantly lower retention rates,[13] perform as well as no-premium-offered accounts, when evaluated in terms of changes in six-month balances.
3. Customers attracted by a free premium offer are just as loyal as those customers attracted to the reduced-price premium.

More recently attempts have been made in the UK to reach an even younger market by giving away free 'piggy banks', etc. to children[14] who win competitions and the TSB has aimed to start at the very beginning by giving away free bibs for the babies of account holders. Obviously the success of such early promotional campaigns will not be known for several years.

Personal selling

Personal selling is another element of the bank promotion mix and as it is associated with the bank manager and his staff, there is almost a traditional reluctance on the part of banking staff to enter this field. At present it seems doubtful that they see their role as sales promoters. Apart from historical explanations this may also be a reflection of the bank training system that may neglect/avoid this potential and/or it may reflect the way in which the organisation of the branch is structured. At the average UK bank, the counter clerk has a number of tasks to perform and perhaps it is unreasonable to expect any more than a prompt service. Personal selling might be more effective if the banker service was less impersonal; the concept of the 'personal banker' has been developed in some US banks with the idea of a better perception of customer needs so that appropriate services can be offered. There is also the possibility of many counter clerks being replaced by more qualified people who can offer advice on the appropriate bank service.

The personal selling in banking plays, however, an important role in two main areas:

1. *'The banked'.* Personal selling is necessary to look after those who already have an account but need help in looking after their money.
2. *'The unbanked'.* Personal selling is necessary to persuade the unbanked to open an account.

Personal selling is defined as the oral presentation – in a conversation with one or more prospective purchasers – for the purpose of making sales. This is perhaps the most important element in the communication process of the banking industry. It can be and is used for many purposes. For example: (i) creating product/service awareness, (ii) developing product/service preference, (iii) negotiating prices and other terms (for example, bank charges are negotiable), (iv) closing a sale, (v) providing post-sale reinforcement and reassurance to bank customers.

The advantages of personal selling are as follows:

1. *Personal confrontation.* Personal selling enables an immediate and interactive relationship between the buyer and seller. This means that each party can observe the other's characteristics, needs and wants and react accordingly. Each party has the opportunity to inspire trust, honesty and responsibility, willingness to help or otherwise, which in turn can help.
2. *Cultivation of bank – customer relationships.* Personal selling permits the growth of relationships to a level greater than a mere matter-of-fact selling. The sales person has the opportunity to win over the buyer.
3. *Response.* In contrast to advertising which is impersonal, personal selling makes the buyer feel under some obligation to purchase the bank's service that the sales representative has gone to some length to discuss. At the very least he has a greater need to attend to what is being said.

In view of the importance of personal selling the salesforce needs to be trained not only in the art of selling, but also they must be aware of all the services available and able to explain clearly what each service offers. They must also be aware of the needs of their individual customers so that they can either refer customers to the branch manager, or suggest appropriate services themselves. Staff must live up to the bank's image of trust, responsibility and friendliness. In order to meet these requirements a mixture of empathy and ego-drive is required. Empathy is vital in order to understand the customers' reservations and problems – ego-drive is required so that the salesperson will make a sale in the end, that is, strike a bargain, as near as possible to the salesperson's goals.

In banking, the customer's needs and motivations are likely to be complex and his ability to assess alternative courses of action without professional assistance is likely to be limited, so the bank's salesperson must know his customer, as well as his product. This is particularly important as the sale of financial services is not based on a floating relationship, but it is the beginning of the development of a lasting relationship between bank and customer. Once a customer has chosen his bank he is unlikely to change and so it is up to the salesforce to enhance the bank's reputation by looking after their customers.

In the age when banking has become increasingly impersonal due to the introduction of computerised systems, Barclays was perhaps the first to see the importance in banking of the personal sale and decided to opt for a more personal touch. They introduced a sort of 'money doctor' system whereby each customer was delegated to a member of staff who was personally responsible for all of that customer's financial affairs. The service was based on the common-sense premise that customers like to think that someone in the branch is personally interested – and responsible for – their financial affairs.

The most important need is to establish a more permanent tie with the large section of the unbanked and this was done by the major clearing banks by opening small branch banks in factories and universities. By concentrating on such a small segment of the market, personal selling has a chance to excel in areas where relative suspicion and distrust of financial services are almost ingrained and where the personal selling effort must be doubled.

The success rate of the personal sell in attracting new accounts is relatively high, particularly in so far as attracting young people is concerned. A younger counter staff helps to eradicate the formidable image; educational leaflets and visits distributed throughout the schools create a financial awareness in young people that was not apparent ten years ago. Young people are actively encouraged into the bank and in Finland, for example, they are seen as such an important market segment that one day per week is set aside for schoolchildren to come to the bank and talk to employees.

The need for personal selling is also an important part of bank communications with those who already have an account. Its importance lies in creating an impression of trust, reliance, friendliness and familiarity. From the bank's point of view it is a means of creating a lasting relationship with a customer and consequently being able to offer services that are appropriate. Emphasis in recent years has been placed on helping small businesses, not only by offering financial services, but also by involvement in the affairs of such customers by bank managers in an advisory capacity. The purpose of this is to give the customers sound practical advice and guidance in the principles of financial planning and control.

In accordance with this policy of helping the small businessman, particularly the self-employed, some useful tools are educational leaflets, for example, Lloyds Black Horse Guides, on starting your own business and making a smaller business bigger, seminars for businessmen and special business centres (such as the one operated by the Midland Bank from 1979 which offers personal financial advice from 9.00 a.m. to 5.00 p.m. on Monday to Friday on an appointment basis).

Personal selling is, therefore, an integral part of the communication process in attracting both new customers to the bank and selling more services to those who are already banked. It can work in conjunction with sales and promotional activities to clinch a deal; it can be used to actively seek out new customers and it can be used to reassure existing ones. It is a technique that demands from the bank's managerial and non-managerial staff the following:

(a) a knowledge of all existing services (or at least a knowledge of to whom the customer should be referred for further information);
(b) an understanding of customer problems;
(c) an ability to solve the customers' problems and persuade the customer to accept the solution.

Publicity

Publicity is perhaps the least controllable element of the communications mix, since it is the media who will tend to decide what is newsworthy. In the so-called quality press banks obtain considerable publicity, although in the popular newspapers publicity is often negative from the banks' point of view. High bank profits usually bring forth adverse comments as do proposals to increase bank charges; seldom is the bank seen as a vital national institution.

The definition of publicity is: the activity of securing editorial space, as divorced from paid space in all media used, viewed or heard by a bank's customers or prospects, for the specific purpose of assisting in the meeting of sales goals. Publicity is part of a larger concept, that of public relations, and it is a tool that is relatively under-utilised in relation to the real contribution it can make. Publicity in many cases can create memorable impacts on public awareness. Probably due to the dramatisation with which it is expressed by the press in this respect, it gains advantages over advertising. One of its main advantages as far as the marketing department is concerned, is the low budget that is required. Although public relations is commonly regarded as unpaid, paid-for advertising has its substantial effect on the public image with which public relations is concerned. An increasing importance is placed on the PR function, so it is increasingly likely that banks will employ staff as press officers, or more generally public affairs officers, whose full-time job will be to actively generate publicity.

Press interest in banks developed in the 1950s and a decade later the banks learned to appreciate that this interest must be intelligently handled or exploited in the banks' favour. The fact that journalists both reflect and influence public opinion makes it important to ensure (as far as possible) that they are well informed. Everyone directly concerned with publicity must be in general sympathy with the press on the one hand, and with the public at large on the other. Information should be objective and accurate.

A similar long-term sponsorship aimed at the young is employed by the Yorkshire Bank. This bank has for some years sponsored sporting competitions, for the young, on a continuing basis. For example, the Yorkshire Bank Trophy and the Yorkshire Bank Squads in swimming have been so successful that Sun Life Assurance has now copied the sponsorship idea on a national basis. Sports sponsorships such as this also obtain free television coverage.

At the Midland Bank the sponsorship programme is planned well in advance and a specific budget allocated. There is a strong link with the marketing side of the bank and projects are agreed that will help to attain certain long-term marketing objectives. The Midland Bank also has an interest in wooing the farming sector through agricultural sponsorship on a regional basis. The bank finds that they are extremely useful in giving the bank local publicity.

Barclays makes a clear distinction between charitable giving, for example, patronage, and commercial sponsorship. With patronage the bank only expects to receive a return in terms of goodwill and no specific business benefit. With commercial sponsorship on the other hand the intention is to see some reward in business development.

Since agriculture is a lucrative sector, Barclays feels that exposure in the farming community, for example, sponsorship of the Royal Smithfield Show, is extremely good for business. On a policy level Barclays thinks it is too restrictive to have a set sponsorship budget and prefers to make decisions on an *ad hoc* basis. One criterion it has tended to use is that of favouring events that move around outside London.

At Lloyds the concept of sponsorship is constantly being reviewed since it considers sponsorship to be a 'blunt' instrument. It is not a precise marketing tool that can be used to achieve a specific objective.

The most widely used opportunities of generating publicity are sponsorship of cultural or sporting activities, competitions, benefit evenings.[15] In the USA banks also sponsor 'walkathons', 'knitathons', bingo games and many other events. By sponsoring such an event the bank achieves three things:

(a) an opportunity to advertise its name via posters (in the sports arena for example);
(b) free publicity (the bank's press officer will call in press photographers to photograph the manager handing over the cheque to the sponsored organisation);
(c) an impression of social responsibility.

This third element is a part of public relations that is used more extensively by US banks than by banks in the UK. Their donations, local and central, to good causes and sponsorship of cultural and welfare bodies are a modest and relatively unobtrusive part of public relations. It is, however, an area to which the main clearing banks are turning attention and which may provide great opportunities for the future. The reasons for broadening their scope in the area of public relations are mainly due to society entering a new era of:

(a) increased consumer awareness;
(b) increased interest in people's well-being;
(c) increasing unemployment.

In the UK, National Westminster, for example, is involved in sponsorship but confines it to socially responsible work, education, charities and the arts. The research done in this field tends to indicate that sponsorship does not have a great direct effect as part of the marketing effort. It does, however, get the name into the right sort of places. For example, National Westminster sponsors the Royal Lifesaving Rescue Skills Scheme, which has been very successful and has made its name known in a very large number of schools.[16]

The banks, therefore, should be looking forward to this newer concept of public relations – sponsorship – that has to do with community involvement and commitment and will represent the sort of activity that can maximise marketing opportunity in this emerging society. Exploration in this area has begun on a fairly small scale by running educational competitions for children, distribution of leaflets concerning information on how to fill in application forms for a job, how to conduct yourself at an interview, etc. Clearly, publicity forms an integral part of such a public relations activity and favourable media coverage and public reaction will reinforce it, if the programme is good. However, it is important that the bank responsible for sponsoring a social programme does not wallow in self-glory, as this will create a bad press release. Unbiased third-party publicity and individual opinion will allow the customer to build up for himself an appreciation of the bank.

Publicity can, therefore, be seen to be a useful means of communications, if it is properly and carefully manipulated. Its qualities include high credibility, it can dramatise the information and it can catch the reader off-guard, therefore creating a more positive impression. If utilised knowledgeably, it provides a free means of stimulating demand for banks' services by planting commercially significant news about the bank's services through various media: radio, television or newspapers. It does require, however, a constant effort by the bank to maintain high standards of customer service and a readiness to answer all inquiries – one slip and the bank can be sure that the press will be just as ready to generate bad publicity.

The contribution of advertising and communications to the bank marketing programme

As in any other industry that advertises its products and services, very little is known in the banking sector about the actual success of individual banks' advertising campaigns, or the overall contribution the advertising and promotions make to the bank's sales figures. Most of the resources budgeted for advertising are spent on pre-testing or on launching the campaign. Relatively little tends to be spent on post-testing the effect of the advertising campaigns. Although tests can be done on the evaluation of advertisements, as far as creating customer awareness is concerned, it is relatively more difficult to relate this to an actual purchase of the product or service advertised – that is, did the customer go to the bank to purchase the service *as a result* of the advertisement?

The fact that the banks do place so much emphasis on advertising and communications alone suggests the need for its continuation. Advertising is necessary if only to compete with other financial institutions. The success of advertising depends on the knowledge of the target segment and extraneous factors, such as economic climate and competitors' activities. An example of how these factors should be understood and manipulated can be seen in the TSB's recent launch of its new trustcard.

The TSB customers have a very different demographic profile in comparison to those of joint-stock banks. The TSB customers are largely blue-collar workers, older and based in the more northern parts of England and Scotland. The characteristics of this segment are: (i) cash orientated, (ii) suspicious of credit facilities and the banks that offer them as they feel they are encouraged to overspend and borrow money, (iii) uneducated in the financial subtleties of credit transfer.

The TSB aimed to create at least some awareness of the trustcard among the public at large. A television campaign was launched that displayed the card and a handshake to typify trust and abolish views that the bank was out to seize money. In order to reinforce the main theme of trust, the commercial employed a number of carefully planned stimuli or signals such as the avoidance of the word 'credit'. The film was also of an educational nature and the campaign was supported by reflecting the same signals in the press, in display material within the bank and also in the direct mail that was sent to likely trustcard holders.

Unfortunately, at the time of the launch, the government restricted the extent of credit card advertising as one means of reducing the growth of the money supply and the TSB had to compensate for this by considerably increasing the concentration of its effort through personal selling. Again, no accurate figures can give account of the actual impact made by the campaign although the ban has since been lifted and the growth of cardholders has been continuous and pretty well in line with the original targets (in two and a half years the TSB put on 1.3 million cardholders most of whom, according to market research, were of the market segment the bank was aiming at). It does, however, serve as an illustration of the importance of considering the various factors that surround communications activity.

It seems to be a fact that once a bank has created an image for itself, prestige and good reputation follow, and services will sell themselves unless this image is shattered. For example, Barclaycard, shown by market research to be the most prestigious piece of plastic after the American Express card, spent only £850,000 in advertising in 1980 and obtained 600,000 new cardholders. However, Barclaycard's image problem caused it to launch the first television campaign in two years, to clarify the misconception commonly held by many that a potential cardholder has to bank with Barclays to get a card.

To conclude, advertising plays an important part in the bank's marketing programme, although it is unclear to what extent it contributes directly to sales. Its functions are, however, as follows:

1. *It keeps a bank's name in the foreground.* In the light of increased competition from building societies, foreign banks and other financial institutions, it is essential that the public should be aware of the bank's existence.
2. *It can create an image for the bank.* Again, increased competition has forced the banks to take the job of attracting new customers seriously. By creating a friendly, caring and yet competent image, they may be able to break down some of the reservations that the unbanked have for the banking industry.
3. *It reinforces the point of purchase communications and personal selling.* Below-the-line advertising enables people to walk into the bank of their choice and pick up leaflets and pamphlets that interest them. It also enables employees to refer their customers to comprehensive guides that lay out in a simple form all the information they require.
4. *It motivates staff and boosts morale.* Employees like to work for a bank that is in the public eye and offers good services to its customers.

A brief example of how one bank – the Ulster Bank (a subsidiary of the National Westminster Bank) – combined the various advantages of advertising, promotion, publicity, personal selling, public relations and employee satisfaction, when it launched an apparently extremely successful painting competition for schoolchildren, is presented below.

The main objectives of the Ulster Bank were to educate children in the importance of money and savings, to abolish the fear that children have of entering a bank and to encourage them to open an account with the Ulster Bank. In support of advertising in the local press, bank staff were deployed around various schools in the province armed with leaflets and specially prepared talks to educate the children in the value and importance of money. The painting competition entry forms were distributed at the same time. One side of the sheet consisted of the bank's savings bank promotion gift 'Henry Hippo' outside an Ulster Bank with the bank's logo clearly displayed. The other side of the sheet was left blank and older children were encouraged to design their own Henry Hippo advertisement. The best advertisements appeared in newspapers with the name of the winner underneath.

Completed entries were to be brought into any branch of the Ulster Bank. Winners of either competition won large cuddly versions of Henry Hippo and substantial cash prizes. All entrants were encouraged to come into the bank and with as little as £1.00 could open an account and walk away with a free Henry Hippo savings bank.

Winners of the competition were photographed beside their huge cuddly Henry Hippos and with a bank representative presenting the money. Although the results of such a campaign, which is being repeated for the second year, will not be known for several years, it has succeeded in the opening of a substantial number of accounts already. Real success will depend on the retention rate of these accounts although it is a fact that once with a bank the majority of customers remain loyal to it. The bank, however, has successfully achieved several objectives:

(a) the deployment of its sales staff into the school has generated employee enthusiasm;
(b) by being in personal contact with the children, bank staff were able to educate them as to the importance and benefits of looking after money;
(c) as well as being of community service, the competition also generated publicity for the bank;
(d) by making the branch banks responsible for collecting the forms, children *had* to come into a bank to deliver their forms; this produced an opportunity for direct relations with the sales staff giving them in turn an opportinity to allay suspicion and fears;
(e) the Henry Hippo prizes were photographed well and constituted free publicity for the bank and again boosted employee morale;

(f) the promotional tool of giving a free Henry Hippo with as little as a £1.00 deposit in a new account attracted additional customers.

This campaign illustrates the thought and planning that the banks are now putting into their marketing strategies. Competition is so great that interest and openings are being concentrated on an increasingly younger market and advertising is becoming more important within the bank's planning and marketing departments.

Product development and pricing

Contents

The special nature of the banking industry creates similar problems with regard to both product development and pricing. Banks offer a wide range of services that consumers use to different extents, in effect creating a product that is customised to the individual consumer. Hence banks offer a highly non-standard product at a highly non-uniform price.

This non-standard nature of product and price creates communication problems that tend to reduce the extent to which either can be used creatively as a marketing tool. Therefore, a common thread running through this chapter is the need to develop both products and pricing systems that are readily intelligible to the bank customers and can therefore be compared with the products and prices of competing banks, building societies and other financial institutions.

Product development and segmentation

Kotler[1] has defined product as 'anything that can be offered to a market for attention, acquisition, use or consumption'. The banks are essentially offering a range of services; these services are generally regarded as intangible although degrees of tangibility have been recognised by Wilson.[2] Thus in relation to banking a cash loan to a customer might be regarded as a different kind of service than, for example, advice on financial investments to a customer.

Initially the service offered by the banks to their customers was a safe place to 'store' their money for which the banks might pay to customers an interest on their deposits, and a service whereby customers could borrow money at a particular interest rate and on certain conditions. Essentially, banks all offered the same service so that product differentiation in terms of these services is difficult. What the banks appear to have done is to add new services (products) to their range so as to make the bank more attractive to a greater range of potential customers and to existing customers. Some of these services, such as credit cards, are directly related to 'traditional' banking, but others like legal advice, tax services, etc. may be regarded as non-banking activities.

These kinds of services may be perceived in a different way by different market segments; thus, for example, the credit card might be mainly considered as a convenient method of paying bills by one socio-economic group (higher income) while it could be perceived as a way of obtaining credit or delaying payment by another group (lower income). In this case a particular service would have attractions for more than one market segment.

The banking product

The 'products' of a bank are essentially services. Any satisfaction the customer gets from the performance of the service rather than from the ownership of a good. Banks are in the business of marketing cash security; cash accessibility; monetary transfers; and time, to enable customers' wants to be satisfied today without waiting until tomorrow when their own savings are higher.

It is no simple matter to define the product in the context of the banking industry. Two extreme definitions might be as follows:

1. Each individual service constitutes a separate product. In this view banks are in the business of marketing some 250 separate products.[3]
2. The entire banking service constitutes a single product.

Clearly the first definition is oversimplistic, in that the consumer tends to perceive and purchase banking services in packages. He would very rarely, for example, use one bank for clearing cheques, and another for standing orders, overdraft facilities, or financial advice. As the services are purchased as a package, it is realistic to view the product as the entire package, rather than as the individual services. In the words of one author: 'It is the overall package of lending facilities, convenience, and other ancillary services . . . on which banks have to compete.'[4] Equally clearly the second definition is too broad, in that a bank may sell aspects of its service range to entirely different markets.

There can be no 'right' answer to this problem of defining the banking product. Any reasonable definition must lie somewhere between the two extremes mentioned above. For the purposes of this discussion a banking product is defined as a service or package of services that: (i) is typically provided for any one consumer by one bank only (that is, the customer does not normally purchase different parts of the package from different banks), and (ii) is aimed at a particular market.

According to this definition, a consumer current account and ancillary services would constitute a single product, as a consumer would not normally purchase different aspects of this package from different banks. A corporate current account would constitute a separate product, in that although it may involve essentially the same services, it is aimed at a quite distinct market. A credit card scheme would also be viewed as a product in its own right, as many consumers will use a credit card operated by a bank with which they otherwise have no connection.

An important implication of this definition is that a banking product is a fluid entity that may alter owing to changes in promotional emphasis or purchasing patterns, without any alteration to the actual physical services offered by the bank. For example, an overdraft facility normally forms part of the overall current account service, and hence does not constitute a product in its own right but rather is a part of a larger package. If however the bank chooses to market an identical credit package to non-account-holders, the service would then constitute a product in its own right.

Aims and means of bank product development

Product development can serve bank marketing ends by:

1. Attracting consumers from outside the present market.
2. Increasing sales to the existing market, by: (i) increasing cross-

selling, (ii) attracting core accounts from competitors, (iii) developing products for sale to competitors' customers independent of the core account.

3. Reducing the cost of providing an identical or similar service.

Each of these aims will be dealt with in more detail below.

(1) *Attracting consumers from outside the present market.* The UK Banks have failed to tap a large sector of the potential market. In 1982 almost 20 per cent of the UK working population did not possess a bank account, the highest proportion in the industrialised world. By way of comparison, in the USA 99 per cent of all wages are paid directly into a bank account, while in Canada, Germany, Australia, and France the figure (for 1980) was 95 per cent.[5]

It is clear that the products offered by the British banks do not meet the needs of a large proportion of the population, and that product development aimed at satisfying these needs could open a potential profitable growth area.

(2) *Increasing sales to the existent market* by:

(a) Increasing cross-selling. Banks typically possess a network of branch offices and a large reservoir of customers who visit these premises regularly, and who trust the integrity and capability of the bank as a supplier of financial services.

Increased cross-selling to existing account-holders represents an attractive means of maximising the profitable use of these physical and market resources.

Product development aimed at increasing cross-selling is very much the soft option, as no product differentiation is required. As long as the service offered satisfies a need felt by some proportion of the core account-holders, the convenience to the consumer of obtaining the service from the bank rather than seeking it elsewhere will probably ensure a market.

(b) Attracting core accounts from competitors. Product development aimed at persuading competitors' customers to switch accounts is very much the difficult option. For most people the choice of banks is a once-in-a-lifetime purchase. Only some 2 per cent of current accounts move banks each year. Research has shown that convenience of branch site and parents' bank are the overriding factors in choice of bank, with product considerations playing only a very minor role. Also consumers see very little difference between the products offered by the major British banks.[6] Any product development aimed at attracting core account-holders from competitors must therefore create a product that is clearly different from those offered by competitors. However, there are no copyrights in financial services and any advantage from product development is fairly short-lived since other banks are likely to introduce the product as well.

(c) Developing products for sale to competitors' customers independent of the core account. It may be much easier to sell some aspect of the banking service to competitors' customers independent of the core account than to persuade competitors' customers to move their accounts. In banking the 'propensity to buy' is much stronger than the 'propensity to switch'.[7] Hence product development with this aim offers a far easier means of increasing sales at the expense of competitors than does development aimed directly at attracting competitors' core accounts.

(3) *Product development aimed at reducing costs.* Automation increasingly offers an opportunity to reduce the substantial labour and administrative costs of providing a banking service. Some automation is behind the scenes, and in no way affects the banks' interaction with the consumer. Banks may, however, be increasingly tempted to automate the actual interface between bank and customer in an attempt to provide an identical or more convenient service at lower cost. This approach may, however, run the risk of ignoring certain intangible needs that can only be satisfied by personal contact, and should therefore be treated with caution.

Product development in banking can be undertaken by:

(a) adding new services to the range;
(b) recombining and repackaging services to produce new products;
(c) modifying or extending existing services;
(d) some combination of the above.

In the following the characteristics of each means of product development will be described, and the extent to which each can contribute to the aims of product development mentioned above will be considered.

(a) *Extension of the service range.* Extending the service range is of itself unlikely to lead to any degree of differentiation between the products offered and those offered by competitors. This is first due to the ease with which competitors can copy a new service, and second, to the fact that the existing range of services is so wide that it cannot be communicated effectively to consumers who are not already customers of the bank, so that any additional services, unless of a most spectacular nature, will simply be buried in the mass of services already available.

Creation of new services may be combined with other means of product development in ways that introduce an element of differentiation, but they are unlikely to do so of themselves.

It has already been argued that the creation of a substantial degree of product differentiation is a prerequisite of any strategy that has as its aim attracting core accounts from competitors. Addition of new services is therefore unlikely of itself to increase sales in this way.

Extending the range of services offered is, however, a powerful means of increasing cross-selling to existing core account-holders. Much of the thrust of recent product development by UK banks has been in this direction. Most of the wide and expanding range of services now offered by major banks are aimed almost entirely at core account-holders. No attempt is made to communicate the existence of most services to non-account-holders and promotion is entirely by personal contact between manager and client, or at least by literature displayed only within branch offices.

The logical extension of this process of service range expansion aimed at increased cross-selling is for banks to offer the entire range of financial and related services required by their clients. This development in the direction of the 'one stop financial centre' clearly represents a major possible product-development strategy for banks, and is dealt with further at a later stage in this chapter.

(b) *Development of 'new' products by repackaging and re-emphasising existing services.* It has already been stressed that the service range offered by a typical bank is very wide, certainly too wide to be promoted effectively in its entirety to the public at large. Within this range there exists a number of combinations of services that have specific relevance to the needs of particular market segments. However, owing to the impossibility of promoting the full range of services, the consumer is probably unaware that a banking product that closely matches his needs can be constructed.

Hence the possibility arises of producing a number of separate banking products, each consisting of comparatively few existing or only slightly modified services of special relevance, which could be promoted effectively to the chosen segement via the media most appropriate and in accordance with the attitudes of the particular group. In this way the bank would be able to create a clear identification in the minds of consumers of the bank's products with the consumers' particular needs.

It has already been argued that a substantial degree of product differentiation will be required if consumers are to be persuaded to switch their core account. It is likely therefore that this market aim can only be served by a process of product development that includes selecting, re-emphasising and repackaging services to produce distinct, readily intelligible products with specific appeal to particular market segments.

A similar process will also form an essential part of any attempt to develop a product that meets the needs of the unbanked.

(c) *Modification or extending existing services.* The banking product may be enhanced without any fundamental change to existing services. For example, an increase in the amount guaranteed by a cheque guarantee card, or increasing the number and type of retailers participating in a credit card scheme, both represent a form of product development that implies no basic change to services.[8]

In the long term this form of product development may be a continual necessity, needed simply to keep pace with competitors. However, because the characteristics of the banking product are so many and so intangible individually, such enhancements seem unlikely to affect sales dramatically. Hence it is difficult to see a process of service enhancement as constituting a distinct product-development strategy.

Special features of product development

The process of product development may be divided into the following five stages: (i) idea generation, (ii) screening of ideas, (iii) business analysis, (iv) technical development, and (v) commercialisation. This five -phase process can be quite complex.

Many banking services have no material aspect and require no special hardware. Hence in many cases the technical development phase is greatly reduced or absent. By contrast, in the case of many manufactured products technical development is the most time-consuming and costly aspect of product development. Because of the relative unimportance of this stage in banking, a new banking service can often be introduced in a very short time and at comparatively low cost. Hence:

1. Any service added to the range can be almost immediately copied by competitors, with the result that product differentiation by addition of new services is very difficult to achieve.
2. There is a natural tendency for services to proliferate, owing to the speed and cheapness with which new services can be introduced and competitors' services copied.

Because a new service can be added with little investment of time and money, full formal market research is frequently not undertaken.[9] The relative unimportance of the technical development phase in bank product development, and the consequent neglect of market research, greatly increases the importance that must be attached to the screening phase, if uncontrolled service proliferation is to be avoided and the bank is not to march in all directions at once. New service ideas should be judged in the light of strategic market objectives, and of the ways product development can serve these objectives. In the ensuing discussion an attempt is made to provide a framework for relating product development options to the various market strategies currently available to banks.

The product range

Numerous services have been developed recently that the banks are hoping will have a wide appeal during the 1980s. Some have as their theme 'money management', for example, Barclays operates the Barclay trust, a 'Money Doctor' scheme whereby experts will discuss monetary problems with clients and prepare personal financial planning, schemes to cover income tax, capital transfer tax, savings and investment strategy. Midland provides a similar service for clients with £20,000 or more to invest. The portfolio management service covers matters like collecting dividends, dealing with rights issues and taxation vouchers and revising the portfolio on an ongoing basis. National Westminster arranges personal loans for season tickets; Lloyds has its series of Black Horse Guides on such matters as 'Buying and Improving Your House'. High-street banks are competing with one another for not only their traditional business, but also areas of commercial activity previously associated with accountancy firms, savings banks, building societies and insurance companies.

A further area of intensive banking activity is that of servicing the small businessman. Banks have always been in this field but arising from the deliberations of the Wilson Committee and the increasing attention being paid by governments to the small business area of the economy, this has been a growth sector and is likely to remain so for many years. 'Getting to know you' has been a major theme of the campaign. Midland has established centres at Newcastle and Southampton where it offers advice services on a 9 a.m.–5 p.m. appointment basis. (Note the change from normal banking hours.) The same bank has also teamed up with the National Enterprise Board to form Newtown Securities (Northern) Ltd. Investments here range from a minimum of £5,000 to a maximum of £25,000 and loans are available with convertible options. National Westminster and Lloyds operate Business Development loans that are usually spread over a period of between five and ten years. The taxonomy of products range in Figure 5.1 offers an indication on the very wide range of product services offered by one of the major London clearing banks. This is not an exhaustive classification of all services offered but it does give an indication of the very wide and diversified range of products that are offered by banks. Other non-banks related services may include tax preparation, personal family counselling, leasing services, advising and offering insurance policies, forwarding mail, legal advice, travel organisation, obtaining and offering financial (and general) references, business (and marketing) research, etc.[10]

Sources of new product ideas

The sources of new ideas for bank products and services can be classified into those coming through internal sources and those from external sources, as shown in Figure 5.2. The figure shows four possible internal and five external groups who may contribute by various means to the pool of original ideas.

Perhaps the most obvious internal source is from the bank's own research and development. That is, the specialists involved in devising

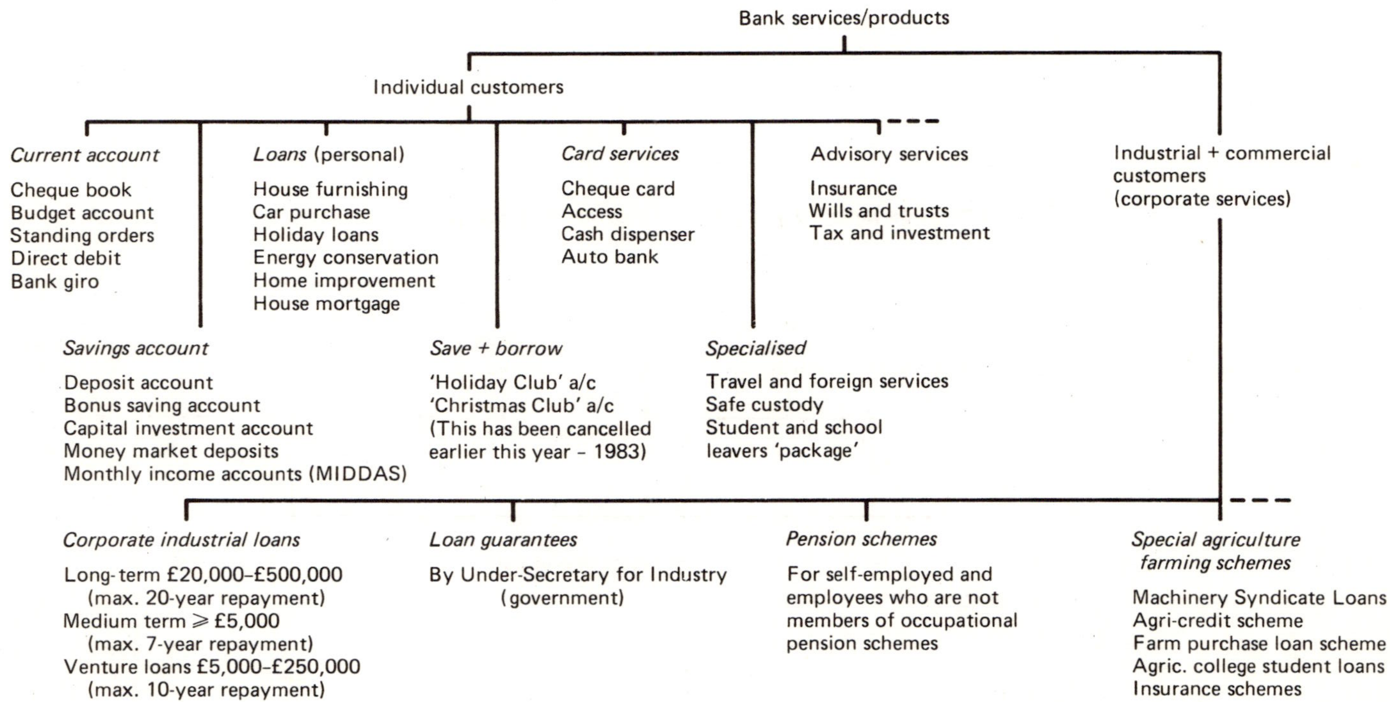

Figure 5.1 A taxonomy of bank products/services on offer

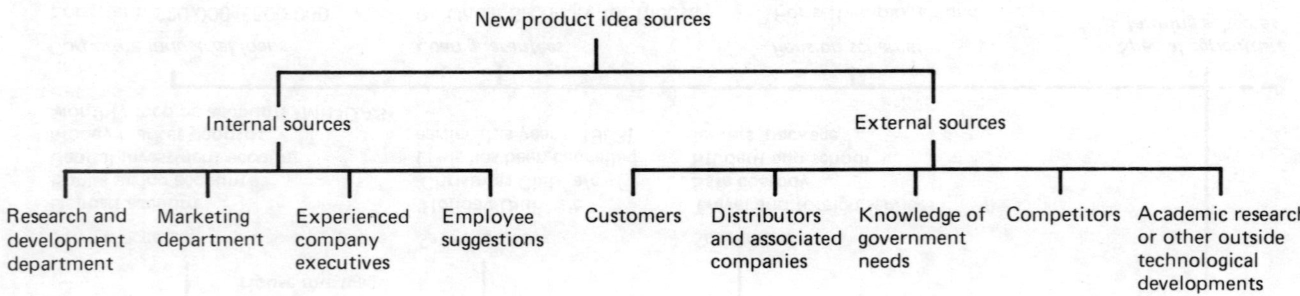

Figure 5.2 Alternative sources of new bank product/services ideas

new methods of corporate finance, personal savings or insurance schemes and so on, to meet changing economic and fiscal circumstances. The second group, the marketing department, may generate ideas by virtue of the fact that it is their job to monitor customer needs and the market place through various research methods and thus are in close contact with the needs and wants of the customers. Third, experienced company executives may provide ideas as a result of a deep knowledge of the market. Finally, employee suggestions may produce ideas because of the close day-to-day direct and indirect contact with customers.

The group of externally derived sources of ideas may comprise up to five different sub-groups as shown in Figure 5.2. First, the customers themselves may make informal suggestions or may be stimulated into idea generation by formal market research methods. Second, the distributors and associated companies may provide ideas. In the case of the Midland Bank, this would include its many subsidiary and associated groups of companies both in the UK and also internationally. For example, the Forward Trust Group, Thomas Cook, Midland Group Insurance Brokers, Joint Credit Card Company (Access), European–Asian Bank, Euro-Pacific Finance Corporation, Trinkhouse and Burkhardt, and so on. Third, a knowledge of government needs warrants special attention, as it is the largest single employer in many countries. Its charging requirements and ample purse mean that this segment merits special study and may be a fruitful source of new ideas. Fourth, competitors may be allowed to make the running with a new product. The bank can perhaps learn from its competitors' mistakes and then launch an improved version of the new product. Lastly, academic research and other outside technological developments may produce ideas.

Product development strategies

Having examined the market aims that product development in banking can serve, the means available for developing the banking product, and the relationship between the two, we are in a position to identify a number of distinct product development strategies open to banks, as follows:

1. *The 'expansion' strategy.* This consists of the expansion of the services offered within the core banking service, with the aim of increased cross-selling. The logical outcome of this strategy is the development of the one-stop financial centre.
2. *The 'differentiation' strategy.* This involves dividing the core banking service range into packages of services aimed at chosen market segments, with the aim of increasing market share in these segments at the expense of competitors.

3. *The 'satellite product' and 'Janus* product' strategies.* The satellite product strategy involves the creation of separate, stand-alone products, marketed independently of the core account, with the aim of generating sales to non-account-holders without requiring that these switch or open an account. The Janus product strategy is an extension of this, in which the same services or packages of services are marketed both as stand-alone products to non-account-holders, and as elements of the core banking service for cross-sale to existing customers.

In the following sections each strategy is considered in more detail, and the future implications of likely technological developments for each is discussed.

The expansion strategy

It has already been argued that this strategy offers an attractive and relatively easy option for the major banks. In addition, it would be expected to bring substantial benefits to the consumer, by greatly simplifying the task of managing his household or business affairs.

A not untypical bank customer might, at various times in his life, need to use a wide range of specialist services in the financial and related fields, including, for example: (i) several insurance companies and brokers dealing in house, health and car insurance, as well as life assurance, (ii) an accountant, (iii) an investment broker or portfolio manager, (iv) a building society, (v) an estate agent and valuer, (vi) a solicitor, (vii) a travel agent, and so on. Clearly, to be able to have access to the services of all the above at a single convenient location, dealing with a single firm whose trustworthiness and competence is assured, would represent a very considerable advantage to the consumer, and would therefore guarantee sales success for the range of services offered.

The expansion strategy appears to be the main theme of recent product development undertaken by the larger UK banks, which now offer a range of specialist advice on personal and business finance, taxation, insurance and investment that would previously have fallen within the province of small specialist firms. The recent move into the mortgage market represents a trespass into the sphere of the building societies, and also may open opportunities for extending the service range into the province of the estate agent, the surveyor and valuer, the conveyancing solicitor and the house insurer.

One author has already warned that by the end of the 1980s the small accounting firm may find itself in the position of the 'corner shop', with the

---

*Janus – the two-faced god of ancient Rome. In this case one face is turned towards core account-holders, the other towards the remaining market.

banks cast in the role of 'supermarket'.[11] The same may well apply to a number of other specialist financial services.

Further service proliferation is not, however, without dangers. It has already been argued that the present service range is too large to be communicated, and further extension would be expected to exacerbate this situation.

A further danger is that the cost of making the full range of services available to all customers will render added services uneconomic. This might, for example, occur if specialised experts were made available at every branch. A prerequisite for further extension of the product range is therefore probably some form of reorganisation along the lines pioneered by Midland in Newcastle and Southampton, in which a number of branch offices offering only a basic service are grouped around a regional central office with facilities and personnel to provide a full range of specialist services.

The differentiation strategy

British banks have largely pursued a policy of undifferentiated marketing, aiming to appeal to a broad spectrum of consumers rather than to particular segments. As a result, the consumer sees little difference between the products offered. Attempts to create a degree of product differentiation have been largely unsuccessful, whereas, in contrast, attempts to increase cross-selling have succeeded.

A move towards differentiated marketing will require the development of distinct products aimed at chosen market segments. For promotional purposes the core of such a product would consist of a group of services selected as being of particular relevance to the segment. This group of services would be kept relatively small, to allow the essentially relevant nature of the product to be communicated, without creating confusion in the minds of consumers. Of course, consumers attracted to open an account by such a simplified product might have access to the full range of banking services. However, any attempt to communicate this full range would be self-defeating, as it would dilute the special relevance of the package in the eyes of the chosen segment.

One might, for example, envisage banking packages aimed specifically at: the affluent, the student, the young married couple, the retired, the shopkeeper, the farmer, the small businessman, the international traveller, and so on.

A strategy of product differentiation might be accompanied by a contraction of the service range, if efforts are to be concentrated on only a few market segments. Abandoning irrelevant services would help to control costs, allowing a service that has been stripped of irrelevancies to be offered at a highly competitive price.

Alternatively, a bank might choose to appeal simultaneously to a number of segments, in effect mimicking General Motors' maxim of a 'car for every purse, purpose, and personality' but within a banking context. In this case product differentiation might imply no contraction of the overall range of services offered.

However, in banking an attempt to appeal simultaneously to many segments might be fraught with difficulties.

It is argued that the result of a policy of undifferentiated marketing is hypercompetition for the largest market segments, and undersatisfaction of the smaller or less profitable segments. This is clearly evident in the UK banking industry, and explains the success of the TSB, foreign banks, and other financial institutions such as building societies in attracting relatively neglected market segments such as the weekly wage earner at the end of the scale, and the affluent at the other.[12]

The major banks have, however, recently taken some steps in the direction of differentiated marketing. Lloyds, for example, has launched a 'Homemakers' scheme aimed at young married couples setting up a first home and considering opening a bank account, which consists of a package of services relevant to this group, plus vouchers for discounts on household goods valued at £300.[13] Midland has designed packages aimed at both the hourly paid worker and the small businessman. With regard to the hourly paid, the package is promoted via Midland's in-factory branches and offers essentially a savings account on which interest is payable, combined with overdraft facilities, but without the full range of facilities normally available on a current account.

Despite the examples quoted above, the UK banks' attempts to create genuinely distinct products have been at best half-hearted. This may be because the larger banks would be unwilling to take the risk involved in abandoning their broad-based approach, and see no way of promoting a number of differentiated products in ways that appeal to different market segments without creating a highly confused image in the consumer's mind.

It has been suggested that the solution to this problem may lie in the proper use of the branch structure, in that each branch office could adopt both its product and its promotional approach to the particular demographic and economic character of its trading area, much as happens in the USA where the banking industry is far less centralised than is the case in the UK. Hence we might envisage branches of the same bank in, for example, and affluent suburb, a working-class housing estate, a rural farming area, and a provincial shopping centre promoting different packages of services in different ways. It is noteworthy that many of the examples quoted above of attempts at differentiated marketing centre on types of branch office that cater to a very clearly defined market segment, such as on-campus and in-factory branches.

There are, however, problems associated with this approach. Firstly, personnel with marketing expertise would be required at branch level. Second, the national image of the bank might be highly confused, and it might prove difficult to use national media to advertise a wide range of locally differentiated products.

The satellite product strategy

The essence of the satellite product strategy is creation of stand-alone products that are independent of the core banking service, with the aim of increasing sales to non-account-holders without the need to overcome the inertia inherent in consumer account-switching decisions. Examples include:

(a) provision of loans to non-account-holders, promoted for example by newspaper or coupon advertising, as practised by the Bank of Scotland, Citibank, and the TSB;[14]
(b) consumer credit cards such as Barclaycard or Access;
(c) retailer-based credit cards centred on department stores, hotel chains, or airlines, and other retailer-based schemes such as the joint venture between Marks & Spencer, Citibank, and the Bank of Scotland in which consumers are provided with a cheque book for use in Marks & Spencer stores;
(d) a variety of investment, savings, and investment management schemes promoted largely via newspaper advertisements, such as the unit trust and portfolio management scheme operated by the merchant bankers Samuel Hill.[15]

Such satallite products clearly represent an ideal way forward for the market challenger or smaller bank that does not have the benefit of an extensive branch network or a large reservoir of core account-holders. In the case of the large clearing banks such products perhaps ideally serve a dual function, generating sales to non-account-holders on the one hand, and enhancing the overall banking service and hence generating cross-sales to account-holders on the other.

Perhaps the best example of this two-faced function of the Janus product is the Barclaycard. On the one hand, the Barclaycard is an independent product available to all, irrespective of location of bank account. On the other hand, the Barclaycard is an integral part of the Barclays' current account service, serving as a cheque guarantee card, with the result that 80 per cent of Barclays' customers hold a Barclaycard.[16] Non-Barclays customers are encouraged to use the card in ways that substitute for services normally provided via their current account. For example, it is possible to pay standing orders by means of the card, and to obtain cash from automatic teller machines at Barclays' branch offices. In this way the Janus product can be made increasingly to attract sales from competitor banks without requiring that the customer actually move his account.

The major problem with the concept of the Janus product is that the message necessary to promote the product to non-account-holders may conflict with the overall image the bank wishes to portray. This is again clearly illustrated by the Barclaycard example.

An important element of the profit generated by Barclaycard comes from interest on extended credit, yet the management of Barclays feels that advertising that overtly persuades the consumer to borrow will be seen as encouraging irresponsibility, and is therefore inconsistent with the bank's desired image. For this reason advertising of Barclaycard has been restrained, and penetration outside Barclays' account-holders has almost certainly been diminished. To quote the manager of Barclaycard: 'One of my prime objectives . . . is to lend money, but one of the things I have not been allowed to do is to encourage people to borrow.'[17]

By way of comparison, Access, which although run by a group of banks does not form a part of any current account package and is not linked by name to any bank, has been allowed a far freer hand in its advertising. As a result, Access penetration outside account-holders of member banks is far greater than that of Barclaycard, whereas cross-selling to member bank account-holders has been less successful than in the case of Barclaycard.

Clearly, the extent to which the satellite product is to be integrated into the mainstream service of the bank and linked to the bank's name has important implications and deserves much consideration. Perhaps the ideal solution would be to offer the same survice to account-holders and to independent users of the product, but under a different name.

To sum up, in planning services/product strategies, there are four alternatives open to the bank, as indicated in Table 5.1:

1. Offering more of existing services to existing customers, that is, market penetration.
2. Offering more of existing services to new customers, that is, market development.
3. Developing new services/products to existing customers, that is, service/product development.
4. Developing new services for new customers, that is, diversification.

The development of new bank services/products should be based on a thorough analysis of the market. There are four ways of developing the bank products – namely, the bank can follow a policy of market extension (or development) through the development of new lending and saving

Table 5.1 Planning bank product strategies

Customers *Products*	*Existing*	*New*
Existing	1. *Market penetration* (via: increasing services usage rate, expanding branch system/EFT points, etc.)	2. *Market development* (via: attracting new customers, deleting expensive service/products, etc.)
New	3. *Services/product development* (via: product/services innovation, accepting lower risks services, special isation, etc.)	4. *Diversification* (via: accepting higher risks, takeovers of smaller banks, developing new market segments)

programmes designed to meet more precisely the needs of various segments. Second, bank management recognises that its facilities can offer opportunities for implementing a policy of product extension, for example, provide commercial billing services for local utilities and handle company payrolls, make the bank computer available to bank customers for electronic data processing and cash dispensing machine, and so forth (cell 2 in Table 5.1). Third, product extension policies, implemented through utilisation of the bank's possession of financial acumen, for example, financial counselling could be offered to existing customers and a means of attracting new accounts (cell 1 in Table 5.1). Fourth the bank may follow a policy of conglomerate growth or diversification by establishing services (where regulations permit) that are clearly outside of the normal scope of commercial bank operations, but that are complementary and are likely to further the use of other bank services. Midland Bank, for example, ventured into travel agency operations, insurance, real estate and housing services, etc. – that is, both horizontal and vertical expansion. The importance of diversification is that a bank that offers a large number of services is ultimately better assured of its continuity as an independent institution than an organisation with a limited range of services. In many European countries the trend for banks to become financial supermarkets that offer a wide range of services such as advice on planning, saving, loans, leasing, investments, insurance and payment transactions has been observed. These services are being sold to 'captive' customers, that is, to people who already have an account at a particular bank. The progress of introducing new services in under continuous review as are existing services that may not be meeting customers' needs. In the latter cases the services may be altered or withdrawn.

The implications of new technology for bank product development

The advent of new, cheap data processing and communications technology has far-reaching implications both in terms of its immediate impact on the banking product, and in terms of the way it may affect the overall structure of the banking industry and hence the advisability of the various product development strategies discussed above.

The 'electronic revolution' has led to a number of very important developments within the banking industry over the past few years. In particular, there has been the development of Electronic Funds Transfer System (EFTS), which in principle is a system for exchanging value via electronic entry, without processing paper. Basically it is nothing more than an exchange of information between consumers, retailers and financial institutions.[18] With a fully developed EFTS two major devices allow consumers to interact with the retail and financial institutions. These are the point of sales (POS) terminal and the automatic teller machine (ATM).

The idea of a POS device is that a consumer comes to the retailer for the purchase of goods and/or services and instead of presenting cash or a cheque for payment, be uses a debit card. The card is fed into the POS device for processing, and a specified amount of money is electronically transferred from the customer's account to that of the retailer. In the UK, there have been a number of setbacks to the development of POS terminals.[19] An inter-bank working party has proposed a scheme (POST) in which 100,000 point-of-sale terminals would be installed in most retail outlets. Each would be directly linked to every clearing bank branch office in the country, allowing instant debiting of customer accounts and crediting of retailer accounts at the time of purchase.[20]

It was envisaged that the scheme would bring benefits to the banks, the retailer, and the consumer. Banks and retailers would benefit by a substantial reduction in adminstration costs owing to the abolition of cheques, credit slips, and transport and secure handling of cash. Consumers were seen as benefiting owing to increased convenience, in that counter service at retailers would be speeded up and neither cash nor cheque books would any longer be required.

The reason for the banks' reticence to act singly on this issue is the fear that such a scheme would be unacceptable to retailers unless it was patronised by customers of all major banks.

In December 1980 it was reported that the banks had decided to drop the POST scheme. Two possible reasons have been advanced for this decision, the first being the clearing banks' 'almost pathological caution when confronted with new ideas',[21] the second being the absence of any hard cost–benefit data to help apportion the cost of the scheme between the banks and the retailers.

Despite this initial setback for EFTS, product development in this direction has not been entirely dormant, and in the end is probably inevitable owing to the escalating manpower and administrative costs of providing the banking service on the traditional basis.[22]

Barclays, for example, has undertaken a highly successful trial of point-of-sale terminals at petrol stations in Norwich, which allows the consumer to purchase petrol at any time of the day or night, and a similar trial has been undertaken by Citibank in California. It is worth noting that the use of point-of-sale terminals for petrol sales overcomes one of the major objections to most EFTS schemes, namely that most of the benefits are to the bank and the retailer with the consumer benefiting only by virtue of a slight increase in convenience. In the case of self-service petrol sales, however, the consumer benifit is obvious, in the shape of 24-hour availability of petrol. It seems likely, therefore, that filling stations will be the first retail outlets at which EFTS will be widely available.

The recent decision by the UK government to initiate widespread installation of two-way communication cables into household and business premises, initially in order to introduce cable-vision, brings the advent of the large-scale application of EFTS a great deal closer. With such a system fully operational it should be possible, for example, to summon a catalogue of goods available from a retailer onto the household television screen, and to order goods and have one's account automatically debited without ever leaving the home.

The probably inevitable advent of home-based EFTS have dramatic implications for the future shape of the banking industry. If cash becomes unnecessary or, in the extreme case, if all banking and other transactions can be performed from a terminal in the home, the need for an extensive network of bank branches will vanish. Such a development would eliminate the present competitive advantage of the large clearing banks, and might also eliminate the opportunity to cross-sell services to core account-holders via the branch system.

Consider, for example, the following quotations from a recent OECD publication on banking:[23] '[EFTS will] . . . probably prove decisive in dissolving the customer relationship whereby banks seek to tie their customers to a whole range of services . . . Potentially the new system can transform the conditions of competition between credit institutions of all types. The key factors are that a branch network will no longer be essential for conducting retail operations, and all kinds of institutions will be able to offer payment services.'

The implications for product development strategy are clear and far-reaching: the opportunity to pursue the 'expansion strategy' described above will vanish. If the consumer no longer needs to visit a branch office to conduct his financial affairs, opportunities for cross-selling will largely evaporate, and the consumer appeal of the one-stop financial centre will disappear. If financial services are available from the home there will be no advantage to the consumer in being able to conduct all his financial affairs under one roof: the one roof will be his own.

We may therefore conclude that the likely future direction of product development in banking will be towards stand-alone products consisting of only one or a few related services. The number and variety of products offered will inevitably increase as the decline in the importance of the branch network allows more institutions to compete for the market, hence product differentiation and specific market segment appeal will assume greater importance. The luxury of broad appeal and a large captive market will probably become a thing of the past.

Pricing systems

Price is important since it represents the only element of the marketing mix that creates revenue. The banking system does not in fact price all its services, since some are offered free to customers. The most important prices in the banking system relate to interest rates; basic interest rates are controlled by the government. There could be limited variations of interest rates charged by banks but, with the oligopolistic position in many countries including the UK, prices tend to be relatively stable.

However, although price may not be a major element, it is still significant for the market-oriented firm in competition with other firms. It has been suggested that the banker should have two main objectives in relation to price setting:

(a) to attract as many customers as possible to the selected segments;
(b) to do this under the most profitable conditions.

Thus prices relate to attracting potential customers and maximising total profit. This explains, to some extent, why some bank services are free or are provided at low cost. It is presumably argued that the low or non-profit on these lines is more than offset by the higher profits on other lines, such as bank loans, so as to maximise total profit. The individual using the low-profit lines is more than likely also to utilise the high-profit services. Another explanation of differential line pricing is that some services may be able to command higher prices from customers than other services. Thus some lines are more price sensitive than others. The effect of these variables is that the pricing of bank services is not necessarily related to the cost of the service offered.

In banking there is another variation since customers are not necessarily regarded as homogeneous, particularly with regard to the pricing of loans (interest rates). Thus a large company with large capital investments is likely to be offered more favourable terms than a small firm.

Price competition does exist in the banking system. During the early

1970s some price competition related to current account charges such that banks varied in their charges on a current account. However, the extent to which prices could be varied and, possibly, the limited effect of this kind of price competition has produced the oligopolistic situation where bank charges on current accounts tend to be very similar as between the main clearing banks. It has been suggested that banks look more closely at the way that they charge for corporate services and the implication is that an increase in service charges is desirable in terms of total profit. This may appear a sound idea, but the establishment of a price for services such as investment and legal advice may be difficult in view of the variety of variables that need to be considered. Perhaps the more important factors that need to be considered are:

(a) the value of the service to the customer (market research needed here);
(b) the cost of developing the service;
(c) the question of whether the service will have a broad or narrow appeal (which market segment(s) does it relate to);
(d) will costs be reduced with volume of use or new techniques;
(e) the pricing of similar services (if any) by the competitors;
(f) to what extent does the bank seek to dominate the market? This seems an unlikely possibility in the UK banking system. If the bank did wish for domination it may have to lower its profit margin to discourage competition;
(g) it may be that the service costs should be absorbed in other costs;
(h) there is the question of whether the service requires capital to be tied up in order to make its performance possible. This involves the problem of determining the basis of capital cost inclusion.

The general situation in the UK appears to be that there is only limited scope for price competition in the field of interest rates and these tend to be very similar among the main clearing banks although there could be short-term advantages gained in this area. Price competition in other banking services has existed, as with bank charges on current accounts, but, again, it is likely to produce only short-term advantages.

Methods of pricing

Banks, both in the UK and elsewhere, have not in general viewed price as a marketing tool. We may cite a number of reasons for this.

1. Bank pricing is frequently subject to government regulation. Until

recently interest rates were regulated in the UK, and this is still the case in many countries around the world.

2. In the UK the banking industry is an oligopoly. Even in the absence of such an agreement, price in an oligopolistic market is notoriously sticky. Economic theory explains this by postulating that firms expect any price cut to be matched by competitors, whereas any price increase will not. As a result, firms expect to gain no additional sales by cutting prices, but expect to lose a substantial volume of sales owing to any price increase.
3. The banking product is non-standard, hence price tends also to be non-standard, and therefore difficult to communicate to the consumer. Price cannot be used as a marketing tool if it cannot be simply and intelligibily communicated to the consumer.

Criteria for a system of bank pricing

A pricing system for a banking product should have the following characteristics:

1. Within a system of differentiated marketing, market segments should be charged differentially according to the elasticity of demand and competitive situation within each segment, with the aim of maximising profit from each segment and hence overall.
2. If a single product with a single pricing system is to be aimed at a wide range of market segments, the pricing system should not unduly subsidise some segments at the expense of others.* If this occurs, penalised segments will inevitably be lost to competitors.
3. Price must be communicable if it is to be used as a marketing tool. Hence it should be simple and readily intelligible. Otherwise, price comparisons are impossible, and price ceases to be a genuine element of the marketing mix.

It should be noted that criteria 1 and 3 above are not necessarily in conflict. Hence within a system of differentiated marketing, a pricing system that meets all relevant criteria is possible. However, within a system of undifferentiated marketing the relevant criteria 2 and 3 often conflict sharply. The need for very simple pricing formulae implied by 3 almost certainly means that certain groups of consumers will be subsidised and others penalised. It might therefore be argued that within a system of undifferentiated marketing, pricing systems will inevitably be deficient in some respect.

---

*Exceptions should of course be made in the case of segments that include a high proportion of new account-openers, when it may be desirable to provide a short-term subsidy in the interests of long-term profitability, as is the case with students.

Cost-based pricing

A cost-based pricing system takes no account of the competitive situation, nor of the willingness to pay off consumers within different market segments. Hence it clearly does not meet criterion 1 above.

Furthermore, any attempt to genuinely relate price directly to the cost of providing the service will inevitably entail a complex pricing formula that will not comply with criterion 3. For example, one author[24] cites twenty cost or revenue components that contribute to the cost or profitability of a basic current account, excluding any charge for the use of specialised ancillary services. Clearly, any pricing system that took account of all these cost and revenue elements would be far too complex to be communicated, or to allow meaningful price comparisons.

A cost-based system does, however, have the advantage that, within a system of indifferentiated marketing, it will at least not penalise some market segments and subsidise others.

Simplified pricing formulae and demand-oriented pricing

Simplified pricing formulae might include, for example, a single price for all, or a single price for all under given conditions.

We have already argued that simplified formulae are essential if price is to be used as a marketing tool. Such simplified systems are therefore a necessary prerequisite of any attempt to introduce demand-based pricing. However, we have also argued that a single simple formula is unlikely to be appropriate for all market segments, as inevitably certain services will be charged for at an excessive rate while others will be provided free.

Ideally, therefore, a pricing system that takes account of demand should involve the following stages:

1. Segmentation of the market into groups that are relatively homogeneous with regard to price sensitivity on the one hand, and service requirements on the other.
2. Development of simple pricing formulae appropriate for each segment.

Pricing methods in practice

In the case of interest rates on deposits and more especially on loans, we see clear evidence of differential pricing according to competitive conditions in the market segment. For example, interest rates on bank mortgages are clearly set according to the need to compete with building societies, whereas a higher rate is charged on overdrafts and personal loans and a yet higher rate on credit card borrowing.

However, the example of interest rates is far from typical of bank pricing in general, for two reasons:

1. Banks practise a form of differentiated marketing in their lending activities, dividing the market according to the purpose for which the loan is required.
2. The interest rate is an inherently simple and communicable price.

In the case of other services such as current accounts and credit cards, the situation is considerably less clear-cut, first, because a single product is marketed to all segments, and second, because in these cases the product (and therefore the price) is inherently less simple and therefore more difficult to communicate.

The history of current account pricing in the UK has shown a steady development towards even more simplified pricing systems, with the aim of allowing the use of price as a competitive element in the marketing mix. However, this has not been accompanied by a process of market segmentation, with the result that segments have been systematically penalised and alienated from the mainstream banking system.

In the early 1970s bank charges were entirely at the discretion of individual branch managers, with the result that these were not standardised even within a bank. Charges were levied according to usage of services and level of balance, but no standard formula or scale of charges was published by any bank.

From August 1973 a form of price war on current accounts took place, which involved the banks progressively defining, specifying and simplifying their pricing systems.

Typically the pricing formulae that evolved have consisted of:

(a) specified charges for each transaction, such as automated credit, and debit, unautomated credit and debit, with all ancillary services provided free of charge;
(b) a nominal interest rate paid to the consumer on balances, which counts only towards offsetting charges; and
(c) specific average and/or minimum levels of balance above which all charges are waived.

More recently, development has been towards even more simplified pricing systems, such as 'free banking if in credit'.

Hence, the recent development of current account pricing may be summarised as follows:

1. *Ad hoc* pricing probably related to both costs and the consumer's willingness to pay.
2. Clearly stated simple pricing formulae.
3. One price for all under most circumstances.

The method by which Williams & Glyn's arrived initially at a formula for current account pricing has been described in some detail.[25] This involved the following stages:

(a) examination of the recent history of a sample of accounts, with regard to movement of balances and numbers of various types of transaction;
(b) testing the sample to ensure that it it representative;
(c) testing the effect of varying possible pricing parameters on overrall revenue;
(d) identifying those pricing parameters that have greatest overall effect on revenue;
(e) developing a simple pricing formula based on those parameters shown to be of greatest importance, with the aim of achieving a target revenue under present conditions.

Two features of this approach are particularly noteworthy. First, no account is taken of the cost of any of the services provided. Second, no account is explicitly taken of the price sensitivity of demand. Given that the pricing systems of other banks are very similar to that adopted by Williams & Glyn's, we may perhaps assume that their approaches also are similar.

It has been argued that the banks simply do not know the cost of the services they provide, that there is an absence of appropriate statistics, and that the true cost position is obscured by the split between the commercial and retail side of the business.[26] It is certain that the pricing systems adopted in general fail to cover the cost of transactions, subsidising these elements from income earned as interest on balances.[27] As a result those who make little use of services, or who maintain large balances, are penalised. One segment that is systematically penalised is those who are paid weekly and in cash. Such consumers tend to have little use for the transaction services, and as a result prefer to use building societies or savings banks.

A rather similar situation may be seen in the case of credit card pricing. With regard to schemes such as Access and Barclaycard, the situation is as follows:

1. The retailer pays a commission (around 2 per cent) on all credit card sales.
2. The consumer pays only for extended credit on balances not cleared within a month.

Barclaycard estimate that every transaction serviced costs in excess of 40 pence.[28] Hence all transactions worth less than £20 incur a loss for the bank. Those who use the card only for samll purchases such as petrol, and who clear their account regularly, are therefore heavily subsidised. This subsidy is paid for by those who use the card for obtaining credit. Perhaps as a result of this, only one-third of Barclaycard holders take extended credit beyond the one-month deadline. One would expect that with increased consumer awareness this percentage would decrease, with the result that the bank will eventually be forced to charge for transactions, and that the potentially profitable lending aspect of the credit card business will be lost.

Banking transactions involve two sides, for example a retailer and his customer, or an employer and his employee. It is essential that any pricing system takes into account the balance of perceived benefit and the willingness to pay of the two sides of the transaction. For example, in the credit card example, if either the retailer or consumer is charged more than the perceived benefits warrant, the scheme will be one-sided, with either two few participating consumers or retailers. The POST scheme of Electronic Funds Transfer ran aground on this very point, as the banks could not agree on any means of apportioning costs between retailers and consumers.[29]

One clear example of the ill-effects of inflexibility in UK bank pricing systems again concerns the case of the weekly wage earner. A change from weekly payment in cash to monthly payment direct into a bank account would bring clear and substantial advantages to the employer, including reduced administrative costs, elimination of the cost of providing weekly secure cash delivery (in 1980 it was estimated that it costs £28 per employee per year to issue weekly wage packets), and greatly improved cash flow equal to several weeks' wages bill.

However, these advantages to the employer are almost exactly balanced by the disadvantages to the employee, at least as perceived by wage earners who have traditionally conducted their financial affairs in cash, and hence see little need for a bank account. Whereas the employer's cash flow is improved, the employee's cash flow is worsened. Whereas the employer is relieved of the cost of cash delivery, the employee is faced with the inconvenience of visiting a bank to obtain cash. Yet it is the employee who pays any charges incurred by his account. It is perhaps not surprising therefore that trade unions have resisted attempts to break the weekly cash payment habit.

Success in persuading weekly wage earners to accept monthly payment into a bank account (which may be the only way of profitably attracting this segment into the banking system) clearly depends on designing a pricing system that allocates the cost of the account more fairly in accordance with the perceived benefits.

The employer would presumably be willing to pay a sum almost equal to the savings he would make on administrative and delivery costs, plus interest on his improved cash position. In contrast, the employee may require a very considerable degree of subsidy, at the very least a free overdraft facility, before he would find the proposition attractive.

This example very closely illustrates the need for market segmentation as an essential element of any attempt to use price as a marketing tool.

Development of a simple, communicable price is essential, but simple formulae will never be appropriate for all market segments. Here there is a clear need for a separate pricing system aimed at the weekly wage earner, in which it is the genuine bereficiary, the employer, who pays.

Price policies: strategic *v.* tactical goals

As mentioned earlier, pricing is only one element of the marketing mix. There may in fact be considerable interaction between the various elements and so pricing should never be regarded as being in isolation from other aspects such as promotion, distribution, and the products themselves.

In terms of pricing, the bank should be very clear about what are its goals that it seeks by means of a particular pricing system. These may be classified into two broad categories. First, there are strategic objectives and second, tactical objectives.

Strategic pricing objectives are characterised by association with a firm's total marketing efforts during a period of time. The main strategic pricing objectives are: (i) maximisation of profit, (ii) rate of return on investment, and (iii) obtaining market share. Tactical pricing objectives are usually related to individual products or narrow product groupings, and its importance is predominant, especially in introducing new products.

As mentioned previously, perhaps the major problem associated with pricing practice in banking is that of the 'production cost' for an individual service. The difficulty is that in an organisation such as a bank, there are high overheads (in people, premises and so on) and relatively low variable costs. The way in which those overheads are allocated between the services has a major effect on the 'cost' of an individual service. A new service can look very profitable, marginally profitably or distinctly unprofitable, depending on the decision as to whether to allocate its share of overheads on the basis of variable costs, proportion of turnover, or estimated load on executive time, space, etc.

McIver and Naylor,[30] suggest that it is useful to differentiate between those services for which prices are fixed centrally, singly or in the form of a range of prices; and those for which prices are negotiated with the particular customer concerned. Centrally fixed services usually include: personal current accounts, deposit accounts, trustee and taxation services, factoring, leasing and personal fixed-term loans. On the other hand, services that may be negotiated individually include: business current accounts, overdrafts, merchant banking, international services and loans (fixed rate or base rate plus).

There are many products offered by banks for which there may be no centrally fixed price or pricing system. In such cases, the bank manager has to negotiate a fee or a charge more or less on the spot. There will usually be some guidelines or precedents for the manager to use, but there will still be elbow room for the individual concerned to decide on the appropriate figure between the various parameters laid down by the bank.

The actual prices charged by the bank should attempt to exploit different price sensitivities in different market segments. However, in order to do this, the bank must ensure that there is no intersegment leakage. Otherwise, customers will merely bypass the higher priced segment and obtain cheaper services by moving into a different market segment.

Future trends in the development of pricing policies will probably be based on the attempt to measure more accurately the costs involved in a particular product or group of products and thus tend to derive some sort of cost plus pricing system.[31] One basic problem facing the banks is that they have relatively little control over the magnitude of their revenue. The government's ability to determine the minimum lending rate means banks may find themselves in a situation of high profits one year and potential loss another. As a result, banks should try to develop pricing policies that shield at least some of their activities from external variables.

The bank marketing programme

The bank marketing programme is composed of the following five elements (Figure 5.3):

1. *Market research* – to identify the needs and wants of the market.
2. *Product development* – to develop financial products and services that will meet the needs of the market.
3. *Pricing* – to determine the prices for the various services/products and different customer types.
4. *Advertising and promotion* – to create widespread awareness about the products/services on offer and to enhance the bank image.
5. *Distribution* – the selection of suitable branch locations and other channels through which to distribute the financial services to customers.

The implementation of the bank marketing programme requires adequate attention to banks' staff education and training which is *very* important.

The first and most basic decision underlying the development of a bank's marketing programme is the type of market to be sought. Each segment of the market had different characteristics. To exploit any one

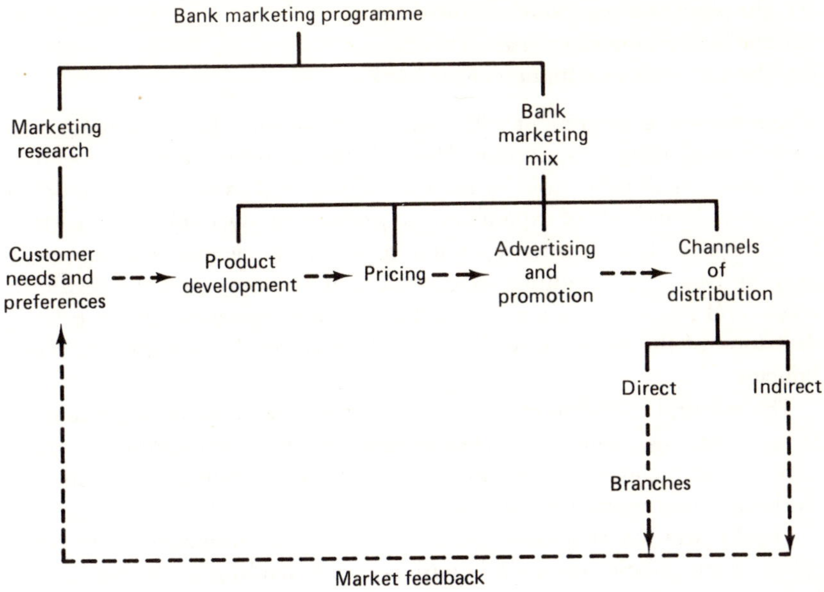

Figure 5.3 The bank marketing programme

segment effectively, these characteristics must be known and the bank's marketing mix adapted accordingly. The 'mix' can be said to comprise at least four basic variables: product, price, promotion and place (distribution). Any one or all of these can be varied to either a greater or lesser extent so that the mix matches more accurately the demands of a particular segment.

In perfecting a marketing strategy, care must be taken to understand how the marketing decisions interact within a single marketing mix. Product decisions affect promotion decisions; place (distribution) decisions may open up new promotion areas; price decisions affect product choices; changes in the target customers affect them all. What the bank must try to do is blend these decisions into a satisfying programme. The full service bank is in business to market a wide range of products. It follows then that the total marketing programme of the bank is really a collection of marketing strategies. Since it is aiming at more than one group of target customers, the bank must develop and manage more than one marketing mix.

The bank must also be aware of the restraints that exist with regard to the marketing decisions that can be made. There are at least five broad areas that influence and often restrain the bank's decisions:

(a) the economic environment;
(b) the cultural environment;

(c) the legal and regulatory environment;
(d) the resources and policies of the bank;
(e) the competitive situation of the bank.

The economic environment will obviously have considerable impact on a bank's marketing programme. Product, price, promotion and location decisions are all influenced by the state of the local as well as the national economy. In periods of expansion and prosperity, the demand for certain bank services is very intense, while in periods of recession the opposite may be true. The condition of the national economy and the resulting levels and costs of funds available have a clear influence on the pricing decisions of the bank as well as an influence on the demand for bank policies.

The cultural environment concerns the attitude of the local population towards saving, spending and borrowing. The traditions and values of the various social classes of target customers are important and may dictate the bank's marketing programme.

Legal restraints may affect price and promotion decisions. In the past, government policy, particularly with regard to lending by the banks, has been one of the principal causes of the past cartelistic arrangement between banks.

Bank resources and policies may affect the nature of the marketing programme. For example, if a bank manager has decided against entry into new areas of home mortgages, credit card, factoring or whatever, then the decisions are a restraint that marketing strategists must recognise in planning their product assortments. The bank's marketing budget may restrict the amount of money that can be spent on promotion, research and development.

The competitive situation will affect a bank's decision about product, place, promotion and price and must be made with a keen awareness of the equivalent decisions made by competitors. Nowhere is this more obvious than in the area of price decisions. Competition is also a large factor in selecting and selling methods, in determining products and services offered and in deciding upon the location at which they will be available.

The areas of product development and pricing systems can be viewed as being two aspects of the marketing function. The above discussion has shown how these fit into both the marketing process and the business of banking and financial service industry as a whole. It is important to be aware of the nature and characteristics of this wider setting in order to appreciate fully the determinants of product and pricing policies and how these in turn may influence the bank markets. In conclusion, it may be said that product development and pricing systems are vitally important in the marketing armoury of banking institutions. However, it should never be forgotten that there are strong interconnections between the elements of the marketing mix and it would therefore be unwise to consider any of these as existing in isolation.

CHAPTER 6

Marketing research

Contents

The roles and functions of marketing research in banking

The word 'marketing research' is used to describe a variety of quite different activities. The complete research function is to provide, analyse and interpret a flow of relevant information about the bank markets, so that management and marketing decisions are made with real knowledge and understanding of all the facts. Marketing research is the search and utilisation of information from all available sources and its adaption to banks' marketing needs.

The concept of marketing research in banking is relatively new. It was not until the early 1960s that the first few banks realised the importance of market research for both their future planning and current activities. By 1973 all the major UK clearing banks had organised and staffed a marketing department and most had a formal market research function. Nevertheless, it ought to be pointed out that the personnel staffing the market research departments were mostly not professional market researchers, but mainly operational researchers or statisticians.

In the following few years, owing to intense competition and banks' changing environment, the banks suddenly wanted answers to questions, such as:

1. What is the number of personal customers? (The number of accounts do not reflect the number of customers, as some accounts are joint accounts while some customers have more than one account.)
2. Who are the current account customers?
3. Who are the deposit account customers?
4. What are the factors influencing bank preferences?
5. How do the images of the major banks compare?
6. What aspect of the various forms of personal credit encourage people to use them?
7. What kind of people apply for personal loans and what do they want to do with these loans?
8. What do students think of the special cheque books provided for them? (And how effective are these in attracting undergraduate students' accounts?)
9. How has Saturday closing of branches affected the way customers and the public at large regard banks?
10. What do individuals (and businesses) require in the way of financial services that the bank currently does not provide?

With the increasing role of computerisation, answers to the questions above, as well as the *why*? question (for each issue), could be handled – via market research – with relative ease.

The roles

Bank market research essentially deals with problem solving.

To understand the roles of marketing research, we should perhaps first examine what marketing research can do for banks. To begin with, banks are dealing with customers every day. This means that banks have to attain a certain level of services so as to keep the customers happy and satisfied. To maintain a high level of service means incurring heavy costs and to maintain a low level of service means loosing business. How do banks then know which level of service to maintain? This is where bank marketing research comes in. Marketing research can be used to gather more knowledge about the market. With the information, services can be developed and existing ones improved. Better and more effective advertising and sales promotions programmes can be designed, in a manner that will be accepted by the public.

As stated above, market research essentially deals with problem solving. The problems almost always originate because the bank is uncertain about the market in which it is operating, or about to attempt to operate. Marketing research serves to structure and formalise the communication channel between the market and the bank. Useful and meaningful data can be fed back to the bank and these enable the bank to analyse the data so that future marketing activities can be profitably directed. Also, current bank activities can be critically evaluated to test their usefulness and effectiveness. The decisions made with the help of these data are then applied in the market by adequate advertising, sales promotions, personal relations, and selling campaigns. Thus, a complete circle, as shown in Figure 6.1, can be drawn to depict the whole marketing research process.

Through the activities listed at the top of the completed cycle (Figure 6.1), the market's knowledge of the bank can be increased. This may induce the consumers to move up the purchase ladder and finally to take action. Such situations will happen when the customers move their accounts to that bank.

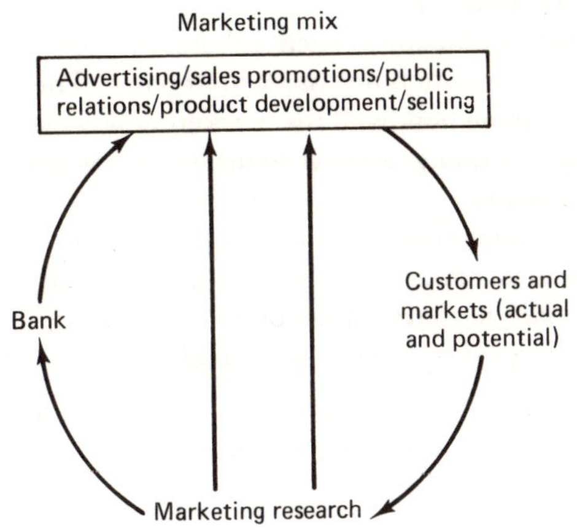

Figure 6.1 The roles of marketing research in banking

Functions of market research

In performing its functions, marketing research has basically four elements that it should perform on a day-to-day and on a long-term basis: (i) market segmentation, (ii) evaluation of marketing programmes, (iii) measurement of results, and (iv) recommendation.

The first function is to describe each market that the bank is trying to serve. Here we try to describe the market in terms of the more common denominators that are prevalent in marketing today, that is, demographics (e.g. age, income, family size, etc.), and to identify these customers' wants, needs and desires in terms of banking services. Thus we get into the realm of attitudinal research and this is where concepts such as bank images and segmentation studies begin to play a role.

The second function that a marketing researcher should fulfil is to ascertain that the programme developed by the marketing department does in fact satisfy customers' needs. This function is achieved by testing products, concepts and advertising campaigns, prior to their introduction or launching into a market. As a result, the risk associated with introducing these new services by the bank will be reduced significantly.

The third function a research department should undertake is to measure the results of the marketing programmes in quantifiable terms. This function is divided into three sections:

1. Tracking all types of accounts (using internal data, for example, number of accounts, openings, closings, balances). With this information, one can determine, for example, how well a specific bank product or service has performed.
2. Tracking external factors, such as bank awareness, advertising penetration, account switching, bank preference. This information can be used to determine how well the marketing mix elements, for example, advertising, are doing, relative to the market as a whole or relatively, in specific segments.
3. Repetition of image and segmentation studies periodically. This effort is necessary to make sure that the structure of the market has not changed, market shares have been maintained, and the bank is 'on track' with regard to its long-term goals and objectives.

The fourth function is to provide recommendations and directions for the solution of each problem that is expected.

The research methodology

There are five main stages (see Figure 6.2) in any bank market study and a failure in any one of these may render the research useless, if not misleading.

The first stage refers to a clear definition of the problem and the objectives of the study, while the second stage is the design of the research

1. Problem definition

↓

2. Design of questionnaire and pre-testing

↓

3. Fieldwork

↓

4. Data analysis

↓

5. Conclusions and Recommendations

Figure 6.2 Main stages in a bank market survey/research

including the size and type of the sample to be used, the framing of the questions and the shaping of the questionnaire(s).

The third stage is the fieldwork in which a team of interviewers contact and interview the sample of respondents. The process of fieldwork can also be carried out using telephone interviews or sending the questionnaires through the mail (mail questionnaires). There are advantages and disadvantages associated with each of these alternative research instruments (see Tables 6.1 and 6.2).

Most desk research for banks falls into one of the three categories, as follows:

1. *Retail banking research,* based on surveys to study banking habits, knowledge, attitudes, expectations and preferences.
2. *Corporate banking research* relates to surveys of financial executives and attempts to study ways in which companies choose between banks, and to identify opportinities for banks to get more business.
3. *General research* on banks, other financial institutions, local authorities, professional firms and other non-corporate organisations that takes many forms, but is always designed to provide both facts and measures of human attitudes in these various markets.

Primary data need to be collected and analysed from 'raw' information, that is, that obtained by undertaking an entirely new research project. There are three types in this category: observational, experimental and survey.

Observational data is that obtained from observing and recording behaviour. The observations are recorded according to a format that is determined beforehand. No attempt is made to modify, change or guide the behaviour of those under observation. An example is the time studies done to determine the average time each teller at the counter takes to serve

Table 6.1 The advantages of some major survey instruments – a comparison

Personal interview	*Mail*	*Telephone*
Full control on respondents' sample distribution	More comprehensive sample distribution	More comprehensive sample distribution
—	No field staff required	No field staff required
The non-response rate is generally low	—	The non-response rate is generally low
—	The cost per questionnaire is reasonable	The cost per questionnaire is reasonable
—	Respondents are franker in completing the questionnaire	—
—	No interviewer bias	Easier control over interviewer bias
A quick way to obtain information	The respondent answers in his own time	A very quick way to obtain information
Two-way communication and observations collection available	—	A two-way communication instrument
Longer interviews possible	—	—
Most flexible	—	—

a customer. The exercise may also be extended to include the time of the day to see if there is any effect due to this.

One major problem encountered in this method is to determine the size and the contents of the sample to be observed. Both factors are significant in the analysis of the data. The observation process may be done mechanically (e.g. by closed-circuit television) or by researcher(s), or by a combination of both. The observation process has the inherent advantage of gathering information on the spot. It often triggers and helps to answer several questions such as 'how?' and 'why?' do people behave in a particular manner.

Like observational data, experimental data are obtained largely by observation. But unlike the former, the situation under observation is being controlled. Thus, by altering the day in which the bank is open after regular working hours, the researchers are able to observe customers' reactions. The data obtained can then be compared with those before the change.

Table 6.2 The disadvantages of the major survey instruments – a comparison

Personal interviews	*Mail*	*Telephone*
Probably most expensive	—	—
Interviewers' control is difficult	—	—
Danger of interviewer bias	Bias due to non-response	Interviewer bias more likely
Slower than telephone	Likely to be quite slow	Interview period affordable is short
—	The questionnaire is usually short	Questions should be short
—	Omissions are difficult to interpret	Non-telephone owners or unlisted numbers are not contactable
—	Certain questions cannot be asked	Certain questions cannot be asked
—	Respondents not always identified and only those interested reply	—
—	Relatively high cost/return ratio	—

Experimental research may be conducted in a natural setting such as the bank counter area, or under controlled conditions, like the testing of a new package of bank services in certain preselected bank branches. The reactions of the customers are then closely monitored. In fact, test marketing is usually done in this way; after all, the best way is still to try it out. This type of data-gathering method is useful, because the marketing variables can be manipulated and this assists substantially in minimising the risks before launching a new package, for example. Despite this advantage, the whole exercise may get very complicated and time-consuming when there are too many variables in the experimental design.

Unlike the above two methods, most market survey studies involve direct or indirect communication contact with the bank customers, and/or the public. This is the most commonly used method in bank research and it often follows an observational or experimental study. Hence, it is basically a hybrid type of study, and has the advantages of both methods. Surveys involve the collection of information on an individual basis, from a set of respondents. The essence of a good survey is good interviewing. Paradoxically, this may be totally out of the hands of the researcher, as it involves interviewers' and/or interviewees' biases. For example, non-response can be due to the method of interviewing, the interviewers, or the design of the survey research instrument (i.e. the questionnaire). The major four types of survey instruments are summarised in Figure 6.3.

None of the four survey instruments mentioned above is without fault. In selecting a particular instrument, the bank market research department will need to take into full account the needs of the individual study. The methodology employed must be able to provide accurate information, and be achieved within a specified period of time and budget constraints. Tables 6.1 and 6.2 summarise the advantages and disadvantages of three out of the four instruments in terms of time and budget constraints. Here we present briefly the main characteristics of the fourth instrument: the hybrid survey. When a combination of either mail, telephone or personal interviewing is undertaken, the resulting method is a hybrid survey. The hybrid survey method is flexible and versatile. The researchers must have imagination and a good understanding of all the alternative survey instruments available, to exploit fully the advantages of their combinations, but also to reduce the disadvantages and problems of the methods used. The choice of the combination depends on the needs and the final objectives/constraints of the market study attempted.

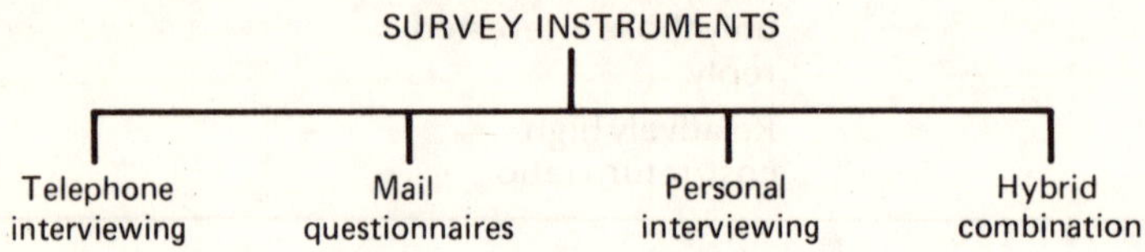

Figure 6.3 The four main types of market survey instruments

Evaluating marketing research programmes

In planning or evaluating market research programmes, it is useful to distinguish between strategic and tactical studies. Strategic marketing research is designed to measure and evaluate long-term shifts in markets and/or consumer behaviour and attitudes that will affect banks' management decision-making in the medium and long terms. Tactical marketing research is to help design short-term projects, for example, how many customers are aware of a current campaign and what they think of it.

The evaluation of research programmes in strategic v. tactical terms can help to optimise the bank marketing research budget and put the various projects in their proper perspective. The ideal research programme should be a blend of the two types of studies.

Strategic research

Before sound decisions can be made, bank management needs to know about the whole banking sector, that is, whether it is expanding, contracting, changing its structure and also the factors that influence these changes. In the financial field, secondary sources of data in the form of published figures relating to advances, deposits etc. are generally accurate, up to date and are readily accessible. The value of these data can be substantially enhanced by relating them to public attitudes and consumer behaviour information. In this way, a much deeper understanding of the market and the factors that can influence it may be acquired.

Strategic marketing research projects fall into three categories: continuous, periodic and *ad hoc*.

(1) *Continuous.* Recently, banks have begun researching changes in accounts structure and on customers' behaviour. However, this cannot provide brand share data and with a product such as a current account for which 'repeat purchase' is almost unknown, it is surely important to know not only who is demanding your product, but also who is buying your competitors' and, more importantly, why. Generally, when a bank's branch shows an increase in new accounts, a shift in age level of new account openers, or in account closers, it is seldom possible to determine (without market research) where the accounts are coming from – or going to – or, for the most part, why.

Continuous audit-type data can assist the banks in a number of different ways by:

(a) accurately measuring the market share at present and predicting it for the future;
(b) telling bank management how it is performing relative to competitors;
(c) identifying movements in individual products/services, for example, students' accounts;
(d) monitoring who is using which type of service, and changes in these patterns;
(e) contributing to long-term profit planning, provided the bank can assess the relative profitability of its various services/products; and
(f) indicating gaps in the market, for which new financial services might be developed and launched.

The method of data collection is through a large enough panel of either the public (for individual customers) or the firms (for corporate accounts). The technique used may be a diary-survey questionnaire combination. It is suggested that this exercise can be combined with a collection of both behavioural and attitudinal data. In that way, the data obtained can be enhanced, as explained earlier. The major problem of this method is the cost owing to the large panel involved. However, the method is straightforward and its feasibility has been proven.

(2) *Periodic.* Financial institutions generally employ two types of periodic surveys: corporate image and omnibus surveys. The corporate image survey is used to measure shifts in public opinion towards the banking sector and the finacial organisations in general. It is used to determine certain characteristics such as: reputation for service, price, financial stability, customer relations, and so on, for the individual banks. These aspects are then linked to the awareness of services offered and services used, demographic details and media behaviour. Questions are included in the omnibus surveys to 'test the water' from time to time.

Although the first of a series of periodic surveys may yield interesting and actionable results, the full value of the series will only begin to be realised when the second and subsequent sets of results are available; that is, when trends become apparent. Periodic surveys, over a number of years, need not be expensive and for bank corporate images it is sufficient to undertake it once or twice every year. The design of public relations and advertising campaigns should utilise these results, and their effects can be measured by *ad hoc* surveys.

Like the continuous survey, the periodic survey monitors trends in the market. But since the survey is done less frequently, the periodic survey has the advantage of cost savings. Moreover, the bank's image is not likely to change drastically over a short period; nor is it necessary to note the change in the population's banking habits (the change is insignificant over a short period). Thus, it will be justified to conduct this kind of survey periodically.

The periodic survey is characterised by the length of time to complete. A bank's 'image study', for example, takes about three to four months to be done properly. The rest of the period is spent on analysis of the data and planning for the next survey. Needless to say, the accuracy of the findings depends to a great extent on the length of the survey.

(3) *Ad hoc surveys. Ad hoc* surveys are done as and when they are required, that is, they are basically of a tactical nature. Nevertheless, studies into the public relations of the bank and into new ventures are considered strategic, because they are of great significance to the bank top management. In public relations studies, public opinion is sought on the likely future issues such as nationalisation, or just simply customers' satisfaction. New ventures studies may be conducted to look into the issues that are not traditional with the banking business. Some examples are mergers or acquisitions of other banks, expansion to overseas markets or bank diversification into other industries.

One obvious point is that all the projects (such as those mentioned above) are of no direct relevance to the marketing department. None the less, they have a great impact on the bank's future strategic decisions and hence are of concern to top management. It is not possible to generalise the cost of this type of *ad hoc* survey and compare it with other surveys. The cost depends largely on the complexity and the time involved in the exercise.

Tactical research

Tactical research covers a wide range of topics – from product research, to advertising, packaging and employees' attitudes studies – and includes extended investigations among corporate, rather than personal, customers.

In undertaking product research, the following questions can be answered:

1. Which types of customers use which services, and why?
2. What is the level of awareness of the various services and how are these in comparison to those offered by competitors?
3. What is the potential for new types of services, for example, cash dispensing machines, advisory services for small businesses, new-style cheque books, credit cards, budget accounts, etc.?
4. Should certain services aim at specific segments of the market, or to the general retail market?
5. What other services would the customer like to have, and what other services might draw additional non-customers to the branch?

Marketing research and planning

Research and planning are two very important marketing activities that work hand-in-hand in the development and introduction of any banking product. According to Stall[1] planning is seen as a process, not a single project. It indicates the directions where the bank should be heading, and the methods of getting there. Marketing research, on the other hand, is a tool for effective planning. In other words, marketing research is employed in order that changes can be detected and fed back into the planning process. The latter can then be adjusted to meet and anticipate any such future changes. In this way the bank's objectives will be more efficiently achieved. In addition, planning keeps the bank in constant awareness of all the variables that might contribute to achievement of the bank's objectives.

The common fault found in many banks is the employment of overdue marketing research programmes. These programmes are conducted mainly because of inertia, with no one actually questioning the usefulness, or the productivity, of the research. Thus, in planning the research programme, one of the methods of checking their usefulness is the use of internal audit. Each research programme is audited to assess its suitability and contribution to the bank in question. any programme that does not meet the bank's requirements will be abandoned. This will release the resources for better projects. When done correctly, planning the research programme will greatly enhance the research function and benefit the bank. This is especially the case when there is a careful interaction of the research plan with organisational plans.

Surveys in bank marketing literature in the USA indicate that most of the bank marketing programmes are badly conducted. This is mainly due to errors of commission (deficiencies in research) and errors of omission (deficiencies in planning). There is a disproportionate emphasis on some marketing decision areas, with negligence on others.

Applications of marketing research in banking

As described earlier in this chapter, marketing research in banking is a tool for problem solving. It refers essentially to two categories of activities: (i) problem solving, and (ii) forecasting results of alternative marketing and business decisions.

There are five major areas in banking where marketing research techniques have been successfully applied. These are: (i) market segmentation, (ii) customer behaviour and bank selection criteria, (iii) customer loyalty, (iv) bank product/services studies, and (v) bank branch research. In this section we will discuss each of these applications in more detail, and will conclude with a review of more recent trends in the role of marketing research in banking.

Market segmentation

Because of the developments on the market place described in previous chapters, one of the first uses of marketing research in banking was in market segmentation. An outstanding study, investigating the private individual behaviour on banking, was the one published by Anderson, Cox and Fulcher.[2] This research indicates the use of various statistical methods to segment a bank market. The research involved a determinant attribute analysis of bank selection criteria. It assesses the principal decision factors used and their relative importance in bank selection decisions. It also examines the usefulness of these factors as a criterion for market segmentation and design of patronage appeals.

Similar studies on market segmentation have been carried out by Barclays in the UK, in Germany by Familien Bank, in France and in

Belgium. At the operative level, the major use of the findings of these studies was in allocating the promotional effort and advertising expenditures.

In a cluster analysis study by Robertson and Bellenger[3] in three geographically different areas in the USA, the researchers have identified six different clusters (or segments) of bank customers. This study present the six major sets of characteristics pertinent to each homogenous group of bank customers, for example, demographic characteristics, financial attitudes, banking habits, media habits, most important factors in the cluster and finally least important factors in the cluster. For each cluster (i.e. homogenous group) of respondents (bank customers actual or potential), a label can be attached that will reflect the typology of customers in that particular cluster. The label is a function of the 'weight' attached by the relevant respondents in the cluster to the various attributes presented to them in the questionnaire. (For a more detailed discussion on the methodology of cluster analysis see Aaker.[4])

There are a number of alternative multivariate marketing research techniques that can be employed for segmentation studies, as indicated in Figure 6.4. Among these are cluster analysis (as indicated in the example mentioned above) and also determinant attributes analysis, linear regression, discriminant analysis and canonical correlation. (For a discussion of the advantages and limitations of each of these methods see Fitzroy.[5])

In canonical correlation analysis the variables are first divied into two sets; (i) the predictor set, and (ii) the usage criterion set. The predictor set consists of three broad types of variables: demographic (including age, sex, marital status and so on), socio-economic (including occupation, education, income, residence length, and general bank account variables), and attitudinal (including attitudes towards various bank characteristics).

The usage criterion set consists of bank services such as: safe deposit boxes, instalments loans, automatic tellers, overdraft checking and bank credit cards. Only the common services are mentioned here and also this set is offered in most banks.

The canonical correlation analysis is used to analyse the relationship between the predictor set variables and the usage criterion set variables. Thus, the main objective of the analysis is to identify the groups of bank services that are associated with groups of respondents' characteristics.[6] The information on the demographic and sociological variables is collected by means of questionnaires sent out to respondents. As for additudinal variables, a measurement of opinions or attitudes towards the bank characteristics is required. This is done by requesting the respondent to rate the bank services on a bipolar scale ranging from very satisfied (score 5) to very dissatisfied (score 1).

The canonical analysis derived two sets of weighting coefficients (a set for the criterion variables and a set for the predictor variables) for each pair

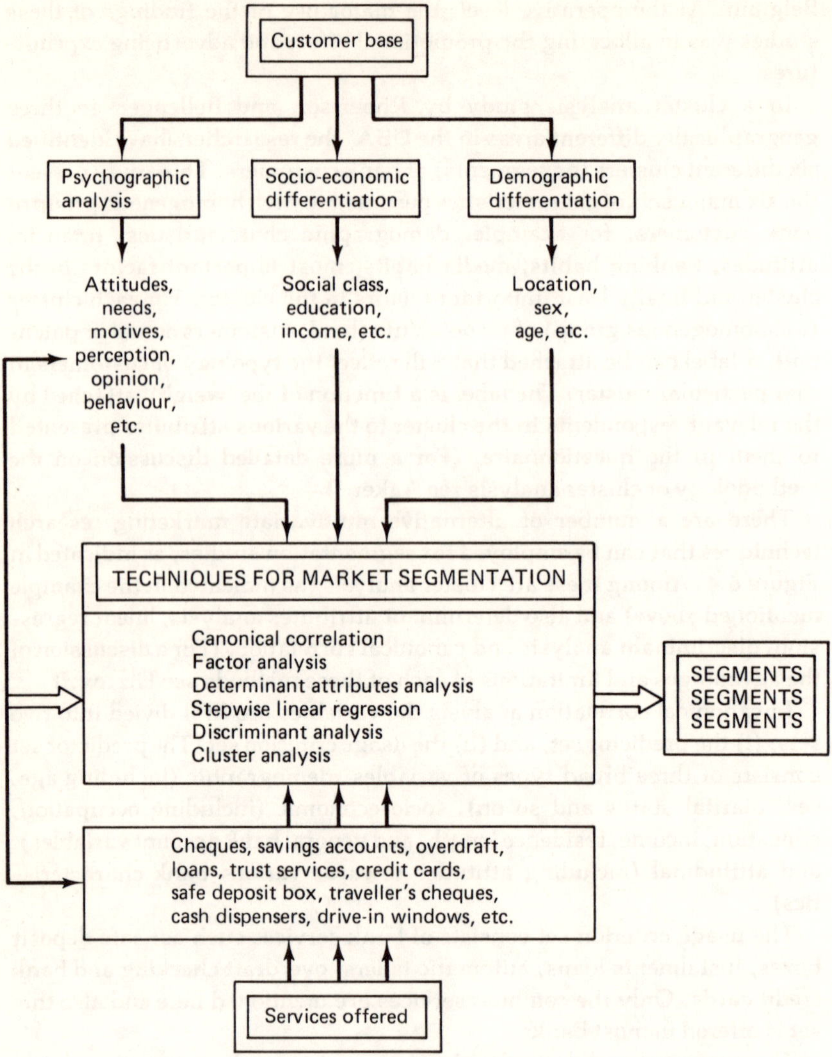

Figure 6.4 The process and techniques for market segmentation

of canonical variables. In fact, a computer program can be used to derive them. The method enables identification of which set of bank services and characteristics appeal to a particular group of bank customers. This, of course, can have some important applications for the bank marketing strategy.

Another investigation provided convincing evidence in support of the real need of market segmentation employing a factor analysis centred around five banks that differed from each other on seven main attributes:

friendliness, quality of service, community spirit, modernness of facilities, convenience, range of services and ownership.[7] The main finding revealed by the study was that on the basis of perception of the overall image of the five banks relative to each other, there existed three distinct market segments: convenience, service and staff friendliness-oriented segments.

The research demonstrated strongly that the bank customer has distinct images of competing banks, and that their images can, and do, vary substantially within the total market to the extent that 'different' market segments do exist. The research also established that the segments differ in terms of the attributes used to differentiate between the banks, perceptions of the relative performance of the banks on those attributes, and in the attributes used to determine preferences. As a result, the segments are so different in their perceptions and preferences that it is critical that market segmentation is seen as an essential aspect of the bank marketing strategy.

To sum up, market research should be required to elicit information about the various segments on these lines:

1. How big is the segment in volume terms? This may indicate whether it was worth pursuing it in terms of profit generation.
2. Who are the clients and customers in the segment? For example, what demographic and sociological features do private individuals have? With corporate customers, what are the growth prospects of the industries and firms in the locality of the branch?
3. What do the bank's clients use the services for? Different social groups may use the same service in different ways.
4. What kind of financial service do the various segments patronise? How big is the researching bank's share of the market compared with other banks, building societies, hire purchase companies, Giro bank, etc? This will help determine whether the marketing strategy should be defensive or offensive.

Bank selection criteria

How do customers select a bank? It is important for banks to clearly identify the process of bank selection and the criteria used in this process. Of course, different customers may have different behaviours and preferences. The preference for a particular bank may be made after considering the range of services offered by the bank. There are two other factors that can affect a consumer choice of a bank. The first is the distance of the bank from home, office and shopping centre, and second, the kind of relations that the customer may have towards the bank (parent, friends, etc.). Hence, we can group the customer bank choosing process into three main factors: distance from the bank, relation with the bank and preference of particular bank services. This has been presented in a significant study on bank customer behaviour that centres round the development of a simulation-based information system for a French bank.[8] The first phase of the simulation, which is described here, considers a customer's behaviour structure regarding their first choice of a bank. The approach considered that each customer has his own behaviour determined by his attitude towards the bank's products and services, the bank's branches and the competition. This kind of behaviour helps the customer to differentiate by a conscious preference analysis between the bank and the competition (e.g. other banks, finance agencies and institutions). Two further factors that the customer considers before making his final choice of a bank are: the distance of the bank from his home or office, and the type of relations that he may have towards a given bank (friend, parent, etc.). The weight that the customer will give to these three factors is obtained by considering the analytical structure of customer behaviour.[9] If the same customer chooses to open a second account at a different bank then this will be primarily due to two reasons. The first would concern a rise in the image of the competing bank as a result of proposing new products or services, or if the quality of certain services improves. If the client considers these services of interest, then he will re-evaluate his preferences and reconsider the triad of distance, preference and relations. The second reason could be a reduction in the bank's own image owing to, say. a decrease of service quality. This will lead to a fall in the customer's loyalty and a reconsideration of the service quality of different banks, resulting in a review of his decision process.

The discussion in this section has been limited owing to the fact that past behavioural analyses have assumed market homogeneity. However, as mentioned in the previous section, it is widely recognised that customer needs can be more meaningfully studied by considering specific segments separately.

The set of characteristics required for bank selection decisions can be obtained by interviewing consumers. The significant product attribute, which plays an important role in determining the consumer choice process, can be identified by multiple discriminant analysis. Each individual indicates the relative importance he attaches to each attribute for different banks. We can now work out the preference indicator for each bank. This can be set best illustrated by an example. An individual weights the attributes (let's take four characteristics: friendly employee, good services, approval of most loans and budgeting assistance) to be 4, 5, -1 and 4 respectively. (The scale ranges from $+5$ to -5.) The preference indicator is: $(4+5-1+4)/4=3$. We can use the preference indicator to predict the preferred bank of an individual as far as service is concerned. (The higher the indicator the more preferred is the bank.)

The final decision as to which bank an individual chooses will depend on the relative importance of the three factors: (i) distance, (ii) relations, and

(iii) preferences. The customer may accord different weights to each factor depending on their importance to him. To illustrate this idea in a simplified and quantified form; let us consider the following; the customer might weigh the three factors:

(a) the distance from the bank to be $N1$;
(b) the relations to the bank to be $N2$;
(c) the preferences of services to be $N3$.

Then the customer might scale the three factors for each bank according to his personal views towards that particular bank. Finally, the total weighted averages of these factors for the various banks are compared and the highest one will obviously be the preferred bank. For example, the scales of the three factors to Bank *A* are:

(a) distance, scaled 4;
(b) relations, scaled 1; and
(c) preference scaled 3, we have

$$\text{The total weighted average} = \frac{4N_1 + 1N_2 + 3N_3}{3}$$

Essentially, we try to quantify the client process in order to have an insight as to how the consumer chooses a particular bank, although in practice the consumer may not go through all this exact 'quantitative' process.

Customer loyalty

The importance of loyalty lies in the fact that it has a significant implication for the bank market strategy. For instance, a bank might decide whether or not to emphasise the moves intended to capitalise on loyalty. Such efforts would include promotion to the young, special locations, and cross-selling to build up business with current customers. Loyalty can be thought of as a continuing patronage at a particular bank by a particular customer, over time. Every customer has a certain degree of loyalty to a bank. The degree of loyalty can be gauged by tracking customers' accounts over a defined time period and noting the degree of continuity in patronage.

Fry *et al.*, in their longitudinal study on customer loyalty to banks, use a simple probability model.[10] The measurements of loyalty used are as follows: assume measures are available for a population of customers indicating whether or not they have a specific account at a specific bank, B, in two time periods t and $t-1$. $P(B_t)$ is the unconditional probability of an individual, randomly drawn from the population, having an account at Bank *B* in the time period t and $P(B_t/B_{t-1})$ is the conditional probability of an individual having an account at Bank *B* at the time period t, given that he had an account at Bank *B* at time period $t-1$. Loyalty exists if $P(B_t/B_{t-1}) > P(B_t)$ and the degree of loyalty is the extent to which $P(B_t/B_{t-1})$ exceeds $P(B_t)$.

In that study, the results were based on the analysis of university graduates' questionnaires, to identify the bank(s) partonised by respondents at specified periods before, during and after their stay at the university. Additional questions were also included to obtain data on respondent location and loan status, the bank(s) patronised by their parents and socio-economic classification. The time periods were classified as (i) the year prior to the respondent's entering the university, (ii) the respondent's year of graduation, (iii) the year following graduation, and (iv) the present time.

The main conclusions of this study on the factors affecting the degree of loyalty to a bank are as follows:

1. *Branch coverage and mobility.* If the respondent does not move from one city to another and stays constantly in one place, or is non-mobile, then the branch coverage of the banks has no effect on loyalty. Other than this condition, mobility in general affects loyalty and the probability of a customer remaining with a bank with relatively better branch coverage is greater than for a bank with a less extensive branch coverage.
2. *Loans.* If the respondent has an outstanding loan at one period, say period 3, then it is more likely for him to remain in the same bank at the next period, that is, period 4.
3. *Sex.* It was found that males have 0.7 higher probability of remaining loyal to the bank than females. One probable reason is that some women, after marrying, tend to shift to their husbands' bank. (The new 'Engaged' package operated by Barclays in England suggests, however, the opposite.)
4. *Prior patronage.* If a respondent had an account in a particular bank at, say, period 3, then the probability of the respondent remaining in the same bank is higher (that is: $P(B_4/B_3) > P(B_4)$).

   The influence of parents on bank patronage of students is also significant. The analysis shows that the conditional probability of patronising the same bank as their parents, $P(B_1/\text{Parent of Bank } B)$ is much greater than the unconditional probability $P(B_1)$.

Product studies

This type of marketing research enables the bank to assess existing products by their usefulness and customers' utilisation rate. For products that are useful to customers, the bank will want to consider how to improve them further. In addition, a comparison is done to rate these products against those of the competitors'. There is also the research into the specific segments of the market using the products. For those products that have a low utilisation rate, this may be due to poor awareness among the potential users, or a wrong choice of the marketing mix.

In short, although the emphasis is largely aimed at customer behaviour, product research still plays a vital part in marketing research in banking. It helps to answer such questions as: which types of customers use which services and why; what is the level of awareness of the various services and what is the potential for new types of service (cash machines, credit cards, etc.); are certain services better aimed at specific segments of the market; what other services would customers like to have; and what services might entice non-customers into the branch. Such research is as much strategic as tactical, and indeed it is often possible to recognise both aspects within the same project.

The importance of market research to banking has led to an ever-increasing growth in the number of investigations and publications in this field, the majority of which have been carried out in the USA. Many banks consider that if the range of services to meet consumer needs is to continue to expand and the associated costs are to be kept within a manageable level then automation and computerisation must play an ever-increasing role in money transmission. Unfortunately the banking industry's active assault on the consumer markets through the continuous introduction of new products combined with a hard-sell approach has met with great consumer resistance. The result of this is that some banks have regressed in their marketing thinking[11] as they are: failing to visualise new products from the perspective of the consumer, engaging in creative research for uncovering unfulfilled needs within various market segments, effectively minimising the psychological discomfort associated with new products, which require substantial behavioural changes for the consumer; and clearly and graphically communicating the benefits of new products to the market segments towards which they are directed. In other words, there appears in many instances to be a failure to look at new products through the eyes of the consumer.

Bank branch research

Owing to rapid expansion that is occurring in a number of bank branch locations, a more systematic approach to market area analysis and site selection is needed. It is important that we should seek to look at a bank's approach to new business development. Some of the most important reasons are:

1. Management science is improving all the time, offering reliable and up-to-date information on bank markets and customers. Because of the high prospects of profits on the financial markets, competition among banks has become keener. Consequently evaluation of data that is

important to the appraisal of new business potential in banking is now critical.

2. The large banking groups attempt to develop new business by offering a large variety of new services in the attempt to open up new markets within the existing customer base (i.e. new services to existent customers).
3. As a result of the greater products/services range offerings, the question of priorities in terms of bank resources allocation becomes increasingly important. Moreover, the question of branch development has to be looked at against a background where banks' services are much the same and therefore rather similar in costs and prices.

Given that there is a resonable spread of services offered by a branch, the development of its business depends on:

(a) Attracting the unbanked community;
(b) selling more services to existing customers (cross-selling);
(c) attracting customers from competitors;
(d) increasing the profitability of existing services.

Past experience shows that if a bank is successful in attracting a new deposit customer, there is a certain probability that the same customer will also avail himself/herself of other bank services by establishing secondary relationships with the bank. These interrelationships among the many services offered to the customers are known as 'cross-sell' interrelationships.

The individual branch, however, has to determine its own priorities in the use of available resources before attempting to achieve any or all of the above goals. To achieve the best results, research on the business potential of the branch bank has to be carried out.

Research for branch development also plays an increasingly important role in deciding whether or not to open a new branch bank in an area not represented by the bank and whether there is any competition or not. It is probable that 80 per cent or more of the business falls within a reasonably defined area, known as the 'catchment area'. Within such a catchment area, there will be a focal point in which the business or community activity of the area is concentrated. This focal point will be determined by a number of factors such as population, industry, shops, traffic flows, parking facilities, pedestrian flows, ease of access by road and rail, etc. It therefore does not follow that the placement of a branch in the centre of the main shopping area will be the best possible site. A subsidiary shopping area or a centre of industry may well prove more suitable. For a more detailed discussion on the various models and qualitative approaches, see Chapter 3.

Recent trends in bank marketing research

Whereas in the past banks have been most successful in employing marketing research techniques in bank business development pursuits – such as market analysis, customer segmentation, products/services development, etc. – recent bank trends have encouraged the senior bank management to ask marketers to focus their attention upon different types of solutions to problems. As can be seen from Figure 6.5, the most interesting development in the role that marketing research is required to play is in the establishment of long-range bank corporate objectives. The newer trend is the bank managers' preferences – and sometimes requirements – of quantitative answers and 'solutions' for better marketing decisions.

Computer technology already offers opportunities for cross-evaluating bank marketing services. The research in this field has recently reached quite an advanced stage both in quantity and in quality terms, attempting

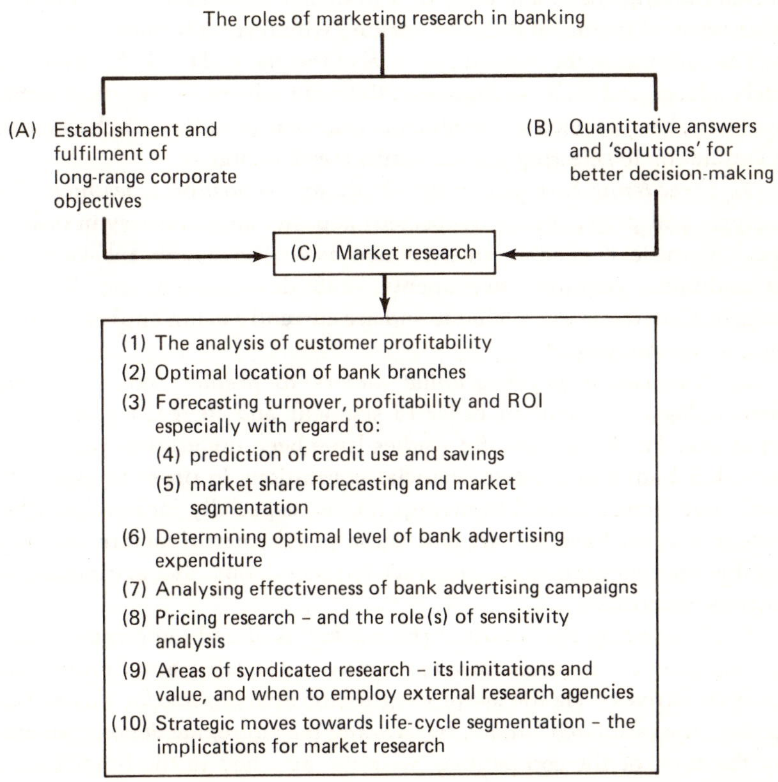

Figure 6.5 Recent trends in the roles of bank marketing research

to supply quantitative answers to some of the most pressing marketing problems facing the banking industry. The major areas in which quantitative tools were very recently employed are as follows:

(1) *The analysis of customer profitability,* via the use of computer-based systems capable of portraying what is in effect consolidated profit and loss statements for each of the banks' customers. The advantages of applying these systems are obvious: they enable the bank management not just to assess accurately the absolute and relative profitability contribution of each major customer, but also provide the necessary information in order to price bank services realistically, generate profitability and performance reports for administrative groups, generate service lines and product managers' reports, and enable control of profit and targets against plans at a high level of reliability and consistency.

(2) *Optimal location of bank branches.* A recent study[12] revealed that about 90 per cent of the respondents banked at the branch nearest their home or place of work. Convenience, in terms of location, was also found to be the single most important factor for selecting a branch.

Determining the 'trade area' of a branch and assessing the impact of other relevant factors of decision-making with respect to bank location, as well as estimating the deposit potential of the planned bank, have received lately a large and increased interest. Relevant advanced statistical techniques have been applied successfully in practical situations, such as the use of simulation in selecting branch banks (see Chapter 3).

(3) *Forecasting turnover, profitability and return on investment.* The analysis and projections of (expected) deposits are necessary in order to check on the level of achievement of new as well as older branches, decide on additional required investments, staff development, etc. Relevant statistical methods are available and are currently being applied successfully in the industry.[13]

(4) *The use of psychographic factors to predict credit use.* This methodology is useful in order to segment and to reach new market segments. Particular specific studies have been undertaken recently by large US banks and other financial institutions in order to obtain the predictive factors related to savings inflow, especially for new branches. Recent studies have shown that these psychometric factors are *more* reliable than the static measures such as: population, average income and savings penetration.

(5) *Forecasting the 'share of the market'* is already in common usage among most of the medium-sized banks in the USA and Europe. This analysis derives – via the use of a regression analysis and/or a hyperbolic model – the estimated 'share', by dividing the aggregate deposit potential by the total of the competitive 'weights' attached to the branch(es) in question.

(6) *Determining optimal levels of advertising expenditure in bank*

management. Some of these models have been applied at operational level by some banks in South California. Usually, the optimal level of bank advertising depends on banks' goals, planning horizon and marketing strategy. Suitable equations that relate these three variables with the other marketing inputs and the environment of the bank can be developed.

(7) *Analysing the effectiveness of banks' advertising campaigns*. The major marketing bank expenditure is on advertising. About 40 per cent to 50 per cent of the total expenditure on bank marketing is on advertising. But still relatively little is being done on trying to assess the effectiveness of advertising and promotional campaigns by banks, although a variety of quite established techniques exist that are successfully employed in industrial and consumer goods marketing.

In addition, life-cycle segmentation and pricing research are two extremely important fields of investigation. The role of market research is strategic – in the case of life-cycle – and tactical – in the case of pricing of bank services. Normally, the investigations on short-term price tactics are conducted via a sensitivity analysis. Finally, all the functions of market research can be performed by the individual marketing research departments in banks, or by external research agencies. In certain cases syndicated research by all – or a number of banks – should be considered.

CHAPTER 7

Controlling the marketing programme

Contents

As the banking industry shifts from a supply or 'production' orientation to one that recognises the significance of the market in determining banking success, three implications for bank management have become apparent; first, bank plans must be built around market needs – not market needs in general – but the identified needs of the bank's branches' own trading area. Thus planning should not only reflect the economic and demographic character of the market segments, but also their attitudes and values regarding money, savings, spending and security; second, incorporation of market variables in bank planning makes possible a balance of market opportunities, bank resources and competitive position in the interests of growth and profitability; finally, with so many marketing activities in operation at one time, the bank runs the risk of confusing customers and alienating prospects. In a full service bank, the problem is particularly acute. A bank must communicate an image that is both secure and prudent, but also progressive and modern. Therefore, planning – however detailed – is not enough. Co-ordination involves control over the activities and the people responsible for them. If the goals are established in sufficient detail at the outset, the control task is made easier because precise goals can be used as measures of performance for control. The process of control involves four steps:[1]

(a) predicting the outcomes of decisions in the form of performance measures;
(b) collecting information on actual performance;
(c) comparing actual with predicted performance;
(d) when a decision is shown to have been deficient, correcting the procedure that produced it and correcting its consequences where possible.

Bank marketing control

An important factor in bank marketing is marketing control, whereby an organised feedback is provided. In dynamic market conditions strategic targets and tactical bank operations should be under continuous control, so that the bank retains the initiative in its markets.

The control of bank marketing performance can be by profitability, by market share, or by business volume. For *each* of these three alternative forms of control, the bank should check and compare the performance of (i) its branches, (ii) various financial services offered, (iii) customer types, for example, retail v. corporate, different types of segment markets, etc. The performance would then be compared against the bank's targets (or standards), *or* past bank's performance on each of these criteria, or/and against the performance of the leading banks in the industry, or the average in the banking industry, if known (Figure 7.1).

The same analyses should be performed for the other major types of control, as indicated in Figure 7.1. It should be emphasised that these three forms of control are not alternative to each other, but complementary. While profitability figures might be of interest to the bank's depositors, shareholders, owners, very large clients, government, etc. as an indicator of the bank's future ability, the business volume ratios relate to the bank's strategic posture, that is, its potential growth and future development in relation to competitive financial institutions. All the nine measures for control are of very great operational importance to the marketing manager in the banking industry. The bank will be able to delete or drop certain financial services that are not 'enough' profitable, or with a 'too low' business volume. In addition, the marketing research section will be able to identify problem areas in order to undertake research with a view to finding out the reasons that underlie these outcomes. However, good marketing performances would be of interest to the marketing manager as much as poor performances. In both cases, marketing control will enable the marketing manager to focus his attention on the problem areas in order to take early constructive action. With the advance of automatisation, most of these control ratios are fairly easily obtainable. They would enable the marketing department to recognise

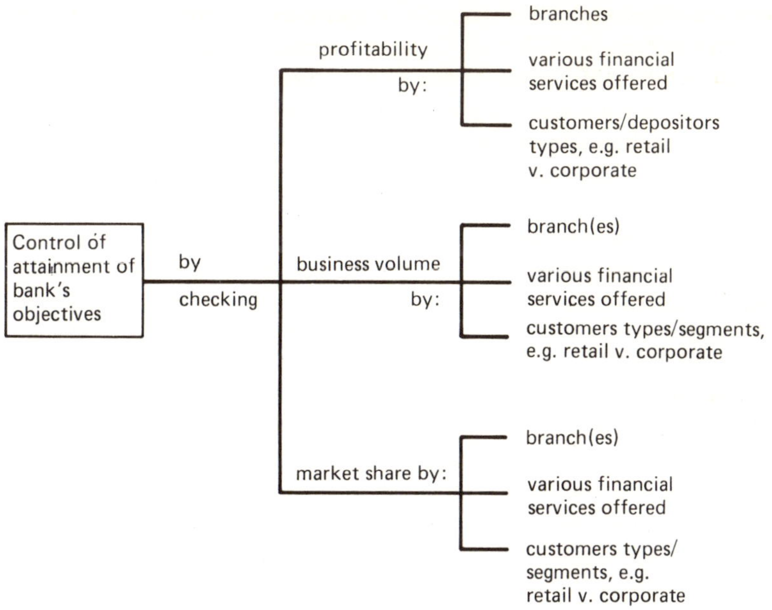

Figure 7.1 Types of bank marketing control

immediately potential 'good' as well as 'bad' products, profitable or unprofitable markets and/or customers' segments, efficient or less efficient distribution channels and branches, and consequently suitable marketing strategies can be developed.

The need for control

Traditionally, the bank's main concern was with total growth. However, currently, the attitude among banks' management has changed, strongly emphasising the need of profits. This is one of the reasons that has led to greater attention being paid to the issue of controlling the marketing programme for a stronger and sounder marketing practice. Another reason is the competitive environment. The banking environment is currently more competitive than in the past and far greater competition can be expected in the future. As we have already seen, other types of financial institutions have diversified their services into the banking business; for example, finance corporations have diversified into consumer credit, checking account services, credit cards, home improvement loans and even trust services. These new financial firms, which had aggressively and successfully responded to the changing market, have drained off business from banks.

In banking, marketing is typically viewed as a staff function. The introduction of new services and products creates a substantial impact upon existing employee resources. Experience resulting from the NOW (negotiable order of withdrawal), non-interest-bearing checking accounts and other types of accounts shows that a new product can have a ripple effect at both the teller windows and the bank office in general. Yet, in total, a branch has some 250 or more services and products it can sell to a customer. The question of what is the optimum number has probably never really been deeply explored. But what is very clear is that the 250 products would be far too many to be merchandised effectively, even if the branch managers were interested. In lieu of the opportunities to display and demonstrate, the merchandiser of services has to rely on his ability to explain and persuade. This in turn requires branch staff time. Moreover, each extra banking service means an increase in costs, which the present bank managements try to lower. Therefore some sort of control is required.

In addition, there are also increasing staff costs. Salaries are rising not only because of inflation, but also because of increasing skills requirements and salary competition from other financial institutions. Not only are replacement costs usually higher, but the substandard performance of a new employee in training affects the overall branch performance. Training costs are rising because of additional training personnel and new training programmes to familiarise new and existing personnel with the new services and products being introduced. Many banks estimate that it takes at least three or four months to achieve acceptable performance from a newly hired teller, and service personnel often require even more time. The total wages and salaries bills account for more than 60 per cent of total operating costs for most banks commercial banks.

In a highly competitive and regulated environment, the critical factor in attracting and retaining depositors is services. Therefore, customer service levels and staffing requirements are critical. Management must ask itself, 'at what price?' The answer to this question will vary, depending upon the respondent, that is, the controller or the branch manager. Quite frequently, poor bank marketing results are the outcome of a lack of basic market and profitability information. Almost as often, such information exists but is simply ignored. Even when new services had turned out to be unprofitable, many banks allow their promotion and advertising to continue virtually undirected at the branch level. Some banks fail to give sufficient attention to planning and the managing of their branch network; others, in attempting to diversify, allow their services to proliferate too much with little regard for their contribution to profitability.

The control process

Weyer[2] suggests that the control process is an integral part of bank marketing management. The general principle of controlling a marketing programme involves the need to know what are the objectives the programme aims to achieve. Once the aims are known, one can set up targets. Failure in achieving these targets will result in investigating the factors concerned. Then corrective action can be taken to identify the causes for failure and to correct the diverged programme results.

An important stage within the control process is the prediction of outcomes of decisions in the form of performance measures. Or, in other words, to develop operational standards or targets. This will very much depend on the market research, since marketing effort and decision must rest upon it. These operational standards could be cost standard, share of the market statistics or some target values that might especially be important when introducing new services.

An example of cost standards for bank marketing is in budgeting the bank advertising costs. Until recently, the banking industry devoted little attention to the study of advertising costs; bankers concentrating their time and talents on solving other pressing problems and therefore the costs associated with 'inefficient' advertising have simply been accepted as inevitable. However, with the significant sums of money that the US banking industry is currently spending on promotions, bank management can no longer ignore the use of cost control techniques to measure the benefits received from advertising efforts. In Rayburn's study[3] it is suggested that the purpose of the advertising and promotional functions is to create demand for the bank's services and to build and maintain goodwill towards the organisation. The manner in which this function is carried out varies from bank to bank. Some banks handle all their advertising on their own. Other banks contract all the advertising to an outside firm. Because of this, advertising efficiency is more difficult to evaluate than most other banking costs (such as personnel or supplies expenses). The use of cost standard allows bank management to examine advertising operations to a greater degree, which can lead to a better understanding of the financial implications of banks' activities. These standards can be used in the development of budgets and for later comparison with actual costs incurred. In fact, most banks do use some type of budgets to control their advertising expenditures. Rayburn stresses that the following steps should be taken in developing cost standards for use in advertising budgets:

1. Break down the advertising function into various elements such as radio media, television media, direct mail, samples, etc.
2. Determine the factors that cause the advertising costs to vary (this is known as the 'unit of variability'). Each factor chosen must fluctuate concomitantly with the activity which is the cause of the cost. For example, newspaper and minutes of television advertisements could be the unit of variability for newspaper and television advertising.
3. Establish a standard cost for each unit of variability. These standard

costs should reflect managers' and accountants' opinions as to what the advertising should cost, assuming relative efficient conditions are in operation.

4. Determine the amount and type of advertising needed for each bank segment. Certainly, the advertising budget should be increased with the introduction of new bank services. However, the starting point for most banks is to analyse actual costs for a previous period and eliminate any obvious excess costs.
5. Compare actual and budgeted advertising expenses with the difference broken down into efficiency and price variances and investigate significant variances.[4]

Thus advertising cost standards and the advertising budget are closely related, because standard costs serve as yardsticks for budgeting. Budgeting attempts to set up a predetermined standard of operation for a period of time, while standards are concerned with cost per unit. Like budgets, standard costs provide criteria by which it is possible to ascertain what the costs should have been in comparison to what the costs actually were. This will enable variance to be computed and analysed.

It is through the variance analysis that the inefficiencies that are found from the factors that caused the differences between the standard and actual costs can be identified and eliminated. Variance analysis can be performed by applying Management Information System (MIS) for banks. According to Limberg: 'The purpose of a MIS is to determine and provide, efficiently, effectively, and economically as possible, what management needs to know. It should facilitate the accomplishment of objectives, prevent failures to reach objectives, and correct conditions which hamper the fulfillment of objectives.'[5] The need for an effective MIS cannot be emphasised too strongly.

Standards and types of bank marketing control

According to Moran,[6] at a recent seminar attended by executive-level representatives of midwestern savings and loan associations in the USA, 150 delegates took part in an industry survey that ranged from economic predictions to branch profitability. Approximately one-third of the replies indicated that the association did not know whether their branches were profitable. Combined with those indicating that branches were not profitable, the survey clearly demonstrated a widespread need for the evaluation and improvement of overall branch performance.

Some comments about the standards for control. Although profitability is a most useful standard against which to measure performance of marketing activities, the bank manager may wish to use other standards as well. Marketing forecast is always a good starting-point. Also, information collected over a long period of time is helpful.

Standards for comparison from outside the bank may be used. Operating data, where available, from banks of comparable size may serve as a measure of overall performance. Studies of other banks, research institutes, etc., may be the source of such data. The total advertising budget or the breakdown of the budget according to distribution to various media may be compared with the expenditure patterns of similar banks. Other indicators, such as economic indicators and (lately) 'social indicators', could also be helpful for setting standards.

Three major types of measurement tools can be distinguished for bank marketing control:[7] (i) marketing audit, (ii) variance analysis, and (iii) ratio analysis.

Bank marketing audit

The level of the bank's ability and willingness to implement a marketing plan effectively is an important consideration in controlling bank marketing effort. The marketing audit broadly takes the form of an independent examination of the whole marketing effort, with a view to appraising what is being done and recommending what should be done in future. It should cover the following:

1. The level of resources allocated to the marketing effort, and how these are divided between market segments, products/services and functions of the mix.
2. The strategies and tactics employed in carrying out the programme, considering why particular choices were made and what alternatives were available.
3. Procedures and systems governing the day-to-day marketing operation.
4. Organisation, authority, reporting lines and management concepts in the marketing department, including the effectiveness of liaison with other departments of the bank.

A marketing audit reviews the marketing operations in the light of its ability to achieve the bank's marketing objectives. Henceforth marketing audit provides useful feedback for decision-making, as well as playing a critical part in the process of marketing planning.

Ratio analysis

Degrees of efficiency, levels of activity and the extent to which capacity and resources are fully utilised are as critical in the bank marketing operation as elsewhere. Ratios relating one variable to another provide a useful method of analysis, enabling the marketing manager to trace and explain developments that would not otherwise be apparent.

Ratios are a valuable early warning guide to possible problem areas in bank marketing performance. They may be used to compare the effectiveness of similar group, such as corporate with retail customers, in relation to various products, or branches; or they can be used to compare the performance of the same bank at different times.

However, it must be remembered that, in many ways, ratios can prove to be false indices, for changes in the environment affecting either variable can destroy the validity of the comparison, and there are the usual problems of deciding what ratio represents an adequate standard. In some cases ratios can be downright misleading. For example, an increase in branch profit ratio may appear favourable, unless it is accompanied by some factor, such as a reduction in total branch marketing expenditure.

Variance analysis

The control element in budgetary control is the determination of variances from the budget. If budget and the standards on which it is based are sufficiently detailed, the magnitude of these variances and the area in which they occur will be the key to management action.

It is appropriate at this stage to discuss the principal differences between standard cost and budgeted costs. Essentially, the differences lie in their scope. While both are concerned with laying down cost limits for control purposes, budget costs impose limits to costs for the marketing department as a whole for the budget period whereas standard costs are attached to various functional activities or processes of the bank marketing department. Marketing budget, it must be emphasised, is a critical element in controlling bank marketing effort.

In addition to variance analysis, there are many other control techniques, for example operational research methods with computer modelling available for controlling the expenditure of marketing efforts such as branch location, personal selling, number of counter clerks, etc.[8] These are of paramount importance to improve the efficiency of bank performance, and bank management should take note of them as the amount of reward in terms of business expansion and/or cost reduction can be of considerable magnitude.

Control in bank branches

Branches have to be controlled as well. In Rossier's study,[10] it is said that in the light of bank branch expansion in many countries, it is extremely unwise for a bank to open a branch without first analysing market potential and determining the expenditure required to obtain a sufficient market share. The risk in expansion is not so much one of opening unprofitable branches, but rather of allocating scarce resources of managerial talent, qualified personnel and capital to marginal projects.

Moran's study[11] previously mentioned, suggests that even though the rising cost of personnel in the branches should be of obvious interest to bank management, there are other factors that are related to the costs, such as: new services, increasing competition, increasing staffing requirements and utilisation of personnel. The plan of economising and improving bank branch performance should relate and include the following aspects:

1. *Define objectives,* that is, areas to be measured and analysed, techniques for measurement and analysis, and responsible for project (branch staff participation).
2. *Develop and implement activity volume surveys,* that is, customer traffic patterns, transaction volumes, and functional allocations.
3. *Develop operations standards,* that is, teller functions, and platform functions.
4. *Analyse branch operations,* that is branch procedures, floor layout, equipment, and security.
5. *Analyse activity volumes,* including average daily transactions, average daily customers, queuing analysis for tellers, and functional analysis of other bank branch personnel.
6. *Prepare recommendations,* in relation to staffing levels, operations improvement, branch classification, and costing data.

In utilising this action plan, the very first step is to define the programme's objectives. This formulation of programme objectives is not solely for the branch, but should include a committee with members from the bank's headquarters in operations, finance and marketing. This committee will evaluate the various needs in different areas and define objectives for the marketing programmes such as determing staff performance; determining staff utilisation; determining customer service levels; determining optimum staff level; developing cost data to be used in product and functional costing; and developing operational improvements.

This programme could be tried in three dissimilar branches on a pilot basis to test it before implementing it throughout the entire bank. An analyst team can be formed comprising of personnel from the branches and other areas to assess and measure performance of the branches.

Doyle, Fenwick and Savage[12] suggest that considerable resources are spent in helping branch staff to develop a greater marketing orientation, stressing particularly the importance of research and market planning. This has presented banks' top management with the need to help branch managers by providing assessments of potential at a branch level and objectively evaluateing the results of their business development effort. They identified that there are two problems that make such evaluations difficult. First, performance in a banking operation is multidimensional, that is, a branch might be in a good area for attracting deposits but not for generating loan business. Thus the exact mix of business is important not only for ensuring that the bank maintains its desired market profit but also because the relative profitability of its different services changes with interest rate movements. Therefore, it is necessary to consider several dimensions of performance separately. Branch profit alone is inadequate for performance analysis.

Second, whatever performance measures are used, these can provide no direct evaluation of the managerial effort imparted. Branch results depend upon both management performance and exogenous factors arising from the branch's local conditions – exogenous factors such as the effects of differences in the size and socio-economic composition of trading areas, the strength of competition, the attractiveness of branch site, etc. Doyle *et al.* suggested, that a model for performance analysis based on identified predictor variables, or determinants of branch performance needed to be built. Predictor variables – like trade area characteristics, location features, branch features, competitive situation, etc. – can be helpful. This will provide a more realistic and accurate analysis of the branch performance. Chapter 10 provides an additional simple discussion on bank branches' performances.

Bank managers and directors with functional duties should be involved in the control of their own functions, but the branch managers are essentially those who control the operation of the bank branches. The word 'control' can be either a noun or a verb. The *Dictionary of Management*[13] defines control (noun) as 'a mean or method, or the process, of controlling', and control (verb) as 'to affect the behaviour of someone or of a group so that it conforms with one's wishes'. The latter refers to the ability of a director or a manager to guide others in the organisation towards the bank's goals, but it is the means of doing this, and the methods used, that are relevant here. 'Control' in this context therefore refers to the responsibility of bank directors and managers for the introduction and use of systems and procedures to enable the organisation's goals to be achieved.

The major controls used in banks are financial controls, but in some cases descriptive rather than quantitative information may be appropriate.

It is obvious that accounting information is not the only means of control, but this sort of information is the most widely used to monitor banks' activities. Budgeting can be thought of as a plan and a control, since actual costs are compared with budgeted costs and variances then explained. Although this tends to produce historical data, modern electronic data processing techniques allow information to be produced in time for corrections to be made to operating procedures. Budgetary control is probably one of the most widely used control techniques in operation today. It can be used also as a motivational tool and also it might enable the identification of variances that allow 'management by exception' to be practised, that is, only variances of a certain significance are commented upon and investigated in any depth. In addition, in many bank branches various reports can be prepared periodically for presentation and discussion by the bank. Such reports are produced for purposes of control and include many already mentioned, for example, ratios, variance to standards and audits, as elaborated earlier in this chapter. The advent of sophisticated computers at low prices allows the effects of changes in one variable to be analysed against other variables. This means that control can become largely an automatic process, with periodic guidance from the bank management to audit the effectiveness and the necessity of the control systems being used.

A major objective of the control process is to improve the bank branch performance. The controllable operating performance at branch level is necessary because of increased competition facing banks, increased staff costs and high inputs of personnel required in bank operations, and the new services developed by banks of late. The various control methods might enable banks to analyse branch operations more satisfactorily, define more realistic bank and branch objectives, develop activity volume 'quota' and operations standards', and prepare recommendations for future plans and proposed activities.

Banks' top management function includes the definition of marketing objectives (fixed and variable), opening and closure of bank branches, development/enlargement/transfer of branches, development of new services, marketing research, etc. In contrast, branch functions are as follows:

(a) to improve services;
(b) to transfer information and advise customers;
(c) intelligence gathering about the customers and the competition;
(d) personal attention and customers' relations;
(e) co-operation and co-ordination of staff;
(f) initiative in increasing the bank's influence, services and line(s) and number of customers.

As will be suggested later, bank branch profitability depends on:

(a) market area potential;
(b) branch deposits;
(c) types of accounts (saving, current, etc.);
(d) branch market share;
(e) branch earning yield v. branch expense ratios;
(f) deposits growth rate; and
(g) capital investment required for branch operation.

It is, however, the responsibility of top management in banks to control the branches' performances – on one or more criteria – and make suggestions for improvement. An example is presented in Figure 7.2. Eight bank branches are compared in terms of $\frac{\text{deposit-generating}}{\text{branch expenses}}$ ratio. The positions of the various branches are presented on the figure, in relation to the consistent expense/deposit ratio (the diagonal). Branches like *G* are particularly expensive to run and relatively inefficient to operate, as far as deposit-generating ability is concerned. In comparison, branch *C* is relatively cheap to operate and efficient in terms of deposits growth. Obviously this type of figure and measurement raises the question on how to identify branch 'expenses' that are related to the deposit-generating effect undertaken by the particular branch, as any accounting method adopted will be largely arbitrary and subjective. In addition, the actual deposits with a branch might change over time, as a result of *other* bank branches' activities, as well as the activity on the market of the 'inefficient' branch over a longer period of time. Indeed, the very same branch (e.g. branch *G*) might be very 'efficient' in lending, or cross-selling, providing foreign exchange services, etc. For this reason this figure – if employed – should relate not just to *one* of the branch's activities, but to several major ones. Only if the branch is relatively 'inefficient' along several dimensions of operation can some more radical conclusions be drawn.

The possibilities of improving branches' performances via adequate control systems are enormous. Banks have developed a teller scheduling model output, suggesting a way to improve and optimise the number of

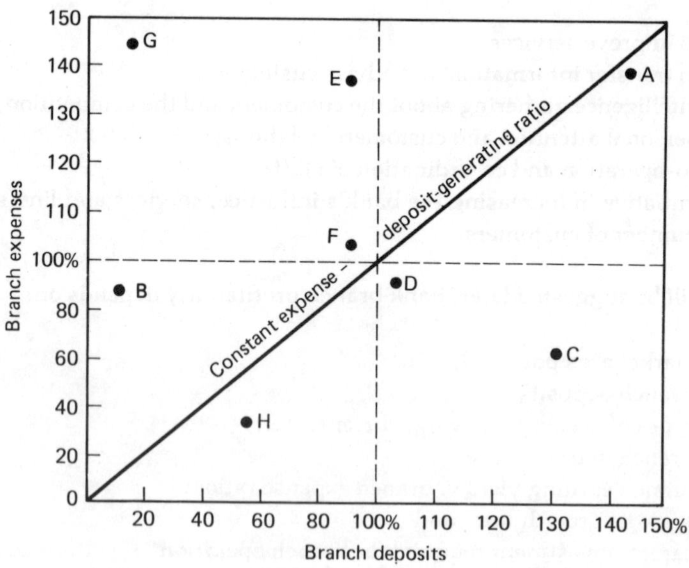

Figure 7.2 Comparison of expenses and deposits/lending ratio 'deviations' by bank branches

tellers in order to avoid too long queues on the one hand, and to employ fewer idle tellers, during slack periods, on the other hand.

Performance appraisal

Since performance is absolutely necessary if a bank is to prosper, today most banks attempt to adopt various formal or informal systems of appraising the performances of their branches, managers or indeed the whole organisation. Measuring performances provides the bank with information necessary for the success of the bank branch's administration (in the short run) and its business policy (in the long run). This information can reveal both the strengths and the weaknesses of a bank and indicate areas where reorganisation, planning, training or recruitment are needed.

The goals of bank performance appraisals in a wider context are:

1. To evaluate branches and bank executives, performers, etc. in order to make: promotion/dismissal decisions, transfer decisions, salary reviews and identify training needs.
2. Allocation of financial, technical, personnel and marketing and resources.
3. Planning and strategy evaluation.
4. Possible changes in organisation and control systems.

However, generally appraisal is intended to serve more than one purpose. In all the bank profits is the dominant criterion. However, there are two 'types' of profit: (i) *windfall profit* – which is the result of very large seemingly unpredictable changes in environment (e.g. sudden evaluation of a foreign currency of which the bank keeps large sums in reserve, and changes in government economic fiscal, financial policies etc.), and (ii) *earned profit*, that is profit earned by sound bank management, planning and control and efficient excutive action.

Generally speaking, three sets of criteria can be used for evaluating bank managerial performance:

1. *Inputs* – The performance of bank managerial activities.
2. *Outputs* – the results achieved.
3. *Personal qualities* – personality traits of bank managers being assessed.

Inputs become appropriate where bank managers have little autonomy, but follow established procedures; outputs are important for bank managers with a higher degree of autonomy or where the decision is to promote, demote or sack; personal qualities and traits are ordinarily not very objective and they might be relevant assessments of how the bank manager affects other employees' outputs.

The most general criteria for assessing banks' performances is profitability. In practice, however, the calculation of branch profits bristles with accounting difficulties involving problems like overheads (for the head office services), depreciation of bank physical and technical assets (i.e. which depreciation method is employed?) and the evaluation of 'inventories' (particularly financial resources). Ordinarily, the calculation of profit is net before taxes and in order to be more exact, one should really employ residual income (= profit – cost of capital employed) as a 'measure' of profitability.[14] There are four major criteria for appraising bank marketing performance (as presented in Table 7.1) and all these criteria should be employed in tandem. The table presents the technique of data collection on each measure, its objectivity/subjectivity and the typical quantitative measures that can be employed.

Bank branch performance

The *main* aim of bank control is to monitor the relative profitability of the entire organisation and its various branches. This is being done *post factum*, that is, *after* the business activity has taken place. Each branch has a profit and loss account in which are entered operating costs, deposits, loans, costs and profits of various services, etc. Bank branch performance, on the other hand, looks at wider aspects of activity than past profitability, for example, prediction of branches market share, branch personnel performance, relations with local community, bank staff levels of activity, the managerial calibre of branches' managers for possible promotion, demotion, training, etc. In addition, one of the major reasons for looking at branch performance is because greater emphasis has been placed recently on the retail customer as a *source* of funds.

The prediction of performance for a bank branch is clearly necessary, but not a sufficient basis for a capital investment decision. Quite apart from the problem of choosing the performance criterion, a marginally 'better' branch may be very much more expensive to maintain and operate. An approach producing an overall ranking of the performances of various branches based on ROI (Return on Investment) would be of interest. One computer-based commercially available model has been reported in the USA.[15] It contains three modules or sets of variables: forecasting business potential, allocation to competing branches, and income and expense analysis variables. This model does not claim to usurp the decision-making function, but to provide additional information rapidly and to answer 'what if'-type questions – such as analysing the effect of proposed rebuilding in the area.

One of the most appropriate techniques for evaluating bank branch performance is probably ABLES (Automatic Branch Location Evaluation

Table 7.1 Criteria for appraising bank marketing performance

Key areas for assessing marketing performance	*Ease of quantification*		*Objectivity/subjectivity*	*Technique*	*Typical quantitative measures*
	conceptual	*Practical*			
1. *Profitability*	Easy	Laborious but routine	Objective but some judgement involved	Routine data collection and analysis	1. Net profit by major service or group(s) of services offered. 2. Profitability per customers' segments. 3. Branch profitability. 4. Expense ratios.
2. *Market position*	Fairly easy	Laborious but often routine with some *ad hoc* investigation	Objective (once definitions decided on)	Business figures, market research	1. Absolute deposits and sales analysis. 2. Trends. 3. Market share (deposits, loans, etc.) 4. Numbers and size of competitors.
3. *Product/service leadership*	Not easy	Not easy	Mainly judgemental	Internal executive panel Market research	1. Ordinal ranking of bank's services offered with competitors'. 2. Ordinal ranking of value of service range. 3. Customer's satisfaction on attitude scales.
4. *Sales and personnel performance*	Easy	Fairly easy	Mixture of objective data and subjective judgement	Human resource accounting techniques Staff inventory	1. Percentage of appropriately qualified staff at all grades. 2. Percentage of promotable staff. 3. Percentage upgrading of qualifications. 4. Percentage ranked 'better than average'.

System)[16] used by Manufacturers Hanover Trust Company in New York City. This model uses a computer to perform calculations of the estimated performance of a great number, typically thousands, of possible branch locations and then uses manual evaluation to rank a number of the best branches. The method works as follows:

(1) Area potential is computed for census tracts using the potentials computed from a local survey of banking habits.

(2) ABLES then allocates share of market and potential to each competing institution and to a hypothetical new institution placed sequentially at each of the intersections of a half-mile grid network. The model is heuristic in nature and it is not possible to test many of the assumptions used to construct it. The survey data used for the balance estimate, based upon consumer interviews, are statistically valid, but the assembly into a model such as ABLES has not – as far as we know – been fully proven. The other limitations have to do with ABLES market definition and market allocation assumptions. ABLES assumes a square primary market area, for which there is no empirical justification. The formula for market share, for savings, in ABLES is

$$S = 1/(B_C + 2B_t + 1)$$

where:

S = market share of the (new branch
B_c = existing commercial banks in the market area under question, and
B_t = thrift institutions in the market area under question

The addition of one in the denominator adjusts for the presence of the new institution. For checking accounts, the formula is: $S = 1/(B_c + 1)$.

It is realistic to allow for the effects of competition. Certainly a market will yield a smaller market share where there are many competitors than where there are few. The major weakness of this algorithm is its lack of grounding in any theory of consumer behaviour. ABLES, as well as Ligaya's[17] approach discussed previously, refers mainly to location of *new* branches; however, the approach can be useful for planning the performance of existent or hypothetical branches and then comparing the branch actual versus planned performance.

A third approach to performance evaluation of bank branches is through the employment of factor analysis. Factor analysis has been used successfully[18] in overcoming the problems of multi-collinearity in branch performance evaluation for a building society. A factor is essentially a linear combination of observed variables and the equation for calculating a factor has the same form as the regression equation, that is:

$$F_j = a_1X_1 + a_2X_2 + , \ldots , a_nX_n$$

where:

> Fj = the factor
> $a_1 a_2$ = coefficients
> $X_1 X_2, \ldots,$ = the observed variables (usually in standardised form)

Ideally, factor analysis that is performed by using a computer package should yield a small number of factors that can then be used as ordinary metric variables in a regression equation and this was successfully done in the case noted above.[19] Another approach was used by Doyle Fenwick and Savage[20] at the Yorkshire Bank, in that the predictor variables were screened for a 'reasonable causal structure' and this appears to have been the case in other investigations.[21]

Predicting bank deposits

Bank executives in the USA, and indeed all over the Western world, regard the long-run attraction of deposits into their local branches as one of the primary limiting factors in this industry's corporate growth and success. By contrast, loan demand of a reasonably good quality has in recent years been adequate to make use of the deposits available, particularly in regions of rapid population growth.[22] Indeed in 1973 a study by Booz, Allen and Hamilton[23] concluded that the primary challenge facing banks in the future would be the acquisition of funds, not the employment of them.

Since the inflow of deposits plays such a crucial role in the measurement of the success or failure of a branch, a performance index would be very useful so that the most promising new locations could be identified. Additionally, such an index would provide top management with an insight into the performances of existing branches so that any remedial action that might be necessary could be undertaken. There are, however, a wide diversity of market segments served by branches and the competitive conditions that each bank faces may well be unique, which would make such an index difficult to use even if this kind of measurement could be achieved. Among the most interesting studies on branch performance is that of Clawson who suggested that multiple linear regression analysis (of branch data) may provide a measure of performance.[24] The dependent variable used in the study was 'net savings gain by the branch' over a twelve month period and the twenty-four independent variables employed could be grouped in three sets:

(a) local competition characteristics (e.g. banks already in the area, banks to population ratio, etc.);
(b) local population characteristics (area population, rate of population change, housing value, incomes, commercial statistics, age groups, household size, etc.);

(c) own branch characteristics (traffic patterns, attitudes towards banking in the area, etc.).

These 'independent' variables are, however, highly interactive and intercorrelated. Although the analysis leaves much to be desired, ten variables were reported as being influential, the most important being the average net gain of competing banks, proportion of depositors in the range 45–64 years, exterior attractiveness of the branch building and income per capita. In contrast, branches located near competitors' main branches or offices were shown to be at a disadvantage as were those located on the approaches to formal shopping centres or surrounded by a large amount of rented accommodation. Therefore, when choosing a location for a branch the previously mentioned factors should be taken into account. Obviously, this approach can be employed where branches already exist in similar sorts of surroundings to planned new locations, so that evaluation of the levels of performance standards can be carried out. This provides further information that may influence the choice of branch location. Additionally, such a model, once validated, has an intuitive appeal since it can be used to hold branch managers accountable for their branch's performance as measured against the regression equation. It could be used to assess the desirability of a merger by taking over a smaller concern to gain 'instant' new branches. The regression model might also be used as a yardstick to investigate branches that had performed exceptionally well or very badly against their calculated performance. This might indicate other areas to which the bank marketeers could address themselves. For example, suppose one branch had a net savings gain that was much higher than expected. Further investigation might show the discrepancy to be due to favourable publicity from bank employees' actions in the local community. It may therefore be in the bank's interests actively to promote these activities among their staff in other branches. Any new performance indicator that is uncovered (either favourable or otherwise) can be incorporated into the regression formula when it is reviewed.

Suppose that it is considered that a branch is doing very badly indeed and this is combined with indications in the formula that this is an inherently unfavourable situation in the area, in terms of population and competitive factors. Any financial outlay in terms of building modernisation, etc. may be ill advised, even if in great need, and it may even be preferable to close the branch and relocate in a more promising area.

The use of target marketing may be a way to profitability for a branch in a poor location. Identification of a potential target market and its subsequent exploitation via, for example, extensive advertising, may produce benefits that could overspill to the more successful branches. It has been often argued, however, that because US banks spend so much money on advertising they have a desire to find the optimal level of such expenditures. If an objective function can be defined, then the level can be estimated by operational research techniques, but to define such a function it is necessary to have a prediction of deposits and loans. Hughes's findings[25] from considering only three savings banks in the Boston area must be viewed with caution because of the small sample. He suggests that models for the prediction of demand reflect the bank's goals, planning horizon and marketing strategy. Other previous work[26] had revealed that banks used different benchmarks for measuring the degree of success of a branch marketing strategy – dollar volume of deposits, market share of deposits, the number of depositors and the share of the depositors.

CHAPTER 8

Bank marketing strategies

Contents

Introduction

The literal meaning of the word strategy is 'the art of the general', deriving from the ancient Greek word for general – *strategos*. In fact, the usage of the word dates back to at least 400 BC, but did not appear in writings until the late eighteenth century. Prior to Napoleon's times, the word had a military connotation implying the art and science of directing military forces to defeat an enemy or to mitigate the results of defeat. Although deriving from an ancient heritage, the term strategy has found its way into bank management literature in the past decade or so. To the banking people the term strategy has come to mean the type of decision made by top executives and members of banks' board of directors concerning the relationship between the bank organisation as a whole and its environment. In other words, strategy describes those critical boundary-spanning decisions that define the framework and direction for overall bank marketing organisation and management, providing answers to questions such as:

1. In what specific business should the bank be, in terms of mix of services/products offered and customers served?
2. What course of action should the organisation pursue, in terms of emphasis, timing, priorities?
3. How should the bank resources be acquired and how should these resources be deployed for more efficient marketing operations?
4. What major market opportunities are most compatible with banks' top management definition of marketing goals, objectives and missions, etc.?

The development of a marketing strategy for a bank must fit in with that bank's overall objectives. Therefore, marketing strategy should be an integral part of a corporate or strategic plan.

Corporate planning

Corporate planning may be defined as 'The planning of the total resources of a company for the achievement of quantified objectives within a specific period of time.'[1] Hence, corporate planning has been developed to meet the management need to take an objective overall view of the total bank operations, and to ensure that the criteria for success are being fulfilled. As such, it involves making careful considered decisions before taking action. According to Gilmore and Brandenburg,[2] corporate planning is a master plan, containing three basic components:

1. *Economic mission,* that is, formulating the kind of business the banking organisation should be in, and what its performance objectives should be.
2. *Competitive strategy,* that is, to find the right services–market–sales approach combination for effective accomplishment of the economic mission.
3. *Programme of action* that involves a search for efficient means of implementing the competitive strategy, that is, developing effective marketing mixes to implement the competitive strategy decided.

Indeed, planning is one of the first and most important functions of marketing.[3] The chief bank executives should expect to look to marketing for help in corporate planning. Similarly, within the marketing function itself considerable planning is required to answer questions such as: What type(s) of customers does the bank want? In what direction is the bank going? How many new employees will be required for servicing new branches, new services, new customers? What will be the most profitable products, services, branches, customers, activities, markets, etc.? The answers to these and many other questions, through planning, will help the bank to create and anticipate rather than follow the more common banking practice of simply reacting to competitor moves and to customers' expected needs. Formal bank corporate planning is particularly essential in the current economic conditions, in order that the banks can realistically consider their use of resources. In addition, an efficient corporate plan is an important tool for decision-making throughout the whole banking organisation.

Corporate planning attempts to integrate two organisational approaches – 'bottom up' and 'top down'. If the approach is *all* 'bottom up' then strategy formulation becomes very difficult. Conversly, if it is *all* 'top down', there is often a lack of realism in the plans and a lack of commitment to the plans by the employees in that bank.

Stages in strategic planning

Before plans are made, a time horizon has to be fixed. This is the period over which the bank seeks to optimize its resource-conversion efficiency. For banks the time horizon is usually five years for long-term (or strategic plans) and one year for short-term plans. Planning (bottom up) can be done individually by the different departments and then submitted to the planning department so that the individual plans can be integrated to form a corporate plan. However, in practice, the more realistic approach in banking today is 'top down', that is, corporate plans will evolve round the main areas in which business effort will be concentrated over the span of the time horizon, and this is decided by the board and communicated to the planning department.

Marketing is part of the central core of management, therefore no really effective marketing plan can be made unless it derives from a business or corporate plan. Banks' planning normally starts with a position audit that appraises the strengths and weaknesses of the bank organisation and notes the current market position. From this, and taking into account economic forecasts and the long-term objectives of the bank, a broad strategy to achieve these ends can be produced.

The bank's strategic planning begins with a statement of financial objectives that looks ahead to a certain period (usually five years) and sets out objectives in terms of certain targets, such as return on assets, return on equity and the equity/asset ratio. Long-term objectives may well alter as a matter of business policy, or in response to political and economic forces. Strategic plans are therefore usually reviewed prior to the preparation of each short-term plan which is often for a period of one year.

A strategic plan of a bank will generally include:

(a) a description of the objectives to be achieved;
(b) a description of the resources allocated to achieve various purposes;

(c) background information essential to the planning process;
(d) any assumptions that have been made;
(e) plans for marketing in all aspects of the bank, by services and the launch of new services, promotional material, press and public relations, pricing if appropriate, research, advertising, training, branch development, local strategies, special audits or projects;
(f) agreed dates for starts and completions, standards of performance and means of reporting and reviewing progress;
(g) agreed budgets of expenditure and methods of control.

Planning must not be allowed to lead to inflexibility. Conditions can alter quickly. Many banks who plan successfully have found that real benefits lie in the *discipline of planning* which makes management consider and understand the factors affecting their business, or the part to which they contribute. Benefit is also obtained in having a system that can be used to adapt to changes as they arise and indicate what the effect of these will be.

Although a bank may identify the best markets within its general field, no bank can serve every market in sight, so it moves from prediction of the environment to selection. A bank chooses by examining its own position. Every bank has certain constraints and certain strengths that it must recognise. These will determine in which segments of each market it can compete profitably, and which markets and segments it should leave to competitors. The constraints affecting the nature of strategic planning for banks are as follows:

(1) *The cost structure.* If the bank is of such a nature that its basic cost structure is largely fixed, it may have priced itself out of certain markets by low cost – more efficient competitors. This is an important consideration today. For example, because of its high fixed costs in premises and skills, a trustee department cannot profitably deal with business under a certain value. Yet more than half of the total business may consist of business below that figure. This prevents the skilled staff from being available for more profitable business, and must eventually lead to a decision either to put up its charges or refuse the business. This is one of the major problems in marketing of bank services. The operational view is to deal with every customer who comes to the bank, whereas the strategic view is that only certain segments of the market are profitable and only these should be served.

(2) *Legal.* The legal environment plays a significant part in what the bank may offer to attract customers, and the effect of the law is to prohibit competition on many substantive marketing programmes. Since banks generally have similar legal constraints, they have a similar narrow latitude for strategy development. This results in intense rivalry, with many banks adopting virtually identical marketing programmes.

(3) *Social or cultural.* These influence bank marketing via customers' attitudes towards borrowing, spending and saving. The public interest in

social problems produces constraints in bank activities and hence limitations in planning.

(4) *Economy.* The decisions on bank marketing are influenced in many ways by the state of the economy. In periods of recession, certain bank services, for example, lending, decline in popularity and demand. In times of prosperity, the demand for loans grows. Growing unemployment, on the other hand, will increase saving. Expansion brings optimism and a demand for borrowing.

Most banks possess some or all of the following strengths and skills:

1. very high financial resources;
2. high credit standing;
3. wide credit and commercial network;
4. a wide branch network that offers deep market penetration;
5. a bookkeeping and money transfer system;
6. international connections, abilities and skills to offer general elementary personal financial advice, cheque processing, foreign transaction handling and certain special services – trustee, income tax, etc.

Consideration of all these factors allows the long-range plan for each service to be determined – growth targets can be defined, as well as market segments and particular target customer groups, industries, income groups and regions. At the same time, a projection of resources – staff, premises, equipment – would be prepared.

When the long-range plans are settled, the more specific short-term plans can be drawn up. The setting of short-term objectives aims at:

(a) making sure that the policies of the bank organisation are followed through at lower levels;
(b) making sure that the managers' efforts are directed at business the bank wants and not at business that is not included in the corporate plan;
(c) obtaining a consistent minimum performance from all branch managers and measuring this performance;
(d) giving the whole bank organisation a sense of purpose.

The relationship between strategy and marketing plans

As mentioned above, the marketing plan derives from the corporate plan. It should be flexible and regularly reviewed and should allow for continuous control, good communication to staff, and regular evaluation. It involves substantial research work and the use of information from the branch network about pricing policy, advertising and promotions, public relations and the use of resources in support, for example, training and development of services.

The short-term marketing plan stipulates the research needed to be carried out during the period to assist in forward planning activities, and to be used to stimulate effort in future periods. Action will be detailed to meet the objectives set out in the bank's short-term plan. It should include a method of monitoring and control, so that results can be checked against targets and adjustments made to the planned activities.

Research is essential to planning and to the entire marketing process. Every successful marketing effort and every sound marketing decision must rest upon research. Continuing and comprehensive research is the useful way to obtain information for planning the marketing activities. Research is carried out on customer use of the bank's products, on the needs of various classes of customers for new types of service, and on the markets that a proposed new service can reach.

One of the effective ways of establishing bank objectives and in turn marketing objectives, is by analysing the strengths and weaknesses and the opportunities and threats. Strengths and weakness are the internal aspects of the banking activities – services, efficiency, staff training, use of finance and promotions – compared with best international standards and national competitors. Opportunity and threat are the external aspects (such as economic and legal conditions). The analysis makes the full use of marketing intelligence, in order to identify and then to determine how best to meet problems that can be expected to arise and exploit any opportunities that are available.

Many banks, for example Williams & Glyn's, use a five-year plan[4] that includes a manpower plan, capital expenditure plan, marketing plan, profit forecast and an estimate of the first year's budget.

An essential part of the market planning is to estimate the current and future size of markets and market segments. Only then can the bank sensibly allocate marketing resources to segments, plan marketing programmes and control marketing effort.

Market sizes can be fairly readily calculated from the banks' own records and published census data. Forecasts must be made for market growth rates. An example of this is given by Hughes[5] who discusses models such as the hyperbolic model, for forecasting the volume of deposits,

$$\text{Deposits} = \frac{1}{(E/P - Dwi)}$$

Where: E/P = earnings/price ratio of common stocks

Dwi = bank divident rate

The equation hypothesises that there are two types of depositors and the formula above should be applied for the two types of depositors, $a + b$, that is insensitive to stock prices, giving constant deposits (a), and one (b) that deposits more when the difference between stock earnings and interest costs narrows. The model is useful for forecasting, if stock *P/E* ratios can be forecasted. Other methods can be used; for example, a demand equation might be estimated by multiple regression and forecasts made on the basis of the known or forecast values of the independent variables.

The corporate plan provides a framework within which the following year's budget is prepared. It is mainly through the budget that the corporate plan is implemented. Monthly monitoring of performance against budget is provided to each cost centre (one of which would be the marketing department). Any change in direction of the marketing effort from the plan requires prior authorisation.

Formulating a marketing strategy

Planning calls for the establishment of objectives and formulation of strategies. While the objectives indicate what the bank hopes to accomplish, strategies follow and attempt to suggest how the bank will reach the objectives (Figure 8.1).

In other words, strategy is the 'connecting' link between planning and action.

There are several definitions of what a marketing strategy is. Perhaps the most popular one is of Kotler suggesting that marketing strategy is 'a set of alternatives, policies and rules that guides over time the firm's marketing effort – its level, mix and allocation – partly independently and

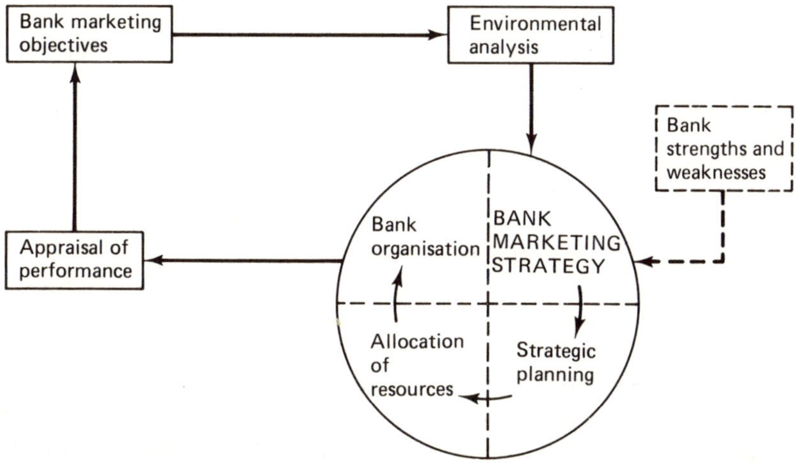

Figure 8.1 The role of marketing strategy in bank management

partly in response to changing environmental and competitive conditions'.[6]

There are three major stages in formulating a marketing strategy:

1. Identification of the target market(s) and their needs, and the formulation of marketing objectives.
2. Defining constraints on achieving objectives.
3. Allocation of marketing resources.

The major stages in formulating a marketing strategy as applicable to a bank is summarised in Table 8.1.

The first stage in formulating a marketing strategy is selection of the target market and the identification of the bank's marketing objectives. Selection of the target market is based on a number of factors: the services being offered; the market segment accessibility and the substantiality of the various (alternative) market(s). The target market needs should be identified and then a marketing plan – as a part of the bank plan discussed in the previous section – has to be developed.

Objectives are necessary to provide the direction with a precise and clear view of the bank's aims and goals, and to provide for the operational managers a firm policy guide to which they can refer. The objectives of a bank may usually consist of the following:

1. *Profit.* A bank's operations are financed mainly by deposits from the public and only a small portion from shareholders. Sufficient profit has to be made to protect the capital and interest of depositors and enhance the capital and dividends for the shareholders.
2. *Growth and size.* Growth may be an objective because size often gives competitive advantages and growth may be an indicator of vitality. Yet size does not always bring economies of scale, nor does it necessarily maintain profit at the required level.
3. *Market share.* An increase of market share often brings competitive advantages; however, usually the objective is a larger share of selected customer groups, and not of the total market.

In addition to profits, growth and market share, many banks might be interested in risk spread and diversification. While some of the objectives may appear of importance in the short term, in the long term they all ultimately contribute to maximise profitability.

In order to identify target markets, the first step is to examine the major environmental trends, opportunities and threats facing the bank, as indicated in Figure 8.1. Each potential market selection should be examined in detail in order to obtain its major characterisation.

Some parts of each market may be more attractive to the bank, either because the customers' special needs have been overlooked, or merely because the bank is more suited to that type of need. Market segmentation should be on the basis of differing customer needs, but it is often necessary

Table 8.1 Stages in formulating a bank marketing strategy[7]

Stages in marketing strategy	*Examples/elaboration*
1. Identification of target marketing and formulating the marketing objectives	Possible target markets: private, industrial, commercial, government/public and international customers. Objectives: profit; growth; market share; spreading risk; diversification of services.
2. Defining constraints	(a) Economic, political, social. (b) Governmental; legal and technological developments. (c) Competitive situation from other banks and/or financial services (e.g. building societies, insurance companies, financial institutions, etc.)
3. Allocation of marketing resources	Via marketing mix: (a) Services (products/services development and differentiation) (b) Price (price policies for the various services the bank offers) (c) Promotion (advertising, publicity and public relations) (d) Place (distribution, coverage, location)

to use less market-oriented variables such as demography, geography or behavioural variables.

Having determined market segmentation, a target must be decided for each market. The choice of target market depends on: (i) company resources, (ii) product homogeneity, (iii) product stage in the life cycle, (iv) market homogeneity, and (v) competitors' strategies in the various segments.

Having selected the target market, the next stage is for the bank to develop a general idea of what kind of offer to make to the target market in relation to competitors' offers, that is, to allocate the marketing resources and this is being done via banks' marketing mix (place, promotion, services and price policies).

The allocation of marketing resources is carried out in the light of an environmental analysis and appraisal of banks' resources.

Environmental analysis is to aid in the formulation of a preliminary set of objectives. Management should first try to identify future opportunities and threats within the bank's existing services and customers. Attention should be paid to signs of change in the customer's needs and desires, expecially as related to legal, technological progress and development. The main aims of analysing the environment are to find (i) new opportunities for existing banking services (with new customers or geographical expansion), (ii) new opportunities to serve existing customers with new bank services or in new geographical locations, and (iii) the major future threats to market position and profit margins.

The appraisal of the bank's resources refer and include financial resources, personnel, market position, management and technical competence and susceptibility to external pressures. The purpose of this appraisal is to examine not only the strengths and weaknesses of the existing resources, but also what resources might be available in the future and possible ways by which future resources might be generated. This provides the basis for the planning of future marketing strategy, as explained in the previous pages.

Most of the banks often offer similar services at similar charges and tend to go in for image building in an attempt to make customers familiar with a particular aspect of their organisation. The Midland Bank, for example, has attempted to promote itself as 'the listening bank' with an intensive television advertising campaign. Furthermore, within this campaign, the potential customer has become familiar with the Midland's symbol, that of a griffin, which helps build an image.

Image building is only part of market positioning. Developing this example, the customer may perceive all banks as being willing to listen and only differing in their symbols. Positioning aims to help customers to know the differences between competing banks so that they can match themselves to the bank that can be of most value to them. It is an attempt to distinguish the bank from its competitors along real dimensions in order to be the preferred bank to certain segments of the market.

The timing and method of entry into a new opportunity are also crucial. To some extent, these considerations may be governed by economic factors or the behaviour of competitors.

Allocation of marketing resources requires also the developing of a marketing organisation, information system, planning system and control system that promises to accomplish the bank's objectives in the target market.

To a large extent the organisation and information system will already exist within the marketing department. Planning and control should be considered within the bank's total field of business and has been discussed previously.

When the target market(s) and the customers' needs have been identified and the marketing objectives have been defined in the light of the environmental and competitive constraints, then in order to meet the target market needs, allocation of the marketing resources should be carried out. This is being implemented via a combination of four sets of variables (called 'marketing mix') as presented in Table 8.1.

We are now in a position to summarise what a bank marketin is. The bank marketing strategy is a plan for action that determ bank can best achieve its goals and objectives in the light of t pressures exerted by competition and other non-controllable variables on the one hand, and its limited resources on the other.

Of the three stages mentioned in Table 8.1, two are mainly the responsibility of the bank's top management. Only the second stage – defining local (or branch) constraints, particularly in relation to competition is – to a certain extent – among the strategic functions and responsibilities of the individual branch manager.

Types of marketing strategies for banks

There are three broad categories of bank marketing strategies: defensive, offensive and rationalisation strategies. These are presented in Figures 8.2 and 8.3. Offensive strategies attempt to penetrate new areas, expand geographically, seize market opportunities and adopt innovations in order to make the bank organisation a leader in its market. Defensive marketing strategies' goal is to protect existing customers and maintain the present market share, either by following the leading bank (i.e. being a market follower) or by concentrating in a specific customer niche. The rationalisation strategy focuses on cost-reduction, either by deleting certain expensive (or 'too high' cost–profit ratio) financial services, or by closing bank branches that are 'too expensive' to operate.

Offensive strategies

There are five main offensive strategies: (i) geographical expansion, (ii) market penetration, (iii) new market, (iv) market leader, and (v) market challenger strategies.

(1) *Geographical expansion.* This strategy seeks to expand sales by extending the physical frontiers of banks' activities. In pursuing this course of action, a bank would no doubt have seriously looked into the commercial viability of establishing new branches or EFT (Electronic Fund Transfer) points in new additional locations. This strategy is also often called a strategy of 'fortification'.

(2) *Market penetration.* This strategy aims at attracting new customers from the market that the bank is already in. It is undoubtedly the most popular strategy prevalent among banks. A bank that had identified its market and the market needs, and has set formal marketing objectives, is

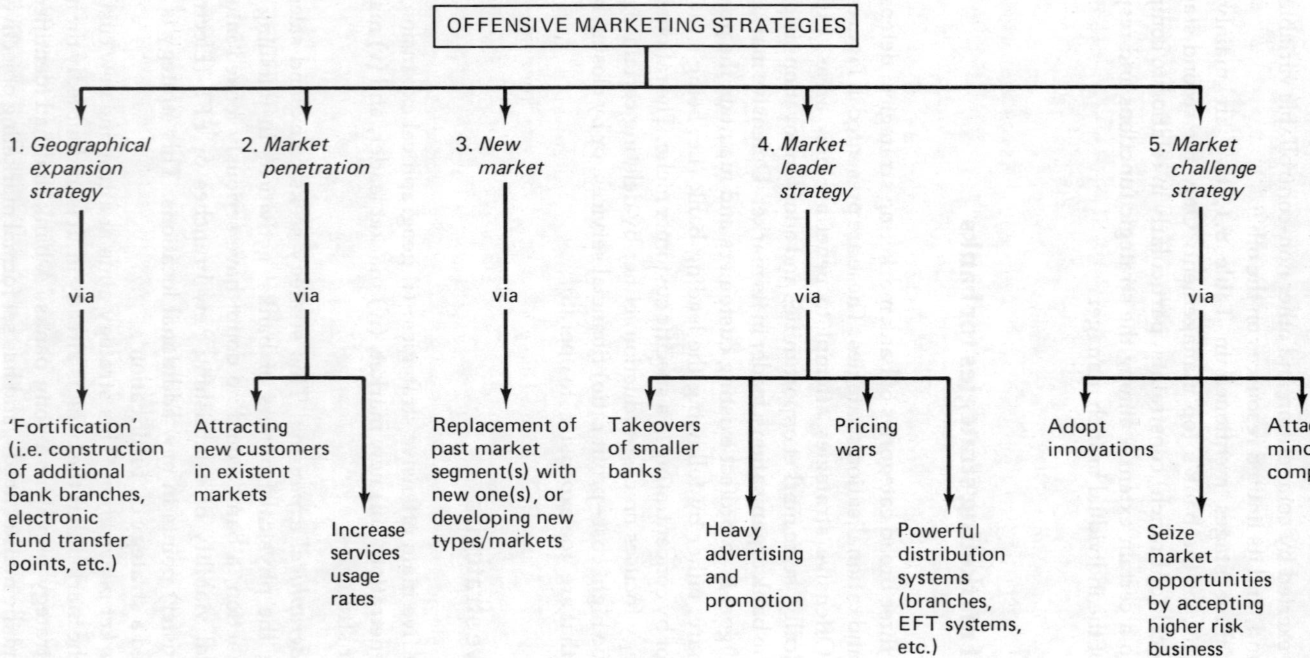

Figure 8.2 Alternative offensive strategies

then able to plan the marketing mix in the best possible way. A well-planned market penetration strategy would also win new customers through its better understanding of their needs, a situation that allows management to work on important matters such as image, to emphasise the right segments and services, and to make better sales contacts. Market penetration strategy refers also to the increase of the 'usage rate' of its branches and services via other new or existent customers in existent markets.

(3) *New market strategy.* This strategy seeks to widen its appeal to attract customers from segments of the market in which the bank in the past has not concentrated upon. Such a strategy may either attempt to receive the new types of customers in addition to its 'traditional' ones, or it may resolve to replace its past market segment appeal.

(4) *Market-leader strategy.* This strategy can only be employed by very large, dominant banks. In addition to having a strong distribution network, being large the bank enjoys the benefits accruable from economies of scale. These in turn allow banks to protect their market shares or indeed to expand and become even more dominant.

These dominant banks have an influential role in the industry by virtue of their size. Their promotional activities based on a well-established reputation put them in the position of 'guardians' of the industry, particularly on prices and promotional intensities.

The market leader has the objective of remaining in that position. This objective can be broken down into three sub-objectives: (i) to increase the total market, (ii) to protect current market share, (iii) to increase current market share. In order to achieve a high market share, banks often enter into confrontation, that is, in promotional and pricing wars.

(5) *Market-challenger strategies.* Market challengers may challenge the market leader by using a 'direct attack' strategy, a 'back door' strategy or a 'guppy' strategy.[8] The direct attack strategy is usually carried out on the major competitors in the same segments, by employing challenging price policies and service innovations. The 'back door' strategy refers to utilising various market segments, channels of distribution, etc. 'Guppy' strategy means challenging minor competitors in the industry, for example by accepting banking business associated with higher levels of risk, harassment (legal or other) of smaller banks, etc.

The major objective of banks pursuing this strategy is to capture the major market share. This can obviously be done by challenging the market leader, other runner-up banks or smaller banks. The decision that banks to challenge will be based on discovered weaknesses of these competitors. Over all, this strategy is characterised by the aggressiveness of the marketing tactics. Typically, banks that follow this strategy are those that are ambitiously trying to grow as fast as they can. They tend to be innovative and opportunistic in their marketing approach and are sensitive to changes and developments in their market and in the trade.

Defensive and rationalisation strategies

There are two defensive strategies (Figure 8.3):

1. *Market follower.* Adopting a market-follower strategy means that a bank has accepted the *status quo*. It will not challenge the market leader(s) but will attempt to maintain its market share by a strategy aimed at retaining customers and winning a share of new ones. This strategy may be carried out by exploiting a set of target markets to which it can bring a distinct advantage, perhaps in terms of location or specialist services offered. In general, market followers possess strong management who give priority to profitability, rather than market share.
2. *Market-nicher strategy.* As the name suggests, such a strategy aims to take advantage of the niches that exist in the market. This is done through specialisation. The markets here are relatively small and tend to be beyond the interests of large banks. To the smaller banks, however, the niche is safe and profitable. The smaller banks may adopt market-nicher strategies to avoid clashing with the major banks. These banks will attempt to find and occupy market niches that may be either overlooked or ignored by the bigger banks.

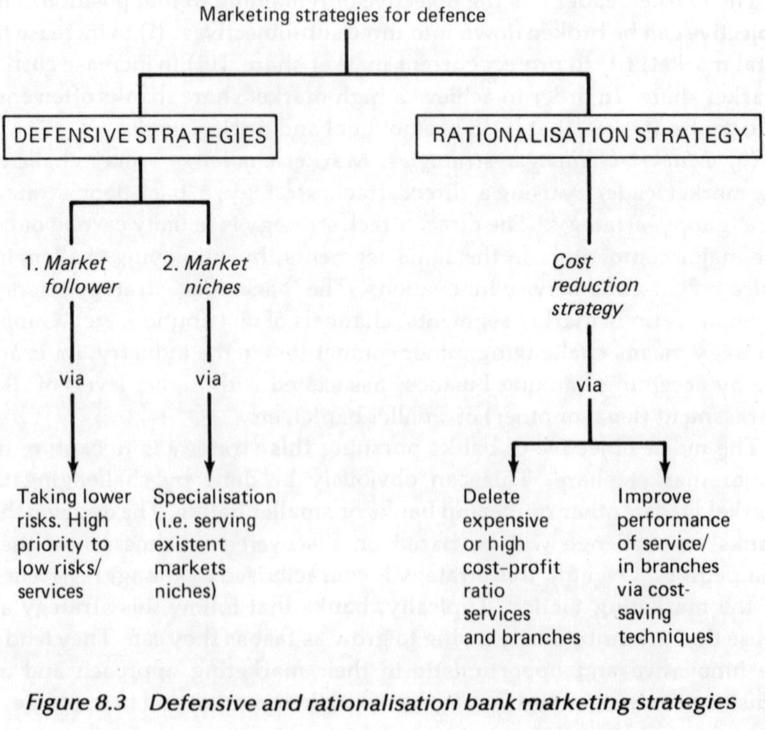

Figure 8.3 Defensive and rationalisation bank marketing strategies

With the increase in competition among banks themselves as well as with other financial institutions, coupled with the world-wide recession, and inflation, the banking industry is more eager to improve performance and to rationalise its operations. This has led to growing interest in the employment of *cost-reduction* (or cost-cutting) strategy that, because of its paramount potential importance to the banking industry today, can be considered as a separate category – the rationalisation strategy. One of the questions that any bank or branch manager would continually be asking himself is – how can cost-efficient operations be obtained so that profitability can be increased? Manufacturing companies can improve operations by leverage, for example, by purchasing faster and more reliable machinery. But most services, including banks, are not able to follow this approach. Nevertheless, there is a misconception about service businesses not being able to obtain operating leverage. Operating leverage exists in any business organisation so long as a change in operations would result in a drop in the relative cost per unit of output. Substitution of capital for labour is the classic method of obtaining such leverage in both product- and service-oriented businesses. Capital is used to purchase machinery, for example, Electronic Fund Transfer Systems, computers, etc. for a bank, which can then sell a service at a cheaper and faster rate, with more consistent service.

K. N. Thomas, an US consultant, has researched on branching strategies employed by US banks.[9] He suggested that in the USA banks employ mainly offensive and defensive strategies. In other countries, including the UK, the rationalisation strategy is also widely used. The situation in the UK at first appears to be against 'defensive banking'. However, the general tenor of banking articles assumes the need for a visible presence throughout the country to maintain the 'correct' image and this can reinforce any tendency to 'defensive branching'.

Offensive branching has been undertaken by the smaller banks in recent years, for example, Williams & Glyn's[10] and the Yorkshire Bank, whereas the 'big four' English banks and the Royal Bank of Scotland have been employing a rationalisation branching strategy. In the 1970s the Royal Bank of Scotland closed 120 branches in overbanked areas and opened up twenty new branches in poorly served areas.[11] Clearly, the different banks are following different competitive marketing strategies; for instance, the Yorkshire Bank and Williams & Glyn's are using market-penetration strategies, where the 'big four' in rationalising are using a cost-reduction approach (among other strategies).

Selecting a bank marketing strategy

Having formulated a bank corporate plan (which incorporates a marketing plan), the next step is to select a marketing strategy that will enable the long-term goals and objectives to be achieved. Ordinarily, a number of alternative strategies are formulated, as described in the previous sections of this chapter. The target group of customers, at whom the banks' services are aimed, is about the same for all banks. The question then arises of how to promote a service if it is virtually identical to that offered by competitors. Marketing efforts emphasise the distinctiveness of a service and banks try to emphasise the individuality of their services by two separate marketing tactics – service differentiation and market segmentation.

(1) *Service differentiation.* This marketing tool emphasises the promotion of differences between a particular bank and its services and those of its competitors. It is easier to differentiate between services if there is some real difference between them. But if there is little or no difference, then by this approach the customer should be made to feel there is a difference. This may be achieved by advertising and stressing brand image or features of the service. In the case where services between banks are identical, then advertising may be the only controllable marketing activity left.

(2) *Market segmentation.* This approach recognises that the diversity of demand for bank services is very wide. Under this approach, a bank would adopt a service to satisfy the distinct wants of selected groups of customers and prospects. The objective is to identify and exploit a niche in the market with a new or modified service. As with differentiation, segmentation involves the use of advertising and promotion but these tools are used to inform the segments of the availability of the services that have been tailored to their needs.

The difference between the two approaches is that differentiation emphasises the characteristics of the service, whereas segmentation aims at emphasising the characteristics of the customer. Banks tend to use both approaches in tandem. There is some discussion in literature about which one is preferable to stimulate the demand for a particular service.[12]

The selection of a bank marketing strategy has been shown to be dependent on a number of factors. First of all, the position of the bank in relation to its competitors must be taken into account – whether it is the market leader or not. Second, the objectives of the bank in both the short and long term will have a great effect on choice. Third, the marketing opportunities that are open to the bank and its potential target market may be a constraint, for example, the budget made available to the bank marketing function.

The selection of an appropriate strategy is based on a careful marketing strategy plan (Figure 8.4). The appraisal of a bank's alternative strategies is based on the internal conditions and external forces facing the firm. These alternative strategies should then be evaluated by the Board of Directors or the bank's business policy team and a selected 'optimum'

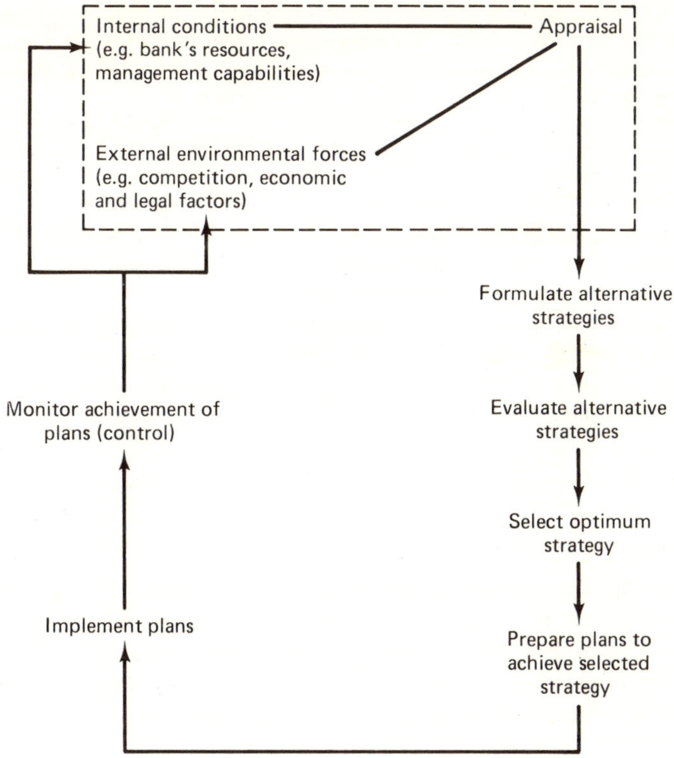

Figure 8.4 Bank's marketing strategy plan

marketing strategy is recommended. If accepted, this recommendation should be carried forward and adequate plans (which involve mainly the determination of means, i.e. allocation of resources) to achieve objectives are undertaken. It is the responsibility of the bank's Board to implement the plan and to monitor its results. Table 8.2 presents some appropriate strategies for small and large banks. Over all, the strategy selected will depend on:

(a) banks' competitive size and position in the market segment;
(b) company resources, objectives and policies;
(c) competitors' marketing strategies;
(d) target markets' buying behaviour;
(e) the stage of the product life cycle;
(f) the state of the economy.

Having analysed the market segment opportunities, the bank can select the segments it will serve on the basis of meeting banks' objectives and is in a position to develop strategies and plans and to allocate its resources

Table 8.2 Appropriate strategies for small and large banks in a given market segment

Strategy to be selected	*Bank size*	
	Large bank	*Small bank*
1. Protecting market share	Yes, but market growing	Yes, but market growing
2. Expanding market share	Yes, but brand loyalty high and there is a danger of anti-trust	Yes, but brand loyalty high
3. Expanding market	Yes, it gains as it has a large market share	No, insufficient resources
4. Market challenger	Yes	No, insufficient resources
5. Market nicher	Unlikely	Yes

via appropriate marketing mixes to serve the selected segments. The marketing mix in a segment is determined by the bank's strategy in the segment. It is that set of controllable marketing variables (services/products, price policies, promotions and distribution channels) that the bank can use to influence customers effectively and efficiently.

Branching and market strategy

The starting point for the marketing of financial services to the customer is his local bank branch. The local branch manager is in a unique position with regard to his customers. No other person can expect to have such an intimate knowledge of others' financial affairs and the information available on customers could be the starting point for a concerted marketing effort. Obviously individual branches can only be given a certain amount of freedom to pursue their own marketing of the bank's services. The bank has to preserve its corporate image and so advertising campaigns and the like must be controlled centrally via the bank's marketing strategy. However, within the scope allowed, much can be done. The branch manager will have some leeway on price since he is the one who will have to judge the creditworthiness of his potential borrowers and fix the interest rate charge to them. The promotion of the bank's services may also be pursued to some degree at branch level by attractively displaying leaflets that advertise the services offered. Also, active promotion of, for example, credit cards, may be pursued over a short period.

To some extent, therefore, individual branches have *some* control over market strategy at a micro level, but perhaps the major marketing variable in the mix is location and they have no control over this. Location selection, which is a function of the centrally planned marketing strategy, has been discussed in Chapter 3.

Because the business of a bank is largely contracted through its individual branches, it is important to select the most promising locations whenever this is possible. The big clearing banks have opted for a deep penetration strategy. The more branches in the high street the more business will be done, seems to be the policy. For the majority of branches, location is a fixed variable (at least in the short term) but where a new branch is planned – either as an additional outlet or as a replacement to a branch that is performing badly owing to its situation – then location is all important.

In 1967 the British Prices and Incomes Board suggested the number of branches was excessive, particularly among those 13 per cent of all branches located mainly in small towns which handled fewer than 1,000 accounts each. Costs per transaction were found to be 10–20 per cent less in the group of the largest branches than in the smallest group.[13] According to the report, banks impose costs on each other through competitive duplication. A reduction in the number of branches could, it was argued, release labour and capital used in the construction and operation of surplus branches for more productive use elsewhere in the banking system. In addition, the costs of co-ordinating the activities of these surplus branches could also be saved if they were closed.

Subsequently, repeated criticisms of overbranching have been made, but the critics may not be fully aware of the evidence and issues in three areas – branch costs, the importance of convenience to the consumer, and the relationship between profitability and branch portfolios.

First, the evidence concerning the operating costs of large branches relative to small and economies of scale must be carefully analysed. One US study[14] has indicated that small and large branches each have cost advantages in the delivery of certain types of financial services. Cost studies generally cannot standardise either for the services delivered or for the other cost and market data that can be altered by management. The aggregation may easily be misleading.

Second, market research studies[15] indicate that banks that compete against one another and as a group against non-bank savings institutions, on the basis of customer convenience, are competing on the basis of a dimension that is of substantial importance to a majority of both business and individual customers.

Banks do, however, appear to find difficulty in coming to grips with the necessity to close a mature branch that has become unprofitable. There are several reasons for this reluctance. First, there is a feeling that closures reflect poorly on the bank's image of financial strength and loyalty towards the affected community. Second, there is an anxiety that not all the business of a closing branch may be transferable to other branches of the same bank. However, if the revenues forfeited by the loss of business to competitors are likely to be outweighed by the savings associated with the closure, such anxiety is less justifiable. Third, a closure involves certain costs, including relocation of personnel and transfers of accounts, which may not appear justified if the losses being made by the branch are not severe. A less severe alternative to closure is the downgrading of a branch in terms of the expertise of its personnel and the range of services provided. However, the size of the branch usually cannot be reduced. Therefore downgrading means that the fixed costs of branch maintenance may have to be carried out on a smaller volume of business.

When a branch is downgraded or upgraded the impact on customer satisfaction must be carefully monitored. Upgrading often involves an expansion of services to cater for a growing business sector. A shift in orientation towards, say, business customers may detract from the personal service valued by the individual customer with the risk that some business might be lost.

CHAPTER 9

Marketing of bank credit cards

Contents

Introduction

The development of the credit card is probably the most significant phenomenon of the modern banking scene. Basically, the use of credit cards enables one to take advantage of the two essential aspects of the banking function: (i) The transmission of payments, (ii) The granting of credit. The development of the bank credit card allowed for the first time the use of these two functions together.

While this chapter deals mainly with bank credit cards operations, in addition there are travel and entertainment credit cards systems, as well as in-store credit cards, that to some extent compete with the banks' cards. There has been significant growth in the number of credit card holders and the use of credit cards over the last ten years. This growth has often been over-dramatised by failing to take account of other factors that put the credit card into proper perspective. Over these years inflation has run at consistently high levels; shopping patterns have changed; the degree and form of competition in the high street likewise, and there have been changes in the pattern of use of the various types and sources of consumer credit.

The credit cards – in a restricted form – initially appeared in the USA about fifty years ago.[1] By 1977 consumer credit cards served 52 million US households and over 2 million merchants, and provided over 100,000 jobs in the services sector. Over 60 per cent of consumer transactions are by bank credit card – much more than in Western Europe.[2] In 1979 credit card purchasing power in the USA exceeded $262 billion, of which bank credit cards have a 31 per cent share.[3] Although a greater percentage of total consumer transactions is by bank card in the USA, this reflects more widespread use of the credit card system there. Of the credit card market, banks in the USA have a much lower share than do bank credit cards in Europe. Mandell's work[4] found that bank credit cards in the USA have only a 16 per cent share in terms of total credit card usage (whereas their share in the UK is over 90 per cent). In-store cards were the most widely used with over 50 per cent of the US families surveyed using one, gasoline cards were second with a 33 per cent share, bank cards third (16 per cent) and T & E cards last, having a 9 per cent share.

In competition to bank credit cards, a wide range of different types and sources of consumer credit are available. There are bank overdrafts, budget accounts, revolving credit accounts, personal loans, retailers' account, retailers' free credit schemes, trading cheques, credit cards and hire purchase. On the UK market the range and types of alternative sources of consumer credit are more limited.

These facilities are provided by the banks, domestic and overseas based, independent finance houses, the trustee savings banks, National Girobank and retail traders, all of whom compete with one another for business. The clearing banks provide, directly or indirectly, virtually all of these consumer credit cards facilities and they also compete with one another for accounts.

The major bank credit cards are Mastercard and Visa in the USA and Access and Barclaycard in Western Europe and the UK.

Within this mix of available sources of consumer credit in Western Europe, credit cards account for a relatively small percentage. Access calculated that its own cardholder outstanding balances accounted for less than 3 per cent of total consumer lending at the end of 1979 and credit cards of all types accounted for less than 10 per cent.[5]

Similarly, in the USA bank credit cards form a relatively small part of consumer lending, but here it is the in-store credit card that is the most important consumer credit facility. In 1978 the outstanding balances of bank cards were less than 6 per cent of total consumer credit, people relying on cheques and other forms of credit cards to make purchases. The banks' share of outstanding consumer credit is small despite the increase in the total amount of consumer credit outstanding in the US economy (from $845 million in January 1968 to $5,603 million in July 1973 and still rising).[6]

The main types of credit cards

There are three broad categories of cards that can be used as substitutes for cash or a cheque in payment for goods or services. They are all commonly referred to as 'credit cards'; However, they do not all provide credit facilities.

Bank credit cards

These offer credit to a pre-set limit. The cardholder has the option of settling the monthly statement in full or taking credit up to a pre-set limit at a monthly interest rate and subject only to a specified minimum repayment each month. The cardholder usually does not pay a joining or annual fee.

There are three quite distinct parties to a credit card operation. These are the cardholder, the merchant and the bank. The cardholder and merchant will be considered in a later section of this chapter. Here, the bank's function will be looked at, the cost and financing of its credit cards.

When a person applies for a credit card he or she will be asked to supply details of his financial circumstances and, subject to references, he will be given a card with an appropriate credit limit. Some limits, for example student cardholders, are small, but substantial limits may be allowed for holders of considerable means. Cardholders apply for cards either to obtain credit, as a means of postponing payment for goods, or in order to have the convenience of a card as a method of payment, and/or as an alternative to cash or cheques. In the early days of credit cards the major banks reported that the majority of cardholders settled their accounts monthly and did not avail themselves of credit. In more recent times, about 70 per cent of cardholders are thought to use their cards to obtain instalment credit. This will be discussed in more detail in the section on consumer use of cards.

There is in any case an element of free credit granted to cardholders because (i) accounts are sent out monthly, covering purchases of goods or services since the last monthly statement, and (ii) the cardholder is allowed twenty-five days from the date of his monthly statement in which to settle the outstanding amount. It follows that if a cardholder's statement is normally sent out, say, on the 15th of any month, any purchases he makes on the 16th of the month could carry the benefit of fifty-five days' free credit.

The costs of a bank's credit card operation can be broken down into four components that are, in order of importance:

(a) the cost of funds to finance the outstanding balances of cardholders. This is borne by the respective card-issuing banks according to the amounts outstanding on the cards they have issued;
(b) for the banks in certain credit cards groups (e.g. the Access group), the costs of the central service company, the Joint Credit Card Company. This cost is shared by individual Access, Visa, etc. banks on an agreed basis;
(c) the costs of running the credit card departments within each bank, which are the responsibility of each bank;
(d) the costs of additional services provided by each bank for its own credit operation, both by the head office and branch network.

The banks' credit card schemes have only two main sources of revenue; there is a small joining fee and service charge paid by retailers and outlets at an agreed percentage on their credit card turnover. However, the real source of income to a bank lies in the interest charge made to customers who use their cards to take extended credit. If all cardholders paid their monthly accounts within the stipulated period, there would be little profit to the companies and indeed they would probably operate at a loss. It is certainly in the interests of the card companies to encourage cardholders not only to make more use of their cards, but to avail themselves of the credit facility.

The rate of interest charged to customers is normally expressed as a monthly rate. In advertising and cardholder conditions of use, notice of the annual percentage rate that the monthly rate represents is also quoted. Obviously, the annual charges vary with the interest rates in the economy. Apart from the costs of funds, which depends also on the Minimum Lending Rate (MLR) and Prime Rate (PR), the calculation of the monthly rate has to take account of a number of other factors:

(a) lending is unsecured and without guarantee;
(b) free credit can be enjoyed for a certain number of days depending on the date that goods are purchased;
(c) there are no mandatory repayment requirements other than a small minimum monthly repayment (for Access in Europe, for example,

this is currently approximately $10 or 50 per cent of the balance outstanding, whichever is the greater);

(d) the credit is of the form of a revolving facility and to be taken to a pre-set limit at the discretion of the cardholder; and

(e) the convenience and service to holders extends beyond just the provision of credit facilities.

But the concept of the annual percentage rate can give rise to misunderstandings. Only in the case of cash advances is the annual percentage rate the effective rate of interest, interest being charged at the equivalent daily rate from the date of purchase. Arithmetic conversion of the monthly rate to an annual rate for purchases takes no account of the interest-free period allowed. There are also other factors that are omitted:

1. Not only are transactions in the month preceding the statement free, but the balance of purchases outstanding longer than twenty-five days after the date of the statement in which they first appeared are subject to the monthly rate of interest for the first month.
2. After that any outstanding balance on these items is subject to an equivalent daily rate.
3. When the cost of purchase is first included on a statement, any payment towards it during the following month decreases the outstanding balance before interest is applied. The arrangements with Access, Visa and Barclaycard are different – if payment does not settle the outstanding balance, full interest is charged before deduction of the partial payment is made.

The sum total of all the factors involved means that the actual rate of interest paid by cardholders will differ appreciably from the annual rate.

A few hypothetical examples will illustrate this:

Assume that purchases are made fifteen days before the first statement and regular equal payments are made fifteen days after the statement date.

Purchases of $100	*Purchases of $200*	*Purchases of $400*
Payment period – 3 months	Payment period – 6 months	Payment period – 12 months
2 payments of $34.10	6 payments of $35.20	11 payments of $37.32
1 payment of $34.08	interest paid $11.20	1 payment of $37.40
interest paid $2.28	total paid $211.20	interest paid $47.92
total paid $102.28	annual rate of interest 20.77%	total paid $447.92
annual rate of interest 14.62%		annual rate of interest 23.77%

In recent times the main card schemes operations have been able to report a profit on their operations. This has not always been the case – in the early years the administration, and to a considerable extent the credit regulations, imposed by governments caused substantial losses to the card companies. In the USA bank credit card operators, however, experienced increasing profitability through the mid-1970s. A large number of bank credit card operators began in 1968 and 1969. A large outlay was initially required for issuing programmes. There are also large credit and fraud losses at first, until undesirable cardholders and merchant accounts have been eliminated. In addition, credit cards are novel institutions with unique management problems and decision-making only improves with experience.

Travel and entertainment (T & E) cards

These cards are not real credit cards since they only offer credit for the brief period between purchase and billing. When billing occurs, the cardholder is expected to settle in full. If settlement is not made in full when required, therefore resulting in overdue accounts, a penalty is normally imposed. However, an interest charge is not made. Instead, a joining or annual fee is applied to the 'travel and entertainment' cardholder. Any additional revenue is generated for the 'T & E' company by charging merchants a commission on sales charged to the card. This tends to be up to 5 per cent and in fact, unlike bank credit cards (where the only source of profit is from interest payments), is the major source of income. Examples of 'T & E' cards are American Express and Diners Club.

Table 9.1 compares the two major international 'T & E' cards with two major bank credit cards and the worldwide group to which they are affiliated.

In-store cards

These cards are issued to customers by a retailer or company and in general can only be used in that retailer's outlets or for purchasing the company's products. Different types of in-store credit cards are available. The common ones are as follows:

(a) *budget* (regular monthly payments are required with the costs of goods purchased being spread over a period);
(b) *option* (payment can either be carried out in full, or at the cardholder's option. However, the latter will be subject to a minimum repayment and then charged interest);
(c) *monthly* (here one has a monthly settlement without any extended credit. Payments in full are required every month and differ from the budget card where outstanding credit can be given up to a multiple of monthly payments, for example, 30 × monthly payment).

Table 9.1 Bank and T & E credit cards activity comparison (all data in millions US dollars)

	T & E cards		*Bank credit cards*	
	American Express (millions)	*Diners Club (millions)*	*Access (millions)*	*Barclaycard/ VISA (millions)*
1. *Cards worldwide* (1978)	$18.6	$6.0	Mastercharge group	Visa group
2. *Turnover*	$2,000	$1,600	$1,560	$1,440
3. *Number of transactions* (per month)	not available	3.3	50	75

The uses of credit cards by retail companies differ from those of the bank and T & E cards. according to Ross[7] only the bank cards and the travel and entertainment cards are intended to return a profit to their issuers. The garages, oil companies and department stores use cards principally as marketing tools, designed to solidify consumer loyalty and increase sales.

There are obvious advantages to the retailer of using such a card – there is little or no cost to him, so that Sears & Roebuck in the USA or Marks & Spencer in Europe can rightly claim that their scheme will not put up prices. On the other hand, if the customer wants to take credit he is likely to be paying a higher real rate than with, say, Visa. However, many of these in-store credit card schemes are developed by traders in partnership with banks or finance companies who undertake the administration and sometimes the financing involved. Barclaycard have done this with the Barclaycare scheme and has just signed up its second retailer, the Snob fashion chain. If consumer spending continues to fall and credit is taken more selectively, this could mean a bigger share for Barclaycard, Visa and Access, which offer cheaper credit facilities, if consumers are convinced that these cards do not put up prices.

The development of bank credit cards in the USA and western Europe

Credit cards were first developed in the USA. Early this century, some US department stores began to issue credit coins or tokens that enabled customers to buy their goods. Oil companies also issued 'courtesy cards' which were to be used only at their respective petrol (gasoline) stations. This may explain the reason why today in-store cards and gasoline cards make up the majority percentage of all credit card transactions in the USA (See Table 9.2.)

In the 1950s 'T & E' cards were introduced in the USA, for example, Diners Club, American Express and Carte Blanche. However, as previously indicated, these are a method of payment rather than a real source of credit. It was in 1952 that the Franklin National Bank issued the first bank

Table 9.2 Comparison of bank credit cards usage in the USA *v.* Western Europe

	USA	*Western Europe*
1. Percentage of adults holding a current bank account.	Over 90% of all adults do have a current account with a bank.	Western Europe including the UK is still mainly a cash-oriented society. Less than 60% of adults have a current account with a bank.*
2. Share of adults holding a bank credit card.	In 1972 a survey indicated that half of all US families possessed at least one credit card.† Currently probably over 80% posses at least one card.	In 1975 80% of adults in the UK did *not* possess any kind of credit card. Only one-half of UK families with incomes greater than £5,000 (about $10,000) possessed one.‡
3. Means of consumers' transactions.	In 1977 6% of all consumer transactions were by *bank* credit card only. No information could be found on percentage of transactions by credit cards in general. However, for total card usage the distribution was:† In-store cards –50%; Gasoline cards –33%; Bank credit cards –16%; 'T & E' cards – 1%; Total 100%	In 1978 AGB Research monitored consumer spending on transactions over £3 (about $6). Results: 2% of transactions by credit card. 61% of transactions by cash. 24% of transactions by cheque. 11% of transactions by direct debt. 2% of transactions by other means. 100% total

*Access Company, *The Credit Card in the UK* (1980). Issued by the Joint Credit Card Company Ltd, Southend, The control service company of Access.
†L. Mandell, 'Credit Card Use in the USA', *ISR* (University of Michigan, 1972).
‡'A UK Credit Card Survey', *The Banker*, vol. 125 (1975) pp. 16–19.

Table 9.2

	USA	*Western Europe*
4. Credit card transactions volume (1979).	Credit card transactions accounted for $262 billion. A far greater amount than in Western Europe, bank credit cards accounted for 31% of this transactions volume.	Of the above transactions, credit cards in the UK had a share of £140 million (about $280 million). Of this, 95% accounted for by bank credit cards, e.g. Access, Visa.
5. The usage of bank credit cards.	It is not known what percentage credit cards make up out of total available consumer credit. However, they are so widely accepted that it is difficult to make transactions without them. By 1977 approximately 52 million US households possessed credit cards. Unlike Western Europe where bank credit cards are the majority credit card, in the USA bank credit cards only form a small percentage. Note, however, they still account for 6% of total consumer credit. In-store credit cards are a most important consumer credit card facility.	Credit cards make up a small percentage of total available consumer credit in the UK. Of this small percentage, most is accounted for by bank credit cards. In 1980 approximately 4.5 million were Access cardholders in England, and approximately 5 million were Barclaycard holders. In Britain credit cards in general make up only 2% of the total consumer credit.

credit card in the world. However, growth in bank credit cards did not really begin until the 1960s; 1969 was the main growth year and between September 1967 and January 1972 there was an increase of 680 per cent in the number of banks with credit card facilities.[8]

Development of credit cards in western Europe began much later than in the USA. The Diners Club card was introduced in the UK in 1951, a year after its launch in the USA. American Express was introduced into Western Europe in 1963. However, Europe has not seen a great increase in the use of these cards and instead bank credit cards were the main growth areas. These were first used in England when Barclays Bank, having come to arrangement with Bank Americard, introduced in 1966 the bank credit card – Barclaycard. In 1972, in response to the success of Barclaycard and not wanting to miss out on the potential market any more, Lloyds, Midland Bank, National Westminster, Williams & Glyn's and the Royal Bank of Scotland launched the Access credit card.

Unlike the 'T & E' cards in the UK, bank credit card usage has been expanding rapidly. For instance, within a year of launching Access, the group had 3.3 million cardholders and 65,000 retail or merchant outlets. However, compared with this, in 1979 in the UK Diners Club and American Express combined had only 550,000 cardholders – a significantly lower figure especially considering their earlier introduction into the UK.[9] An important factor that may account for the low usage of bank credit cards in the USA has been put forward by Malechi and Brown.[10] In the USA the banks were initially reluctant to adopt even a local credit card, much less a national one. The reason for this was the difficulty in overcoming the conflict in philosophy towards consumer credit. With the credit card system, there is only a minimal qualification for being a cardholder. Instead, the cardholder is given a credit limit within which he or she controls the amount, use and timing of loans. However, this is the opposite to the concepts bankers have been accustomed to for years. Bankers have been used to maintaining complete control over credit, approving it in an item-by-item basis. Because of this there is obviously a greater risk to credit cards, but these risks tend to be compensated for by quite high interest rates. Nevertheless, despite this compensation, it was mainly the competitive atmosphere among banks that finally brought about acceptance of national credit cards.

In Western Europe the situation was completely different. Barclaycard was introduced and later it was the major banks themselves who initiated the pooling of resources to establish Access. Introduction was based largely on the realisation of the success in the USA and the fact that there was a large market for credit cards waiting to be tapped.

Unlike the USA, bank credit cards, as opposed to in-store cards, were to become the most widely used type of card in Europe. Having come to an arrangement with Bank Americard, Barclays launched Barclaycard as a credit card in 1966. Lloyds, Midland, National Westminster, Williams & Glyn's and the Royal Bank of Scotland introduced Access in 1972, by which time Barclaycard had over 1.7 million holders in England only and over 52,000 merchant outlets, in direct competition with existing credit card schemes. Within a year Access had 3.3 million cardholders in Britain and 65,000 merchant outlets. The group negotiated an agreement with Eurocard in 1973, giving it a link with a further 60,000 shops, hotels and restaurants throughout Europe, and in 1975 Access became a member of the Interbank Card Association (now Mastercard) with then 32 million cardholders around the world.[11]

It is only recently that there has been rapid expansion in the number of in-store schemes in Europe as competition for consumer loyalty has increased. However, there are only a limited number of these at present, most of which are backed by the major banks.

Western Europe is still a largely cash-oriented society. A quarter of the working adult population receives pay in cash and less than 60 per cent have a current account with a bank.

In 1975 80 per cent of adults in the UK did not possess a credit card of any kind and only half of those with incomes over $10,000 owned one,[12] whereas in the USA research in the early 1970s showed that half of families there use at least one credit card.[13]

In 1976 the Interbank Research Organisation estimated that in the UK 94 per cent of total consumer transactions by value were in cash, 4 per cent by cheque and only 0.35 per cent by credit card.

AGB Research launched a service called Index in 1978, monitoring consumer spending by a 10,000 survey on transactions over £3 ($6). In July 1978 when the survey first began, 2 per cent of the value of such transactions was paid by credit card, 61 per cent by cash, 24 per cent by cheque, 11 per cent by direct debit and 2 per cent by other means. The total value of these transactions was £6.9 billion, giving credit cards a share of £140 million. Assuming that hardly any credit card transactions are below £3, this gives a fairly reliable figure for monthly credit and turnover. Of the £140 million, 99 per cent accounted for by Barclaycard, Access, American Express, and Diners Club, and some 95 per cent by the first two. This suggests that Barclaycard and Access together had a turnover in 1978 of around £1,500 million.[14]

Advantages and limitations of the credit card system

To the cardholder

The advantages to a cardholder under the bank credit card system can be summarised as follows (see table 9.3):

1. A card is a convenient method of payment as opposed to cash or cheques. it is simple to operate convenient to carry and reasonably immune to financial loss.
2. It is a convenient source of credit if desired, to be taken advantage of when the holder wishes, for any amount up to his limit.
3. As all monthly purchases are covered by one payment, activity on the customer's bank account is diminished with possible decreases in commission charges.

Table 9.3 Advantages and limitations of bank credit cards – to the cardholder, retailer and the card company/bank group compared

	To cardholder	*To retailer*	*To card company/bank group*
Advantages	1. Convenience as a method of payment. 2. Simplicity to operate, to carry, and immune to financial loss. 3. Decrease in the bank commission charge, as all the monthly purchases are dealt with by one monthly payment. 4. Aids budgeting and planning. 5. Acceptability in many countries by banks and businesses as a means of payment. 6. Protection to cardholders as the credit card company (together with the retailer) is jointly liable for any purchases made. 7. Hedge against inflation (buy on credit now before prices go up).	1. Protection. The card is a guarantee of payment. 2. Aids to increasing business turnover. 3. Reduces the possibility of customer's bad debts. 4. Lessens the security risk of dealing with cash. 5. Aids in the bookkeeping process and increases cash flow. 6. Certain free advertising/ promotion from credit card companies or banks.	1. Revenue from the joining fee and service charge paid by retailers and outlets, at an agreed percentage of their credit card turnover. 2. Income from the interest charge made to customers taking credit.
Limitations	1. Payment of interest, if credit taken, generally the rate is quite high.	1. Bad debts (in case of own store/bank cards). 2. Payment of a certain fee and service charge.	1. Monetary control may restrict bank credit cards, credit limits and operations. 2. Risk of frauds. 3. Risk of bad debts.

4. It is an aid to budgeting as the holder pays a fixed amount each month according to his circumstances and can plan accordingly.
5. The acceptability of leading cards in so many countries is an aid to business and holiday travel.
6. The ability to draw cash from any branch of the major banks worldwide.
7. Protection is given to cardholders because the credit card company is jointly liable with the retailer for any purchases made with the corresponding credit card. This regulation holds for purchases between £30 and £10,000 in Europe (around $60 to $20,000).

Whichever of these advantages proves to be most important after market research, it will aid banks in knowing which attribute of credit cards to emphasise in their marketing strategy.

The credit card business is not without its risks. The original risk was that conservative customers might not respond to the vastly expansive campaigns launched to introduce credit cards. However, the operation was well timed and well executed and proved highly successful. The hazards that remain are those inherent to this type of business, vis. legislative controls, fraud and bad debts.

To the retailer

From the merchant (retailer's) point of view there are obvious advantages in operating a credit card system, as follows:

1. If a retailer accepts a credit card (bank), it obviously signifies a guarantee of payment and therefore is an excellent form of protection.
2. Accepting bank credit cards in particular, and introducing in-store credit cards, should help in increasing turnover for the retailer. This will be especially so as more retailers and consumers accept the idea of credit cards.
3. A retailer, by accepting credit cards and therefore having protection against the purchase, will also reduce the possibility of having bad debts.
4. Accepting cheques or credit cards instead of cash lessens the security risk of cash with retailers.
5. Overseas visitors may purchase more and therefore this is a market that the given retailer will now find open.
6. As well as reducing the security risk, the acceptance of purchases with a credit card can, as well as easing the difficulty of handling cash aid in the bookkeeping process, admittedly at a cost to the retailer.

In 1979 *The Banker* carried out an opinion survey,[15] the results of which suggested that retailers preferred methods of payment such as cash or cheque or budget accounts. These are obviously methods of payment over which retailers have greater control, incur the least delay in payment and consequently maximise cash flow in their favour. It was also obvious that retailers in general believed that customers have similar preferences. If this is true then obviously retailers will not lose out if they do not provide in-store credit cards or bank credit cards. However, if they do not keep abreast with the market trend in terms of credit cards they may well lose potential customers. More market research, particularly now as credit card usage is increasing, needs to be undertaken by retailers so they do have knowledge of up-to-date trends and consumers' opinions.

The study[16] also found that retailers were convinced of the value of operating bank credit cards in their bid to win new customers from rival stores, as opposed to developing consumer loyalty through the development of their own credit schemes. They saw American Express and Diners Club as too expensive to operate and believed that Visa, Access, etc. have significantly more advantages than any other forms of credit.

Retailers do not experience the same risks with bank credit cards as they do with their own cards – as the banks guarantee payment and themselves bear the cost of fraud and bad debts. This advantage outweighs the advantage of in-store cards that build up customers' loyalty, and leads to bank cards being the most popular form of credit card in many countries.

These disadvantages of bank credit cards as seen by retailers are very important to know because these are the factors that need to be overcome in any bank credit card marketing and advertising campaigns.

Monetary controls, either restrictive or expansive, imposed by governments can affect lending rate and consequently interest rates on bank credit cards. In fact there is little any credit company can do to minimise the effect of this.

Fraud, theft, etc. is also a problem. Anti-fraud organisations exist, however, within each major credit card company and have been successful in combating this type of misuse. Nevertheless, much risk is still an unwanted disadvantage to credit card companies.

Obviously one major risk is that of bad debts. As we have seen, retailers are protected from this; however, the companies themselves are not. Nevertheless, Visa, Access and Barclaycard lend well in excess of $20,000 million a year and bad debt experience is low despite this. American card companies have been found to experience fraud losses as high as 4 per cent, in Western Europe this figure has not yet been reached for fraud and bad debt combined.

Credit cardholders' profiles

A cardholder profile is basically an outline of the cardholder background in terms of education, income, residence, family and age. In addition, it should include frequency of card usage, types of purchases made by the cardholder and the number of cards a cardholder possesses.

Analysis of cardholders' profiles, pattern of activity and use in extremely important for effective marketing policy. In addition, market research should be used to identify market segments that could be potential areas for credit card companies to 'attack'.

Who uses credit cards

Both in the USA and Europe the profile of cardholders has been influenced by the way in which card schemes have been launched and promoted. On both sides of the Atlantic credit cards have been marketed to high-income groups from the beginning and these groups have always found credit-card facilities easier to obtain.

The banks initially issued their credit cards to their own customers, but since then there has been considerable growth in the number of bank credit card holders and the profile is no longer confined to account-holders of the banks. However, an 'average' bank cardholder tends to be a middle-class person who has a bank account already. In fact, 70–80 per cent of Visa, Access and Mastercharge holders are believed to be in the A, B and C socio-economic groups.[17] The European experience is that bank credit cardholders' outstanding balances remain well within their total credit limit. Over the years cardholders have used only 40 per cent of their credit at any one time. On 1 September 1980 Access calculated that the average credit limit for cardholders was about $800, and the average outstanding balance was $400. Mandell's survey in the USA[18] found that families living around the largest cities are the most likely to use credit cards. Three-quarters of such families used credit cards in 1970. Both in the USA and Western Europe, there is obvious room for bank credit card development away from capital cities.

The other determinants of card use were found to be:

1. *Income.* High income was found to be positively correlated to credit card usage. This is because high-income groups purchase more goods, so will be inclined towards a mechanism that facilitates these transactions. In addition, a great proportion of the goods that are possible to buy by credit card are luxury goods, more likely to be bought by those with higher incomes.
2. *Education.* The more highly educated a person, the more likely he is to use credit cards. This is obviously highly correlated to income and many US credit card companies use education as an indicator for soliciting preferred customers.
3. *Age of family head and family life cycle.* Families that are in an age range that characteristically makes many expenditures – that is

younger families, especially with children – are more likely to use credit cards than other groups. Also, income will not have reached its peak at this stage and this group also makes the greatest use of the credit aspects of the cards.

Research by Access in Europe indicates that less than 20 per cent of Access holders also hold a Barclaycard and only 5 per cent have one of the other T&E or in-store cards. Thus there is a tendency in Western Europe to use only one type of credit card. This is in direct contrast to practice in the USA where, if a family owns one type of credit card, then it is very likely to use another type too. Of families who use a credit card, the median number of cards used is three, with 14 per cent of families using six or more cards.

How credit cards are used

Social class has been looked at to find out if this affects bank credit card usage in order that the marketing of credit services can be improved. Mathews and Slocum found that for the USA different social classes exhibit different credit card use patterns.[19] Members of the lower socio-economic classes tend to use their cards for instalment financing much more than the higher socio-economic classes. One reason put forward to explain this is the difference in deferred gratification patterns between social classes in the USA. In effect, lower classes are characteristic of more impulse purchasing and being less sales resistant than the middle classes who feel they should save money and postpone purchases. On the other hand, the upper classes have a greater tendency than the lower classes towards convenience use. The upper classes do not need to save and defer gratification, but as there is no reason to use instalment credit they use credit cards for convenience.

As in the Western Europe, where it is estimated that 70 per cent of credit card usage is for instalment credit, most credit card usage in the USA is also to obtain instalment credit – although this does change with income and other demographic variables. However, in a second study carried out in 1970[20] it has been found that social class was not the most useful predictor of credit card usage. Variations in income cannot be overlooked in any market analysis.

One of the most important marketing aspects of a credit service is to determine what merchandise and/or services the consumer considers chargeable. Once a group of goods has been identified as a potential market, the credit card company has a frame of reference within which to plan and develop its marketing strategies.

Data obtained from a US study[21] suggest that the majority of card users favour purchasing goods like appliances, furniture, clothing and gifts on credit. Fewer bank card users find it acceptable to purchase items like meals in restaurants, holidays and antiques on credit. The graph also shows differences in acceptable items to charge between convenience and instalment users. Convenience users felt petrol, meals, entertainment, luggage, groceries, hobbies and swimming pools are more acceptable to charge than instalment users. Instalment users, from the lower socio-economic classes, are more in favour of purchasing consumer durables on credit.

No similar analysis has been done for the European market between goods or between convenience and instalment usage – except that groceries are not commonly bought on credit – partly because profit margins are too low to bear a service charge and also because of a lingering view that people should not be encouraged to buy food on credit.

In the UK the typical credit card holder uses his or her card about fourteen times a year according to the *Daily Telegraph* (14 November 1977) – the average purchase being between £11 ($22) and £14 ($28). Mandell's US research[22] found that, of families with bank credit cards, 31 per cent used their cards every month and an additional 11 per cent used their cards every other month, thus 42 per cent can be said to be regular users. But 9 per cent did not use their cards at all in the year prior to the survey. Regular or frequent use was found to be positively related to income and education, and inversely to the age of family.

In a USA study in 1977[23] it was found that two-thirds of the 52 million people owning credit cards use their cards every month. A typical consumer household with one or more credit card uses between twenty and twenty-five cheques per month versus seven or eight credit card transactions. Of these, only two or three were performed with bank credit cards.

What determines whether a card user is active or inactive?

Awh and Waters[24] carried out a study after remarking that a significant portion of cardholders had never activated their accounts. They related card use to economic, demographic and attitudinal variables, but unfortunately ignored the fact that a bank or other credit institution can affect use by its own marketing policy.

The following is a brief summary of the factors that they found to influence card use, in order of importance:

1. *Attitude towards bank charge cards* was by far the most differentiating factor distinguishing active from inactive cardholders.
2. *Age.* Increased age reduces the likelihood of an individual being an active cardholder (this is consistent with other studies, such as that of Mandell).[25]

3. *Socio-economic standing* also differentiates between active and inactive holders. An individual with a relatively high social standing is more likely to be a user of a bank charge card than is a person of relatively lower social standing – this in contention with the view that lower socio-economic classes utilise credit cards beyond their means, engaging in 'free spending'.
4. *An individual will be more likely to use his card if he also uses other types of credit cards.* Perhaps this implies that credit card use is a matter of habit.
5. *Attitude towards credit generally.*
6. *Education.*
7. *Income.*

Interestingly, although Mandell found education and income to be critical in determining credit card use, Awh and Waters's study finds such items to be of minimal importance. This apparent conflict is still to be settled.

The conclusions on credit card holders' usage can be summarised as follows:

The factor that differentiates the most between active and inactive cardholders is attitudes. Unfavourable attitudes were due to (i) fear that cards may make users (holders) rely heavily on credit, (ii) their belief that card usage should only be to cope with emergency needs. As we shall see later, this finding has an important implication for marketing strategies, that is, the convenience aspect should be stressed because many inactive holders may be convinced that this is an acceptable reason for activiating their accounts. Other conclusions reached were: (i) increased age reduces the likelihood of a cardholder being active, (ii) higher social-class cardholders tend to be more active than lower social-class cardholders. This is quite an important point because lower socio-economic classes could possibly be a potential market. However, at present credit card companies are very cautious because of the bad debt risk, and tend to assume that the lower socio-economic classes will spend too much on credit, far beyond their means. In addition, individuals with more than one card were obviously more active in their usage.

Bank credit cards' market segmentation

The introduction of bank credit cards was a major marketing operation and despite the enormous initial costs it must be rated as a highly successful exercise in terms of the market penetration that was achieved and the ultimate profitability. In broad terms the marketing effort of the credit card industry is pointed in three directions. There is the market among merchants, the market among potential cardholders and the marketing drive to encourage existing cardholders to make greater use of their cards.

(1) *The market among merchants.* The view here is that the market is approaching saturation point. With very few exceptions, all the major retail trading groups in North America, Western Europe and Japan accept payment by credit card. There may be expansion of the market into, for example, the food trade and certain non-trading areas such as payment of rates to local authorities in Europe; small retailers usually have such a small turnover, making profit margins narrow, that they are outside the card market. Therefore the main marketing thrust as far as merchants are concerned lies in servicing and developing existing outlets. Each of the major card groups has several hundred or more of sales persons who pay regular visits to the merchants to assist with the administration problems and the training of staff. The card companies (including bank card firms) also take a close interest in the marketing of the trader's merchandise and will assist with advertising campaigns or displays in order to improve the merchant's turnover and thus enhance the return to the credit card company.

Market segmentation from the point of view of the regional retailer has recently been performed in the USA[26] Bank cards are only just beginning to be accepted by the major retailers in the USA and the market has by no means reached saturation, as is perhaps the case in Western European countries. By late 1976 thirty-four stores among the 100 top volume US department stores had begun to accept bank cards, which has opened up a new market for bank credit card services.

The growing importance to regional retailers of bank credit card users has arisen because of the mobility of the population and the relationship of the mobile sector to retail chains. There are three market segments that a local retailer may be able to attract more effectively by accepting bank credit cards. These are:

1. Newcomers to a marketing area will not only have cards issued by major retailers but also bank credit cards. Newcomers tend to make initial purchases at a local branch of the national chain store with which they have established credit. Because regional retailers lack this national credit base they are at a disadvantage in attracting newcomers unless they offer bank credit facilities.
2. Tourists and business visitors are an important source of revenue and will patronise local shops. They will gravitate towards those shops accepting American Express, Master Charge or those accepting bank cards.
3. There is a segment of the market that prefers not to be overburdened with credit cards. People in this segment prefer to carry one or two multi-purpose cards and often a bank card is one of those carried.

This study[27] aimed to find out what kind of retail store bank credit card users found most appropriate to their shopping needs, so that the retail shops could define this market segment more precisely to develop marketing strategies to attract it.

The profile of bank card users can help to provide regional chain department store retailers and other local retailers with insight into the social activities, store characteristic preferences and demographic characteristics of cardholders. It has been found that the tendency of bank card users is to shop at stores with a wide variety of merchandise. Socially, they play more tennis, do more gardening, and do more entertaining than non-users. They also affiliate with religious, social, community and business organisations more. With regard to demographic variables, bank cardholders have a greater disposition to possess credit cards and have credit at a variety of retail outlets. Typically they have fewer children, higher incomes and are more highly educated. In addition they tend to be white and male.

Benefits will accrue to regional retailers who accept bank credit cards for purchases:

1. They will attract newcomers, travellers and those wishing to carry a minimum of cards.
2. The customer is pre-screened as a credit risk and the cost of giving credit is reduced.
3. By encouraging the bank cardholder to establish a credit account with the store, the retailer will increase consumer loyalty to that store.

In order to do this the retailer will base his strategy on the above results; he can sponsor organised clubs in gardening, bridge and tennis or may provide cooking classes and home decorating lessons – to attract a high proportion of people from the bank card user segment of the market. He could also try selling theatre tickets in the store and even sponsor local productions, and maintain a bestseller section in his book department.

By catering to lifestyles, activities and the characteristics of card users, regional retailers will increase market penetration.

(2) *The market among potential cardholders.* There is no question here of reaching saturation point, but some researchers believe that the number of cardholders may have reached a plateau for the time being. A whole new marketing strategy would be required to try and change attitudes towards credit cards, and as these attitudes are so deep-rooted it is doubtful that it would succeed. However, it has been noted that scope exists for expansion away from capital cities. In addition, in the USA the population age group 25–54 is expected to increase by 10 per cent over the next five years or so, and as this is the prime credit card market the banks will no doubt be able to recruit new customers here.

(3) *The market among existing cardholders.* As has been shown in the section on frequency of card use, which tends to be fairly low, there is

great scope here to increase both the average amount spent on credit card purchases and the number of times they are used, as people make fuller use of their credit limit. Thus this is probably the main growth area for the companies. If the banks could encourage the average use of credit cards merely to double to two purchases a month, the effect on profits would be dramatic. Administration costs would not increase proportionally and even if the average credit period did not increase past the present figure of four to six months, the interest earnings would double. It is very much in the interests of the bank credit card companies to increase activity among their existing users.

Finally, it is extremely important to develop credit schemes among retailers. This is an important growth area for the banks, as most in-house schemes are administered by themselves and the major card companies. In August 1978 Marks & Spencer in England announced their credit card scheme in association with Citibank. Barclaycard have launched a special service, called Barclaycare, for the purpose of running in-house schemes for companies who wish to have their own cards. Many US, Japanese and European firms do the sme.

It is also possible, as we have seen, to segment the market further, particularly in the area of existing users, in terms of social class, income, attitudes and so on in order to devise better promotional activities and increase market penetration.

Marketing strategies for bank credit cards

The purpose of the market segmentation studies and the extensive research among users and non-users of bank credit cards and into their attitudes, economic well-being, income and so on, is to establish criteria for marketing strategies so that target markets may be reached more efficiently and more effectively. Previous research has ranked the advantages of credit cards to holders, as follows:

1. The advantage cited most frequently was that the use of credit cards enables one to buy now without having funds for purchase. Thus the credit aspect of cards is their most important facility.
2. Second was the safety of the cards as compared with cash or cheques.
3. Third was the convenience aspect of cards as a cash or cheque replacement (see Table 9.3).

This ranking varies among sub-groups, as has been shown, with high income groups emphasising convenience and so on.

The use of credit cards can basically be split into two categories: instalment credit or convenience. As this splits the market into two, different marketing strategies can be used to appeal to different groups.

Traditionally, credit cards have always been marketed to the relatively rich, emphasising the convenience of using them – for example American Express, in building up to its launch in the USA in 1958, sent 22,000 personal letters to business executives; and in addition over 12 million account-holders of co-operating banks received letters announcing the comprehensive 'passport to the world of service'.[28]

It seems quite likely that the high-income groups have probably just about reached saturation point with bank cards, and it may be time for the banks to switch their advertising and promotion strategy to encourage instalment use by the middle and lower classes. This is by far the most profitable aspect to the banks of the credit card system, and effort could be made to induce not only potential customers to use it, but also either convenience users to use the instalment credit facility too, or existing instalment users to increase their use. Although the banks would do well to aim at instalment users, there is an increased risk that such promotion would attract lower income groups and lead to more bad debt and in fact decrease profitability instead of increasing it. As 70 per cent of users already use this facility, it is in any case the most popular aspect of credit cards. Safety is also important and the security of using credit cards, as opposed to cheques or cash, would also encourage increased use.

As the attitude towards bank charge cards is the most important factor in differentiating the active from inactive cardholders, advertising could perhaps be used to dispel some negative aspects of the attitude of non-users. Unfavourable attitudes stem primarily from (i) a fear that credit cards induce people to rely heavily on credit, and (ii) the belief that credit card utilisation should be confined to emergency needs. This is important for *activation strategies* – non-users may find the convenience use for credit cards acceptable, so advertising could centre around this. Research such as that done by Slocum and Mathews[29] in the USA to discover which goods are considered chargeable, and by whom, is useful when formulating advertising policies.

Research in this field has to be done for Western European countries as well, to find out what sort of strategy will be the most successful in the European countries to increase the usage of cards. With the introduction of in-store cards, for instance, attitudes towards having only one card may be changing, making the potential credit card market size very large indeed, and promotion could take advantage of this. Experience in the UK would suggest that credit card users are remarkably insensitive to interest rate competition between card companies, suggesting that other forms of competition, such as advertising and promotion, are more important – convenience (distribution) and product being fairly similar between the different companies.

For the USA, it was found that instalment users seek out stores honouring their cards, whereas convenience users do not – they use another method of payment if cards are not acceptable. So a bank's strategy should here be for stores to extend the number of outlets offering credit facilities in order to aid the transactions process to instalment users.

Although, as already pointed out, credit card companies have in the past been very 'conservative' about new markets for cardholders, it may now be time for these companies/banks to change their marketing strategy aiming towards the lower to lower-middle classes. This in fact could prove to be even more profitable. As seen, upper- to middle-class cardholders do tend to use their cards for convenience and not so much for instalment use. Profit is made if cardholders do not pay their bills within the credit-free period and instead pay interest. In fact it was in 1971 that Ross stated in the USA that, 'a successful credit card programme requires a card holder mix that is heavily weighted on the side of the gainfully employed at the lower end of the income scale, to whom a $500 line of credit is a great boom'.[30]

Advertising should then emphasise the instalment use of the card as opposed to the convenience aspect. In addition, effort needs to be made to attempt to encourage earlier convenience users to use the instalment credit facility. However, it should be remembered that aiming at this market means that more risks will be attached, that is, there will be more possibility of bad debts.

Previous research indicated[31] that attitude was an extremely important factor in differentiating between the active and the inactive cardholder. To summarise briefly, unfavourable attitudes stemmed from fear that credit cards could cause people to rely too heavily on credit and therefore credit cards could only be used for emergencies. The first point is also probably a major factor preventing many people from using credit cards. Consequently, advertising should aim to dispel these fears. Emphasis could be made on the convenience aspect and almost certainly goods that generally people find more acceptable to use on credit should be used for illustrating in advertisements.

In a recent example of a Barclaycard advertisement, the following message has been presented:

1. A barclaycard does not necessarily lead you to use excess credit – simply to manage or budget one's money.
2. The convenience aspect, for example, use spontaneously to buy a bunch of flowers.
3. The instalment aspect (e.g. for goods that have already been shown to be acceptable for buying on credit, e.g. cars, washing machines).
4. Its use in emergencies.
5. The fact that one can, if correctly timed, make use of up to seven weeks' free credit.

Conclusions: the future of credit cards

The market for credit cards is expanding both in the USA and in the rest of the world. However, the growth areas are completely different.

In the USA in-store credit cards have reached saturation and bank credit cards are only beginning to expand.

It has been estimated that by 1985, the number of all credit cards will have reached 700 million.[32] At present, in the USA there are 15 million users of bank cards, that is, active cardholders, and predictions for bank credit card users in the USA for 1985 are around 255 million. It is also predicted that by 1985 over 50 per cent of the population will be cardholders and that bank cards will overtake in-store credit cards in numbers and may take as much as one-third of the sales volume currently charged to retail cards.

On the other hand, in Western Europe the growth areas will be bank credit cards and in-store credit cards. For instance, we have just recently seen the introduction of the new TSB bank credit card in the UK. Literature is not available on predictions for increase within the UK but Nilson[33] predicted that in fact European countries, and possibly Japan, would see faster growth than in the USA. Whether this is so remains to be seen. There is much controversy at present in Europe as to the role of banks. Many economists believe that in fact too much saving is being channelled into consumer credit (unlike Japan at present) and more should be used for investment for industry. They would like to see restriction on the amount of consumer credit available. However, at present until the economy revives, there is little demand for investment so it seems unlikely that such views will be enforced. But if they were, this would affect future growth of credit cards.

Obviously, with the use of more and more sophisticated computers, memory capacity, etc., new areas for credit card and money transmission services are opening up. However, the speed with which these new technological developments occur and result in credit card growth will be also partly affected by the consumer. As pointed out by the Access company, most of Western Europe, unlike the USA, is still largely cash-oriented. Consequently, much will therefore depend on consumer attitudes and habits. This will in turn very much depend on the marketing strategies adopted by the different credit card companies. Continued market research is required about the changing state of the market segments, for example, retailers, active and inactive cardholders, and the changing influence of factors such as income, age, etc. on these market segments. Only if this is undertaken will effective marketing policies be carried out and new potential markets identified. This will influence future growth rate just as much as technological innovations.

Cardholders react rationally and responsibly to the general economic climate. When the economy is depressed or turning downwards, cardholders generally reduce their outstanding balances, and vice versa when the economic situation is improving or buoyant.

There are fears that extensive credit card use may be proven to be inflationary owing to the fee that merchants pay to card companies leading to an increase in their costs and thus to price increases. But there appears to be no evidence to support this; credit cards do not add to inflationary pressures or indeed encourage greater consumer borrowing. In fact credit cards can even be a hedge against inflation, enabling the customer to buy now before price increases and use the instalment facility to pay. In inflationary times this could be useful in advertising and promotion policy.

There is also the effect of credit card use on the demand for money. The use of a credit card should enable a consumer to keep a lower average balance in his current bank account. This has implications for inflation, the demand for money, the velocity of money and the monetary policy of government, but as yet there is no evidence that credit cards do actually reduce the amount of money consumers hold in their current accounts – either in the USA or anywhere else in the world.

Finally, in the USA it has been found that the use of credit cards has changed the pattern of consumer debt – yet this is only among the higher-income groups who are making increased use of their cards. However, most of this debt can be viewed as a convenience feature (cheaper credit can be obtained by other means such as loans), rather than as traditional, longer-term consumer debt.

It was the advent of the computer data processing systems that provided the impetus for the development of the credit card. It enabled fast and economic processing of thousands of consumer and trade transactions and their associated accounting requirements.

Whether by accident or design, the credit card business has usurped some of the older and more routine functions of traditional banking – helped by cash dispensers and credit cards, customers can now receive statements, cash, etc. without even having to enter a bank.

Thus credit cards are increasingly replacing cash and cheques, but the speed with which these new technological capabilities are accepted – such as credit cards as a means of instruction to computer terminals in shops, airports, hotels, etc. – will not just depend on the availability of suitable equipment, but also upon consumer and social attitudes to (i) plastic, (ii) technology, (iii) point of sale systems, as well as on the extent to which banks and credit card groups will find some mutual system(s) of development and integration of their ideas to penetrate the existing market.

CHAPTER 10

Bank marketing administration

Contents

In essence, administering involves the following activities:

(a) delegating authority to 'line' manager;
(b) selecting appropriate staff personnel to work with programme;
(c) communicating purposes and appropriate details of programme to employees;
(d) establishing performance evaluation and reward system.

Bank marketing can often be seen to play a function role in the marketing department. At the branch level, however, it is mainly seen to play a supporting role. The point is that the administration of the bank marketing programme will vary according to the organisational structure of the bank in general, and the organisation of its marketing department in particular.

At any rate, the organisational structure of a bank will, to a large extent, depend on its historical development. Certainly this is true for 'big four' banks in the UK, where the organisational structure varies tremendously among them. Although there are, in general, three major types of organisational structure: by-products, markets and function, a *mixed* form of marketing organisation prevails in most of the large modern banks. This particular form of organisation is suitable for banking, because banks offer divergent products and services to divergent markets.

Administering the marketing programme

In order for a bank marketing programme to be successful, the bank needs to define and delegate the responsibilities related to the various aspects of its marketing programme, as well as the implementation, feedback and corrective actions – if necessary – to various bank marketing executives. In order to delegate responsibilities, clear knowledge on how the bank is structured is required.

In addition, in order to administer the programme, one needs to know to whom the delegation should be? In other words, who are the controllers? The controllers are those personnel in the organisation responsible for planning and monitoring the activities and use of resources within specified functions of the business. In this case, the controllers are in the marketing department in the central division/headquarters – as for example in the case of Midland Bank Ltd. There, the marketing department will plan out the market programme for the bank including developing new services/products, testing these and gathering information from such tests to set up some targets for lower management (like branch managers) to achieve. In the formulation of such targets, it is required that the participation of the persons involved, for example, the branch managers, have to agree on specific targets for their branches. In addition, controllers have also responsibility for providing information to operating managers, that is, branch managers and supervisors, so that they have all the facts on which to base corrective actions, if required. That is to effect changes, as they deem appropriate to the circumstances, in order to achieve objectives for which they are accountable.

How, then, is the control implemented? This can be achieved by the dissemination of information from the control systems within the administrative function. It is important to appreciate that the administrative sections collect, record, process and provide information to the various levels of branch management who effect corrective action as deemed necessary from the information provided. The administrative sections do not themselves affect action directly.

As mentioned above, it is the branch management who affect corrective action as deemed necessary, from the information provided. Consequently, there is a need to know the span of control that refers to the number of subordinates who report to and are controlled by a superior. It is the span of control that serves the basis of any organisational structure. When delegating responsibilities the span of control should always be considered. In order to establish the most effective span of control for each function, the appropriate bank manager should consider building the organisation structure from the operating staff upwards, establishing for each activity the number of personnel involved and the degree of supervision and control required for effective operation. Having planned the organisational structure through the span of control basis, the administration of the bank marketing programme is much more effective since everybody in the organisation will know what his/her responsibilities are.

When administering the marketing programme in an organisation, the human aspect should also be considered. It is this human element that reacts to environmental changes in different ways depending upon the various individual characteristics and points of view. People's reactions may clash with regard to objectives, as the organisational objectives may not correspond with the individual objectives. For example, the attainment of company objectives may require additional personnel to achieve specified outputs that are greater than the outputs that individuals wish to achieve. Thus the need to motivate and provide incentives will be required and financial rewards are by no means the only motivating force. In fact, Midland Bank for example used this as an incentive to motivate their branch organisation. On achieving a target, the branch will be given some percentage of the profit to be shared by everyone in the branch organisation network. Some other additional forms of motivation force may be when money is a marginal 'disincentive', because of taxation rates for example. The incentives can be a greater level of participation in decision-making, more status, etc. In fact, the participation in decision-making is very important as marketing in banking needs the support of top management and also participation of those managers involved in setting the targets. In Berry, Kehoe and Lindgren's study[1] it has been found that the most frustrating aspects of bank marketing work are as follows:

(a) lack of management support;
(b) lack of interdepartmental co-operation;
(c) crisis management;
(d) government intrusion;
(e) advertising and media problems.

After knowing the organisation structure and the relevant information, the next step is the design of communication channels. Information is only useful if it is communicated, thus a communication system is just as important as the relevance of the information provided for an effective management information system.

The criteria needed to design an efficient communicating network within the organisation are:

1. *Relevance.* The system must be relevant to the specified bank business requirements. It is necessary to present clearly the objectives of the system, to specify who will use it, how the users will relate it and

describe the manner in which the system will satisfy the stipulated objective.
2. *Timeliness.* This is important as it defines the response-time criterion in advance of the system's implementation.
3. *Cost-effectiveness.* The effectiveness of the system, both in respect of tangible and intangible benefits, should be related to the cost of installing and operating the system, in order to determine its feasibility.
4. *Accuracy.* Basic control, checks and balances, should be applied to data sources and system components, to ensure that the system is not only efficient but also that its output is correct and usable.
5. *Flexibility.* A system should be flexible enough to handle (i) normal activity growth for a foreseeable period ahead, and (ii) inevitable changes in the planning process or the organisational operations.

Feedback and decision-making are fairly easy if the communication system is effective and the organisational structure and its span of control reasonable. Once the symptoms have been identified by the operative management in-charge, the diagnosis will be carried out to find out the factors causing variance in bank performances. Having diagnosed, prescription or recommendation on corrective decision will have to be implemented, and all these steps can be systematically undertaken if a systematic and organised structure is available.

Marketing department organisation

An efficient marketing organisational structure is really a function of the marketing strategy adopted by the bank. Objectives for the bank marketing department are established in the form of descriptions of the marketing department responsibilities in terms of deposits and borrowing volumes, market share, advertising, promotion, services development, market research, etc. This analysis leads to a preliminary estimate of the number of marketing persons required given the opportunities in the market. The statement of marketing objectives leads also to an estimate of the marketing budget required which must also consider the availability of financial resources and other bank constraints.

The next step in the decision process for the bank marketing manager is to develop the basic control units from which he plans to organise and control the marketing efforts. He must decide the basis for these units (branches, regions, etc.) as well as the span of control to be used. Using some estimates of market potential and expected deposits, borrowing, profits, etc., the bank marketing manager must allocate sales effort to control branches' operations. Here he must consider the individual branches' locations and potential and how the branches should be organised.

Generally, the marketing department is just one of the several major departments in a 'typical' bank organisation (Figure 10.1). In the past, most of the marketing emphasis in a bank was on the tellers' functions, the other major functions and sections in the marketing department were marketing research, advertising and promotion and services planning. This type of marketing department organisation is called functional organisation, and its advantage is that it leads to a better utilisation of specialist resources in the various functions, and therefore is a more effective form of organisation. Its limitation is, however, in the ability of the management to control or assess performance in the individual sections, for example, marketing research.

In large and modern banks it is generally recommended that the marketing function must be organised along customer group lines. This is so, because the key tasks involved differ among customer groups. To illustrate, pricing differs significantly between corporate and retail banking. Corporate account pricing should be based on some measurement of the overall relationship – the return on assets or capital employed or some similar measure taking into consideration the risk involved – and looking at incomes and costs from all sources including the cost of funds and the credit for funds supplied. In contrast, retail services should be priced *en masse*, on the basis of standard costs and then with some reasonable mark-up adjusted to reflect competitive conditions, and then marketed *en masse* at specific prices.

Similarly, packaging also differs significantly from one customer group to another. In general, packaging for the corporate market has to take a very tailored approach – customer-by-customer type. In the retail markets this is just the opposite.

The segmentation into corporate and retail markets entails the decentralisation of the organisational structure of the banking system. However, the decentralisation should not be confined to the branch or affiliate (multibank) level, but to the retail banking division, the corporate banking division, the trust or consumer finance level.

Problems in bank marketing administration

There are a number of problems facing the implementation of bank marketing administration, as follows:

(1) *Lack of support from bank managers.* In Carroll's 'Ten Commandments for Bank Marketing',[2] the second commandment deals with *top* management support. He stresses that in common with most new and significant programmes, marketing success or failure is directly traceable to the support that top management gives or withholds. In a similar tone, to ensure fruitful marketing effort, bank marketing should be well received by the top bank managers. Many studies have pointed towards a

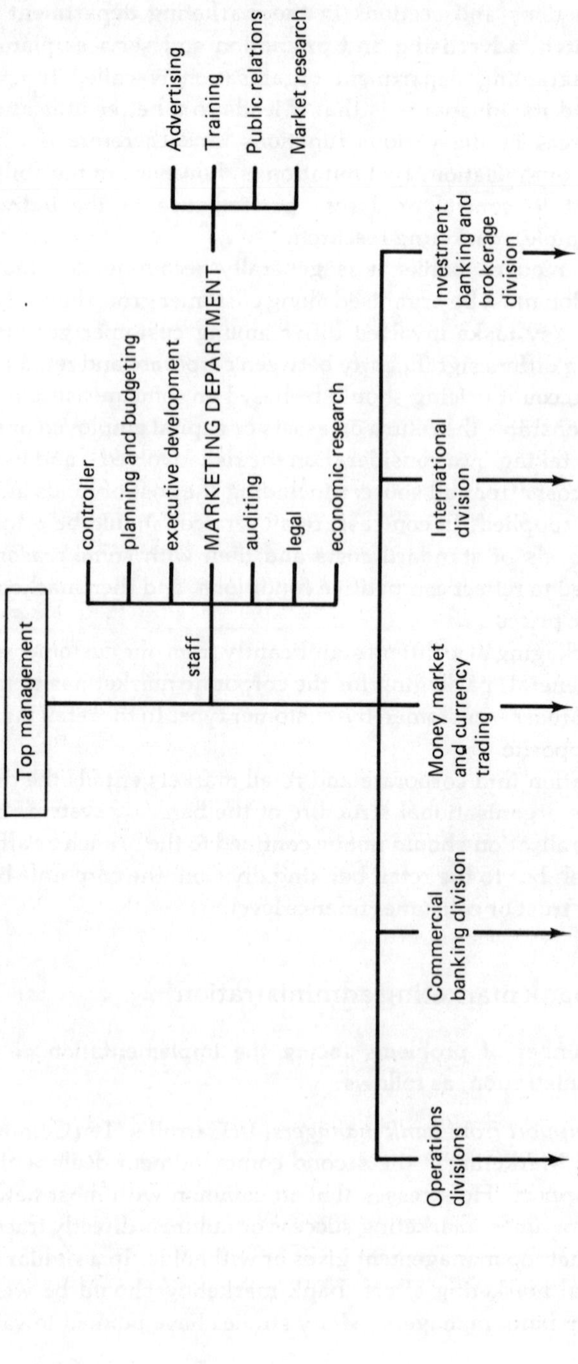

Figure 10.1 Typical banking organisation: staff functions and main divisional lines

'lukewarm' attitude of the bank managers towards bank marketing. The following responses suggest the scope of frustration of bank marketers:[3]

'Getting the CEO and other executive managers to view advertising/sales promotion as part of the overall marketing concept rather than as an expensive luxury.'
'Low level of importance in overall bank management as viewed by senior management. Relegated to low priority in budgeting.'
'Convincing a conservative Board that new ideas should be tried.'
'Even in a "marketing-oriented" bank (declared so by management) marketing is often separated apart as something done in addition, not vital to the central process and functions of banking.'

This is a very serious problem, because the bank managers are the most important people in influencing the bank marketing effort, especially the personal selling.

(2) *Branch manager limitations*. Nobody is going to suggest that a bank manager can equally become a 'marketer' or that he can acquire sufficient marketing knowledge to be able to give off-the-cuff advice to the customer on all his financial problems. He is merely the general practitioner who will listen to the case put to him by the 'patient' and then refer it to the specialist for diagnosis and treatment. To illustrate, say, on insurance, half the inquiries will be passed over for further attention to the local office of the insurance broking subsidiary. The other half, or perhaps a good deal less, can be dealt with at the branch, where instant cover is available on schemes for straightforward insurance – mainly short-term life assurance and household insurances. Another point is that even though the branch manager may be very keen on promoting 'Bank marketing', he may not have the time to devote to it. The branch manager will be a busy man. He may have anything from 1,000 to 15,000 customers and a staff to serve them. He may have one or more assistant managers, a manager's assistant, and an accountant, and hopefully, all will be able to handle inquiries from customers on insurance matters. The average branch manager, or assistant manager, meets in the course of the year only a fraction of his customers to whom he may have the opportunity of presenting services the bank can offer, say, in the insurance field, or pension plans. He has therefore to contact his customers with personalised letters offering appropriate products.

(3) *Lack of bank marketing knowledge* As aforementioned, 'marketing' is a relatively new concept in banking. Even today, many branch managers do not fully understand their bank marketing programme. We can expect even less from the bank employees. Many of them consider advertising alone will do well for all the marketing effort, plus, maybe, public relations. Rarely do they realise the importance of their role in the process of marketing.

The above points towards the relative lack of marketing knowledge. Although marketing training and education is an element of bank marketing today, a more vigorous drive is suggested in order to educate the bankers in general, and bank employees in particular. More seminars, and in-bank contact talk on bank marketing, should be encouraged. It is generally acknowledged that most banks in Western Europe, for example, lack strong professional marketing teams. Unlike their US counterparts, most UK and European banks are somewhat reluctant to employ more business graduates in particular those in marketing management – although this has changed recently. This is particularly needed in the light of foreign competition. Although many may argue that the banking habits in Europe and the USA are vastly different, few will deny that the US banks are more aggressive and at the same time well ahead in the knowledge of bank marketing management. In addition, at the very least, training and education should make bankers more customer-oriented and efficient.

(4) *Use of outside services.* Another aspect of European banking is a general reluctance to use outside services. A lot of literature on bank marketing has confirmed the fruitfulness of US banks in hiring the services of outside agencies. It has been asserted that an innovative and aggressive marketing organisation will almost certainly have great need for outside professional services. Specifically, it could very well need an advertising agency, a public relations firm, consumer research services, management consulting services, and so forth. Without going into specific needs that each outside administration might answer, it is probably sufficient to say that even the most developed bank marketing organisation is unlikely to be able to justify the kind of talent mix and reservoir of experience that these firms can supply.

(5) *Staff motivation.* There are two important trends that the banks have to examine and their effect on actual and prospective bank employees. First, because the climate of employment has changed markedly in the past twenty years or so, and with it the motivational pattern, there is evidence that some of the older motivators have lost their vitality. Second, the forces of competition present through the banks' marketing and businesss development sectors many new challenges to the staff; these challenges must be met by the banks. It is therefore the responsibility of top management to consider the following: (i) banks' top management – and also regional, area and branch managers, for that matter – should themselves be highly motivated, that is to say, they should personally have a strong need to achieve, (ii) banks' top management has the duty not only to clarify the aims of the business, but also to control and manage a system of working relationships that reflects the business's particular style. For instance, acceptance of modern concepts of MBO (management by objectives) and similar management styles whereby the bank and branch employee is not only required to perform, but he or she also

participates in some of the decisions affecting his/her work, (iii) communications to employees and a degree of involvement needed for motivation throughout a widely spread concern requires effective business organisation leadership, both at the bank and at branch levels. It also requires an efficient two-way communication system.

Some of the steps that can be taken to motivate staff are as follows:

1. Account for the basic human wants and the individual's response to his/her needs and enviroment.
2. Refinements for the banker-salesperson. First, the individual must be allowed to take personal responsibility for finding solutions to problems. Second, he/she should take part in the setting of goals/functions which, while stretching, are inducing extra achievement.
3. Incentives – can be in term of awards, cash, holidays or status.
4. Clear and acceptable objectives to provide a framework for a commonsense of purpose through mutually shared bank/branch objective(s).
5. Adequate training, to identify the training needs of individual bank branch managers and their subordinates.

(6) *Personal selling.* The prime part of the marketing mix in the banking industry is the personal activity of the branch manager. Personal selling, in essence, is face-to-face presentation of the bank's sales message to prospective users.

Administration of retail *v.* corporate bank markets

Broadly speaking, the markets in which banks operate can be analysed along two major dimensions or categories of activities: (i) the retail v. the wholesale (or corporate) banking markets, and (ii) the domestic v. international banking markets.

The retail market

Over the years wholesale banking (including international banking) has received considerable attention by the banking industry. However, recently there has been an increasing awareness of the risks involved, the strengths of competition, and the smaller margins available in the corporate and international markets. Although banks' activities in these markets seem to be growing, it is also true that banks are giving more attention to the importance of traditional retail operations. To a very large extent the retail banking objectives are mainly achieved through the intensive employment of promotional tools.

Among the various marketing promotional tools, premium promotions are the most widely used in the banking industry. In the USA more than one in four banks have tried premium promotions since the Second World War. Recently banks are the largest users of direct premiums among incentive-using industries. The range of premiums differs from bank to bank. For instance, a Chicago bank's prepaid-interest plan offers a Mercedes 450 SL Sports Coupe to a depositor with $150,000 or over, and a Minneapolis bank offers a free house plant for a $100 depositor.[4]

In Europe, in response to increasing pressures and competition from foreign banks in the retail market (especially from large US banks), banks have introduced various premium promotions, especially to students, women and young married couples.

In spring 1980 Lloyds launched a major incentive scheme for a limited period aimed at young married couples setting up a first home by offering vouchers worth over £300 in the form of cash discounts. This is an example of the increasingly important role played by premium promotions in bank marketing. There are several major objectives for using premium promotions, as follows:

(a) to attract new accounts;
(b) to increase the level of deposits and increase the bank's market share;
(c) to lower the cost of acquiring new deposits by seeking to avoid direct price competition with other financial institutions;
(d) to reach specific market segments;
(e) to modify banks' images; and
(f) to obtain deposits quickly when needed for banks' loan operations.

In attracting new accounts, bank premiums are useful for two reasons: (i) the banking industry is to a large extent regulated by the government and regulations limit the pricing latitude in order to protect the financial strength of the banking industry, and (ii) product and service differentiation in banking is rather difficult.

In European banks the recent use of bank premiums aims generally at reaching specific market segments (e.g. the young married couples market). However, it overlaps and coincides with the more general objective of attracting new accounts to the bank. Thus the use of premiums as marketing tools seems to be quite widespread in the banking industry. However, there are many banks that reject premium promotions as 'undignified' and because they are rather expensive marketing tools. In fact, there is a debate whether or not premiums create customer loyalty to the bank. A study conducted by Preston *et al.*[5] indicates that there is no significant difference between the retention rates of premium-attracted and of non-premium-offered deposit accounts. Consequently, the conclusion is that customers attracted by a free premium were just as loyal as those customers attracted by a lower-price banking service premium.

In any case, it is essential to evaluate the effectiveness of a bank premium with respect to both its benefits and costs to the bank, when it is introduced as a marketing promotional tool. Taking all the arguments into account, the marketing programme for introducing bank premiums can be summarised in the five stages shown in Figure 10.2.

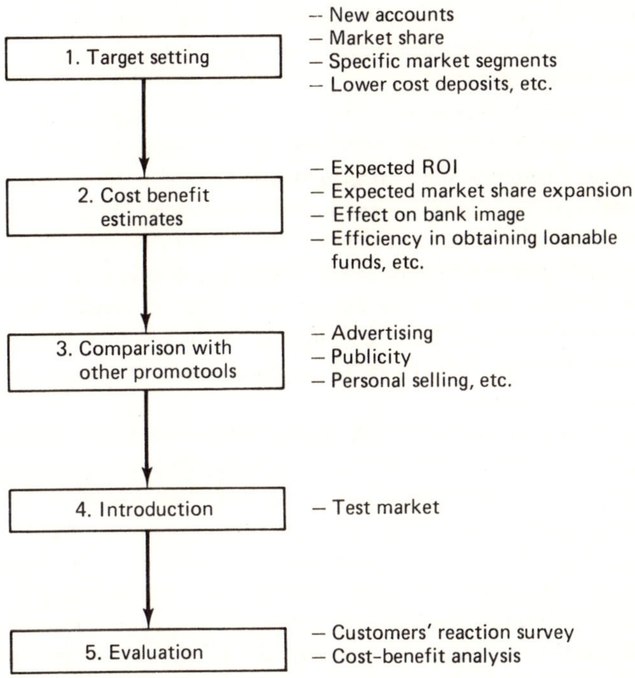

Figure 10.2 Introduction of bank premium promotions

The corporate banking market

During the last decade the nature of corporate services offered by banks has changed very rapidly. Brown and Cohen[6] suggest the following factors that have made corporate banking services much more comprehensive, and that have created a much more competitive market:

(a) the growth of the banking industry;
(b) the size and importance of banks' corporate clients;
(c) the widespread use of computer systems in the banking industry;
(d) the increasing competition from non-banking financial institutions;
(e) the growth of other financial markets.

Currently, the generally available major corporate banking services are: (i) financing services, (ii) cash-management services, (iii) agency services, (iv) international services, and (v) management counselling services. The availability of the above-mentioned services varies from bank to bank, depending on their size and specialisation. Over all, the corporate services offered by banks recently have become far more diversified and sophisticated than they were in the past. As cash-management and international services (especially services to the multinational corporations) are the most important in the corporate banking markets, they will be discussed separately.

(1) *Cash-management services.* The rapid expansion of cash-management services in corporate banking is largely the result of recent technological progress and consequent development of electronic banking. Basically, cash-management is the practice of obtaining the maximum use of cash by commercial enterprises.[7] Traditionally, the objective of a cash-management system in any corporation was to accelerate cash collection into its various bank accounts, and then transfer these funds into the central corporate bank account. In this way, the combined funds could be used to pay debts, to lessen autonomous borrowing or to support short-term investments.

Recently, more sophisticated cash-management techniques have evolved, and the new objective of cash-management is to optimise the corporation's liquidity position so that cash is available when needed. In other words, cash-management has reached new levels of performance from controlling the payment and receipt processes of a company, to maintaining its liquidity objectives. In response to these changes in needs of corporate customers, the banking industry has created a number of new cash-management services. At present, the following services are commonly being offered[8] by banks, mainly in the USA:

1. *Terminal-based information services.* Inquiries about deposits, balances and other account activities, as well as the entry of instructions for transfer of funds, are feasible through the computer terminals that are connected to the bank's computer.
2. *Automated-lockbox.* Information about the receipt of payments into lockboxes at bank locations is transmitted electronically to the corporation's computer centre, for posting accounts receivable into records.
3. *Individual-to-business pre-authorised debits.* Through an automated clearing house, the individual is able to pay bills without a cheque, and the corporation receives payments directly into its bank accounts.
4. *Business-to-individual-direct-deposit of payroll, dividends and pensions.* Through automated clearing houses, corporations' payments such as payrolls, dividends and pensions are directly transmitted into receivers' accounts.
5. *Automated depository transfer cheques.* Funds are transferred from local banks into a central corporate concentration account using automatically generated depository transfer cheques.

These new cash-management services that fully utilise computer technology have become money-savers for the banks' corporate customers, by speeding up cash-management processes and cutting down the hours of work that corporate employees must put in. In this way, these services have increased the utilising efficiency of corporate customers' resources. However, it is often argued that banks have not exploited the opportunities that had resulted from offering these services. It is argued that although banks with long-established cash-management services departments are aggressively marketing their products, the majority still seem to approach cash-management only in response to customer inquiries or some other outside stimulus. Obviously, banks that do not initiate cash-management miss the opportunity to increase their profitability for the following reasons:

1. In the current stagnant economic conditions coupled with high inflation, cash-management is a highly saleable service. Banks that aggressively exploit the need for sound cash-management advice and technical assistance have made substantial inroads in the corporate markets.
2. In a period of high interest rates when banks cannot extend further credit to some firms, the application of sound cash-management within the firm can sometimes generate those sums of cash that were formerly sought on credit. Thus the marketing of cash-management allows banks an additional option, whereas in the past they had simply to turn the borrower away.
3. Through the promotion of cash-management services, unprofitable accounts can become profitable and potential borrowers may become more creditworthy.

For these reasons, it had become highly important for banks that offer cash-management services to adopt an appropriate marketing approach.

In the first place, banks should recognise the big potential benefits of marketing cash-management services. Second, they should analyse the needs of each corporate customer. This analysis will enable banks to re-examine cash-management services from the perspective of the corporate customer, so that the available techniques can be integrated into individual corporations' set of cash-management requirements. In fact, since corporate customers' needs for cash-management services vary considerably depending on their own management system, banks should place greater emphasis on tailoring the services to the specific customer's needs. In order to accomplish this, what is required from the banks is more communication, co-ordination and understanding of the users' perception of these services. As a result, they will be able to tailor the best package of cash-management services that the customer requires. To summarise the above discussion, the most important aspects in marketing of cash-management services can be described as illustrated in Figure 10.3.

In addition to the aspects mentioned in Figure 10.3, the other important

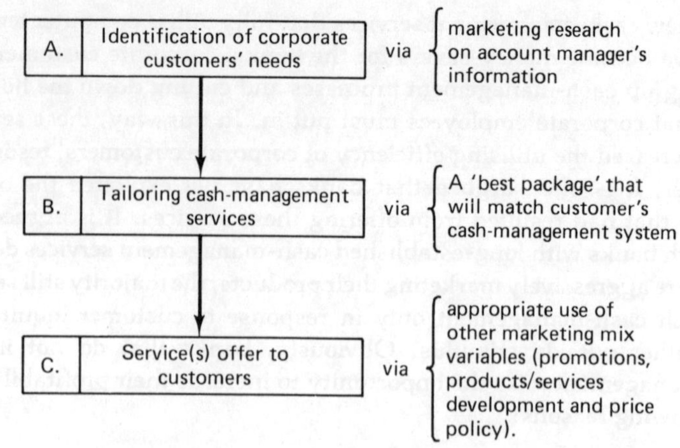

Figure 10.3 Important aspects in marketing of cash-management services

issue is the profitability of these services. In general, banks will be somewhat restricted in their pricing of cash-management services, owing to outside competitive forces. However, as we have seen, these services provide a number of potential benefits both to banks and customers. Therefore, the pricing decision should be made by taking all the potential benefits into account.

To sum up, from the bank's point of view the cash-management service means exchanging balances in non-interest accounts for service charges, but against this, the bank is seen to be providing a worthwhile service and more business can be generated. Cash management services highlight another reason for the changed position of banks. Once a main source of funds for loans and investment was the interest-free balances in current accounts. However, due attention must be paid to the needs of the customer and in the case of cash-management the bank must also consider the impact on company operations, because the ability to fit new systems into the corporate accounting structure may decide whether these services are needed.

International services

So far, the discussion has been concentrated on domestic banking. However, over the past decade the growth in banking has been associated mainly with the international side of the business, rather than with domestic banking operations. All the leading banks in the USA, Europe and Japan have set up their networks of branches and representative offices in the main financial centres. The expansion and the importance of international banking can be seen in the recent accounts of some of the top world banks. For example, in the USA, the leading multinational bank, Citicorp, reported recently that it raised 68 per cent of its total income before taxes and securities from its international operations.[9] The banks' international operations consist of various banking services ranging from simple foreign exchange services for the individual customers, to sophisticated international financial services for the multinational corporations (the MNCs).

Recently, many leading banks in search of ways of expanding their international operations have devoted increasing attention to the MNC market. Generally, this market is considered of interest to the banking industry for the two following reasons:

1. The sheer size of the MNC market and its rapid growth. For example, in 1976 MNCs owed an estimated $285 billion in short- and medium-term debt.
2. The number of services that MNCs require and the possibility of duplicating these services around the world make the multinational accounts extremely profitable.[10]

However, although the market is very attractive, the standard of service required by the MNCs is very high. Therefore, the bank's business should be extensive enough to meet their requirements. G. R. Thomas[11] suggested that the most important requirements for successful entry into the MNC market were as follows:

1. *A sufficiently large size bank.* The MNCs often require a large size of loans, therefore only banks with substantial resources can hope to make a real impact on the MNC market. Of course, a second-tier bank may be able to secure a share of the market by concentrating on fewer clients or specialising its services.
2. *Worldwide network.* Because of the MNCs' nature, a bank that has wider geographic coverage will have better service opportunities for the MNCs. However, geographic coverage alone is not enough. The network should incorporate branches and other financial subsidiary units sizeable enough to provide a substantial operating capability, where multinationals are likely to be active.
3. *Customer base.* Generally speaking, it is considered to be advantageous to have a bank's head office in the same country where the MNC customers are based.
4. *Skills.* The quality and skills of the bank staff who serve the MNCs is considered of primary importance in determining a bank's long-term position in the MNC market.

For this reason, it may be essential for banks that aim to enter the MNC market to undertake a feasibility study before any major marketing operation on this sector is initiated. The study should at least examine the following two aspects: (i) whether the bank can provide relevant services to the MNCs, and (ii) whether the bank's resources match the client's needs. If the feasibility study results are satisfactory and it is confirmed that the bank can cope with the MNC's needs with adequate profits to itself, then it can initiate marketing operations in this market segment. In general, the marketing activities should be planned by taking into account such factors as the MNC customer's financial performance, customer's account profitability, the MNC's financial decision-making structure (whether it is centralised or decentralised), and the possibility of expansion for the bank (whether the bank could offer other services). However, and most importantly, the marketing approach should be based on a global scale in order to provide a co-ordinated worldwide service to MNCs.

Consequently, it becomes very important for the banks interested in serving MNC to structure the marketing mix in such a way as to be effective in worldwide operations and bank–customer relationships. The essential aspects for each of the four major elements of the marketing mix can be summarised as follows:

(1) *Product.* The bank should offer an appropriate package of services so as to meet the multinational customer's needs. It should seek to maintain a consistent range and quality of services for the customer in each of the countries in which it operates.

(2) *Price.* The MNC market is highly competitive and the client is a sophisticated customer; therefore, services should not be overpriced. However, it is also important to evaluate the risk and return from this business. Another important requirement in servicing this market is to maintain a consistent pricing policy throughout the world.

(3) *Place.* A diversified overseas branch network with on-the-spot facilities for customer contact are necessary. Consequently, the bank's international expansion plan should take into consideration the MNC's potential geographical interests.

(4) *Promotion.* Personal selling is the most important and effective promotional tool. A competent worldwide management team should be formed. This is perhaps the most important element in the mix. It should include a worldwide public relations manager (responsible for this total relationship and who will assist and co-ordinate the activities of the account managers throughout the world), account managers (responsible for all the current and potential local business), and product managers (responsible for the specialist services such as merchant banking, foreign exchange, project financing, and other highly technical areas). This is because only a team extremely well structured can effectively serve the complicated and complex banking and financial needs of the MNCs. The basic relationships between a bank's worldwide management team and a MNC is schematically described in Figure 10.4.

The MNC market is probably the most complicated and sophisticated market in which banks operate. On the other hand, if the banks serve these customers well, their rewards will be great. In adopting a marketing approach towards these customers, the basic approach of 'the customer comes first' is a must. In addition, as we have discussed, the quality of bank staff who are in contact with multinational customers is a key element in the marketing approach. Hence the first priority of bank marketing in the MNC market is to set up a competent worldwide management team.

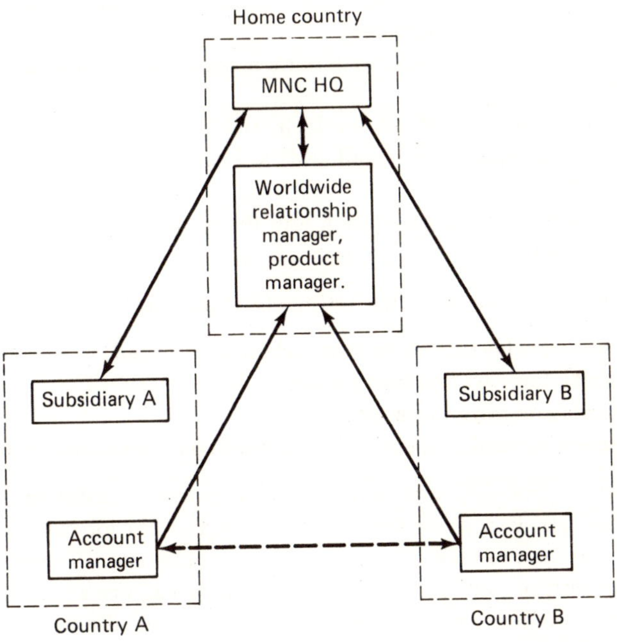

Figure 10.4 The relationships between banks offering international services and multinational corporations (MNC) customers

Future outlook

One point can be made with certainty about the banking industry as one looks ahead: the banking environment will – in the future – be far more competitive than in the past. To all financial institutions, profits will be harder to come by in this more intense competitive environment. Therefore, better services will be anticipated and expected from banks. It is in this context that more than ever before, has marketing been considered so important for the banking industry. And the trend is that it will increasingly be so. As the success of the bank will depend on what extent the bank marketing effort is successfully co-ordinated, it is evident that efficient administration and control systems of the bank marketing programme will be prerequisite.

In administering the bank marketing programmes the following are the more pertinent issues:

(a) the need to educate and train the bank employees to the marketing concept;
(b) the need for a stronger marketing team internally and more use of outside professional services;
(c) acceptance and commitment of bank managers and chief executives to bank marketing;
(d) active participation at all levels in the bank and dissemination of marketing programmes to all staff at branch manager or equivalent level;
(e) an efficient 'sales' organisation and therefore more need to motivate bank employees.

Efficient control of the bank marketing effort include the following:

(a) provision of relevant information when it is needed;
(b) marketing forecast and budgeting;
(c) standards and criteria for control;
(d) implementation of cost control; standard cost and variance analysis.

Delegation is probably one of the most important duties of the bank branch manager. Except for the smallest branches, the job covers too wide a field for one man to take sole responsibility. Delegation of responsibility is the main purpose of having an organisation structure at all. It enables the branch manager to use functional specialists, and allows him to stand back from these functional operations and study the overall operation of the bank.

Motivation is another important facet of the bank branch manager's job, which includes both the motivation of the branch manager himself by the bank Board, and the motivation of the other employees in the bank.

As far as the bank manager is concerned, his reward system is often determined by the success of the bank. For example, a bonus dependent on results, profit-sharing, and share incentive schemes are now prevalent throughout the banking industry. The employees are also given a share of the profits in more enlightened banks, and this method can be used as a 'self-financing' productivity scheme, especially in times of wage restraints.

Although not legally necessary, many banks provide a large amount of information for bank employee digestion, both verbally and in written form. Communication is therefore an important management tool in the pursuit of harmonious industrial relations. Any bank director has a duty to communicate with his employees – what he communicates is another matter, and depends on the confidentiality of the information, the communicative skills of the director, and the interest shown by the listener.

Most bank directors should believe in Theory X, put forward by Douglas McGregor, that is, the human being is basically willing to work, and merely requires guidance. Therefore the director has a duty to his workforce, not least of which is the responsibility for continuing to provide jobs. This can be achieved by making the best use of the skills available to the bank, and applying these in the interests of the organisation, the employees themselves and society in general.

Since bank marketing activity is mainly conducted in branches, effective marketing will inevitably mean more delegation to the branches. Branches must penetrate the market independently, dynamically and systematically. To do so, they require good planning and control instruments as well as well-trained executives. Rossier[12] suggested that the ideal marketing staff will consist of a small group of well-qualified people who will work closely with the line staff on a few, well-defined priority tasks, such as: (i) test-marketing new services, (ii) training the line in marketing planning method (identifying key accounts, assessing the potential of different market segments, and so on), and (iii) developing a marketing information system and guiding line personnel in the selective analysis of market data. All other marketing activities would normally be left to the line.

Owing to the great increase in competition with other clearing banks, as well as with other financial institutions, the marketing concepts, tools and techniques will have to be more efficiently employed in the banking industry. Particular attention will have to be given to branch management, personal selling, public relations, product and services departments, and their contribution to the bank's profitability. Consequently, some control systems – to check on bank marketing programmes' profitability – will have to be more readily and effectively adopted. This will inevitably lead to some forms of delegation of responsibilities, and administrative systems, and organisational structures to be implemented by the bank. This all means that a more systematic organisational structure and clearly defined communication channels will be required.

Notes and references

1 THE ROLES OF MARKETING IN BANK MANAGEMENT

1. W. D. Reekie, 'Marketing in Banking', *The Bankers' Magazine,* (UK) (Aug. 1972) pp. 56–60 and (Sept. 1972) pp. 97–100.
2. A. Meidan, 'The Roles of Marketing Management in Banking', *Quarterly Review of Marketing,* vol. 8, no. 3 (Apr. 1983) pp. 11–18.
3. R. Hodges and I. Tilman, *Bank Marketing: Text and Cases* (Addison-Wesley, 1968) p. 2.
4. P. Kotler, *Marketing Management: Analysis, Planning and Control,* 4th edn (Prentice-Hall, 1980) p. 31.
5. R. B. Stall, 'Marketing in a Service Industry', *Atlanta Economic Review* (May – June 1968).
6. Reekie, 'Marketing in Banking'.
7. R. H. Brien and J. E. Stafford, 'The Myth of Marketing in Banking', *Business Horizons,* vol. 10 (1967) pp. 71–8.
8. G. M. Wasem, 'The Triple Dilemma of Bank Marketing', *The Bankers' Magazine* (USA), vol. 152 (1969) pp. 65–9.
9. M. Everett, 'See the Banks Selling', *Sales Management* (USA) (9th July 1973) pp. 16–26.
10. A. Meidan, 'Marketing for Banks – The State of the Art', *Proceedings of MEG Conference,* London Business School (May 1978), pp. 189–208.
11. R. A. Kirk, 'Coordinating the Marketing Effort', *Burroughs Clearing House* (June 1969) p. 67.

2 CUSTOMER BEHAVIOUR AND MARKET SEGMENTATION

1. P. Martineau, 'Social Classes and Spending Behaviour', *Journal of Marketing,* vol. 22 (Oct. 1958) pp. 121–30.
2. R. H. Evans and M. D. Beckman, 'Phychographic Analysis: An Aid for Bank Management', *Magazine of Bank Administration* (Jan. 1974) pp. 32–40.
3. R. Y. Awh and D. Waters, 'A Discriminant Analysis of Economic, Demographic and Attitudinal Characteristics of Bank Charge Card Holders – A Case Study', *Journal of Finance* (Nov. 1974) pp. 973–80.
4. Evans and Beckman, 'Psychographic Analysis'.
5. J. N. Fry, 'Customers' Loyalty to Banks – A Longitudinal Study', *Journal of Business* (Sept. 1973) pp. 517–25.

6. W. T. Anderson, E. P. Cox and D. G. Fulcher, 'Bank Selection Decision and Marketing Segmentation', *Journal of Marketing,* vol. 40 (Jan. 1976) pp. 40–5.
7. A. A. Pool, 'Attitudes Towards Consumer Banking Packages: An Empirical Analysis', *Journal of Bank Research,* vol. 7 (Spring 1976) pp. 88–92.
8. R. L. Fitts and M. J. Karson, 'Canonical Correlation in a Bank Segmentation Study of Commercial Bank Services', *Journal of Economics and Business* (Winter 1977) pp. 116–21.
9. Fry, 'Customers' Loyalty to Banks'.
10. M. Badoc, 'Banks' New Marketing Wave', *European Research,* vol. 2, no. 3 (Autumn 1974) pp. 88–93.
11. J. Pattison and J. Quelch, 'Branch Banking Strategies', *The Bankers' Magazine* (UK) (Jan. 1979) pp. 16–17.
12. P. Kotler, *Marketing Management: Analysis, Planning and Control,* 4th edn (Prentice-Hall, 1980) ch. 9.
13. L. L. Berry, 'Marketing – The Time is Now', *Savings and Loan News* (USA) (Apr. 1969) pp. 60–1.
14. R. W. Haas and L. L. Berry, 'Systems Selling of Retail Services', *Bankers' Monthly* (USA) vol. 139 (July 1972) pp. 276–83.
15. S. J. Levy, 'Consumer Views of Bank Services', *Journal of Bank Research,* vol. 4 (Summer 1973) pp. 100–4.
16. D. H. Robertson and D. N. Bellenger, 'Identifying Bank Market Segments', *Journal of Bank Research,* vol. 7, no. 4 (Winter 1977) pp. 21–30.
17. N. Gee, 'Banks Tap the Women's Market', *Public Relations Journal* (Aug. 1975) pp. 14–16, 30.
18. D. Bannister, A. P. Brown and B. Dormand, 'The Effectiveness of the Major Clearing Banks in Attracting New Accounts – A Case Study', *Managerial Finance,* vol. 5, no. 3, pp. 277–89.
19. P. K. Chandhury, 'Marketing Bank Services to Blacks', *Journal of Bank Research* (Spring 1978) pp. 52–8.
20. J. Watson, 'Crucial Issues in Bank Marketing', *The Bankers' Magazine,* (UK) (May 1973) pp. 205–9.
21. P. Martin, 'Savings and Loans in New Submarkets – Search for Predictive Factors', *Journal of Market Research,* vol. 4 (May 1967) pp. 184–90.
22. L. Mathews and J. W. Slocum, 'Social Class and Commercial Bank Credit Card Usage', *Journal of Marketing,* vol. 33 (Jan. 1969) pp. 71–8.
23. Pool, 'Attitudes Towards Consumer Banking Packages'.
24. R. L. Fitts and J. B. Mason, 'Marketing Segmentation Research – An Application to Bank Services', *Omega,* vol. 5, no. 2 (1977) pp. 207–14.
25. H. Geiger, 'Standard Surveys for Analysing Local Bank Competition', in *The Use of Market Research in Financial Fields* (ESOMAR, 1975) pp. 85–95.
26. Ibid.
27. Levy, 'Consumer Views of Bank Services'.
28. Pool, 'Attitudes Towards Consumer Banking Packages'.
29. Chandhury, 'Marketing Bank Services to Blacks'.
30. T. S. Campbell, 'On the Extent of Segmentation in the Municipal Securities Market', *Journal of Money, Credit and Banking* (Feb. 1980) pp. 81–2.

3 BRANCH LOCATION AND DISTRIBUTION

1. A. Meidan, 'Distribution of Bank Services and Branch Location', *International Journal of Physical Distribution and Materials Management,* vol. 13, no. 3 (July 1983) pp. 5–17.

2. J. A. Rossier, 'The Coming Crisis in Bank Management II', *The Bankers' Magazine* (UK) (Aug. 1973) pp. 53–7.
3. J. H. Donnelly, 'Marketing Intermediaries in Channels of Distribution for Services', *Journal of Marketing*, vol. 40, no. 1 (Jan. 1976) pp. 55–7.
4. P. Kotler, *Marketing Management: Analysis, Planning and Control*, 4th edn. (Prentice-Hall, 1980) p. 31.
5. L. A. Soenen, 'Locating Bank Branches', *Industrial Marketing Management* (July 1974) pp. 211–28.
6. C. Maurice, 'The Co-op Bank – The Sleeping Giant', *The Bankers' Magazine* (UK) (Jan. 1974) pp. 46–9.
7. M. Everett, 'See the Bankers Selling', *Sales Management* (July 1973) pp. 16–20.
8. D. Bannister *et al.* 'The Effectiveness of Banks in Attracting Students Accouts', *Managerial Finance*, vol. 5, no. 3, pp. 277–89.
9. P. Doyle, I. Fenwick and G. P. Savage, 'Management Planning and Control in Multi-Branch Banking', *Journal of Operational Research Society*, vol. 3, no. 2, pp. 105–11.
10. A. Losch, *The Economics of Location* (Yale University Press, 1954) pp. 18–19.
11. W. Isard, *LOcation and Space Economy* (MIT Press, 1956).
12. M. M. Ali, and S. I. Greenbaum, 'A Spatial Model of the Banking Industry', *The Journal of Finance*, vol. 31, no. 4 (Sept. 1977) pp. 1283–1303.
13. L. L. Lundsten, *Market Share Forecasting for Banking Offices* (UMI Research Press, 1978).
14. L. M. Olsen and J. D. Lord, 'Market Area Characteristics and Branch Bank Performance, *Journal of Bank Research* (Summer 1979) pp. 102–10.
15. Doyle, Fenwick and Savage, 'Management Planning and Control in Multi-Branch Banking.
16. Soenen, 'Locating Bank Branches'.
17. J. F. Devaney, 'A New Way to Choose Bank Locations', *Bank Marketing* (Feb. 1973) pp. 44–7.
18. See Lundsten, *Market Share Forecasting for Banking Offices*, pp. 47–8.
19. Ibid.
20. Olsen and Lord, 'Market Area Characteristics and Branch Bank Performance'.
21. K. W. Alexanderson, 'Branch Bank Location Feasability Analysis', *Burroughs Clearing House*, vol. 54 (Feb. 1969) pp. 26–7.
22. W. B. Wentz, *Marketing Research* (Harper & Row, 1979) p. 456.
23. Lundsten, *Market Share Forecasting for Banking Offices.*
24. Bannister, 'The Effectiveness of Banks in Attracting Students' Accounts'.
25. W. D. Reekie, 'Marketing in Banking', *The Bankers' Magazine* (UK) (Sept. 1972) pp. 97–101.
26. P. Stahel, 'Finding the Best Bank Site', *Banking*, vol. 61 (Mar. 1969) pp. 54–92.
27. Reekie, 'Marketing in Banking'.
28. EFMA Seminar, 'Creating a Bank Image', *The Bankers' Magazine* (UK) (Feb. 1979) pp. 38–44.

4 ADVERTISING AND COMMUNICATIONS

1. N. W. Pope, 'A Philosophy of Bank Advertising', in L. L. Berry and L. A. Capaldini (eds), *Marketing for the Bank Executive* (Leviathan House, 1975) pp. 162–78.

2. F. Hammar-Brown, 'Do the Banks Make Good Use of Advertising?', *The Bankers' Magazine,* (USA) vol. 222, no. 1607 (Feb. 1978) pp. 13–16.
3. R. King, 'The Alcatraz Image that Haunts U.K. Banking', *Marketing* (July 1981) p. 13.
4. B. Cox and M. Hughes, 'How Banks and Building Societies Communicate', *ADMAP* (May 1977) pp. 227–30.
5. Hammar-Brown, 'Do the Banks Make Good Use of Advertising?'.
6. J. Prince, 'Increasing Television Support for the Financial Sector', *Viewpoint* (Autumn 1981) pp. 15–17.
7. R. W. Lawson and D. R. Netherton, 'The Roles of Advertising in Banking', unpublished research paper (University of Sheffield, 1980).
8. P. Kotler, *Marketing Management: Analysis, Planning and Control,* 4th edn (Prentice-Hall, 1980) p. 467.
9. D. Bannister *et al.*, 'The Effectiveness of Banks in Attracting Students' Accounts', *Management Finance,* vol. 5, no. 3, pp. 277–85.
10. H. Thomson, 'All Change for Cornflakes, Detergents and Banks', *Incentive Marketing and Sales Promotion* (Mar. 1980) pp. 31–2.
11. R. H. Preston, F. R. Dwyer and W. Rudelius, 'The Effectiveness of Bank Premiums – Do they Pay Their Way?', *Journal of Marketing,* vol. 42 (July 1978) pp. 96–101.
12. R. M. M. McConnell, 'Do Premiums Pay? How? Where? A New Look at the Pros and Cons', *Banking* (Sep. 1973) p. 74.
13. G. M. Dupoy and W. J. Kehoe, 'Comments on Bank Selection Decision and Market Segmentation', *Journal of Marketing* (Oct. 1976) pp. 83–90.
14. 'Banks Toy with Free Gifts', *Marketing* (25 Nov. 1981) pp. 25–7.
15. M. Thoren, 'Bank Sponsorship – A Corporate Strategy', *The Bankers' Magazine* (UK), (Apr. 1980) pp. 12–15.
16. R. Roter, 'Attracting People Who Don't Bank at all', *Campaign* (23 Mar. 1979) p. 14.

5 PRODUCT DEVELOPMENT AND PRICING

1. P. Kotler, *Marketing Management: Analysis, Planning and Control,* 4th edn (Prentice-Hall, 1980) p. 351.
2. A. Wilson, *The Marketing of Professional Services* (McGraw-Hill, 1972) p. 8.
3. E. Shankleman, 'Marketing by the Clearing Banks', *Industrial Marketing Digest,* vol. 4, pt 2 (1979) p. 156.
4. M. Blaniler, 'The Changing Face of the Future', *The Banker* (Sept. 1980) p. 87.
5. 'Banks Fight for Consumers', *Marketing* (May 1980) p. 24.
6. J. S. Winter and E. H. Nelson, 'Launching New Financial Services to Customers', *Journal of Market Research Society* (Jan. 1978) p. 30.
7. Ibid.
8. D. Monasian, 'Making Amends at Amex', *Management Today* (Apr. 1980) p. 76.
9. J. H. M. Cockayne, 'The Creative Role of Market Research in Developing New Marketing Opportunities', ESOMAR Seminar Proceedings, *The Use of Market Research in the Financial Fields* (Banking and Insurance) (Jan./Feb. 1975) pt I, p. 107.
10. A. Meidan, 'Marketing for Banks – The State of the Art', MEG Conference Proceedings (London Business School, 1977) pp. 189–208.

11. M. Brandenburg, 'The Changing Face of High Street Banks', *Accounting* (Aug. 1979) p. 50.
12. J. M. Rathmell, 'Research for Financial Marketing Decisions', *Journal of the Market Research Society*, vol. 20, no. 1 (Jan. 1978) p. 14; R. Roter, 'TSB: The Asset that Turned into a Milestone', *Campaign* (26 June 1981).
13. 'Banks Fight for Consumers'.
14. 'The Scots Dig for Gold in their own Backyard', *Financial Times* (14 June 1981) p. 13.
15. Cockayne, 'The Creative Role of Market Research in Developing New Marketing Opportunities'.
16. 'Barclaycard Set to Branch Out', *Marketing* (22 Apr. 1980) p. 14.
17. Ibid.
18. C. R. Martin, 'The Future of Electronic Business Systems', *Business Horizons* (Oct. 1975) pp. 69–74.
19. R. Cox, 'Why the Banks Dropped POST', *Marketing* (10 Dec. 1980) pp. 6–7.
20. Ibid.
21. Ibid.
22. J. R. S. Revel, 'Costs and Margins in Banking', *OECD Report* (Paris, 1980).
23. Ibid.
24. G. C. Naylor, 'Seeking a Balance Between the Needs of a Bank and the Demand of the Marketplace – A Multidimensional Study of the Pricing System', ESOMAR Proceedings, *The Use of Marketing Research in the Financial Fields* (Jan./Feb. 1975) pt 1, p. 107.
25. Ibid.
26. Revel, 'Costs and Margins in Banking'.
27. Blaniler, 'The Changing Face of the Future'.
28. 'Barclaycard Set to Branch Out'.
29. Cox, 'Why the Banks Dropped POST'.
30. C. McIver and G. Naylor, *Marketing of Financial Services* (London: The Institute of Bankers, 1980) pp. 149–57.
31. R. W. Lawson, A. W. Watt and D. R. Netherton, 'Marketing Oriented Pricing for U.K. Banks', *Proceedings of European Academy for Advanced Research in Marketing* (Mar. 1981) pp. 261–73.

6 MARKETING RESEARCH

1. R. B. Stall, 'Marketing in a Service Industry', *Atlanta Economic Review*, vol. 28 (May/June 1978) pp. 71–8.
2. W. F. Anderson, E. P. Cox and D. G. Fulcher, 'Bank Selection Decisions and Market Segmentation', *Journal of Marketing*, vol. 40 (Jan. 1976) pp. 40–5.
3. D. H. Robertson and D. A. Bellenger, 'Identifying the Bank Market Segments', *Journal of Bank Research* vol. 7, no. 4 (Winter 1977) pp. 21–30.
4. D. A. Aaker, *Multivariate Analysis in Marketing Theory and Application* (Wadsworth, 1971).
5. P. T. Fitzroy, *Analytical Methods for Marketing Management* (McGraw-Hill, 1977).
6. R. L. Fitts and J. B. Mason, 'Market Segmentation Research – An Application to Bank Services', *OMEGA*, vol. 5, no. 2 (1977) pp. 207–13.
7. C. R. Laurent, 'Image and Segmentation in Bank Marketing', *The Bankers' Magazine* (UK) (July/Aug. 1979) pp. 32–7.
8. A. Thabor, 'The Bank New Customer Behaviour and Communication Simu-

lation Models', *The Use of Market Research in the Financial Fields* (ESOMAR, 1975) pp. 1–16.
9. Ibid.
10. J. N. Fry, D. C. Shaw, C. H. V. Lanzeauer and C. R. Ripchand, 'Customer Loyalty to Banks: A Longitudinal Study', *Journal of Business* (Spring 1979) pp. 16–24.
11. L. L. Berry and J. S. Hansel, 'Why Do Some New Products Fail?', in L. L. Berry and L. A. Capaldini (eds) *Marketing for the Bank Executive* London: Leviathan House, 1975) pp. 125–35.
12. A. Meidan, 'Branch Managers' Attitudes on Bank Objectives and Operations', *Proceedings of the European Academy of Advanced Research in Marketing Conference* (France: Instead, Apr. 1976) pp. 215–28.
13. D. P. Stegall, 'Projecting Deposit Potentials for a New Commercial Bank', *The Bankers' Magazine* (UK), (Summer 1977) pp. 16–28.

7 CONTROLLING THE MARKETING PROGRAMME

1. J. M. Rothmell, *Marketing in the Service Sector* (Winthrop, 1979) pp. 147–8.
2. D. V. Weyer, 'The Marketing of Financial Services', *Journal of General Management*, vol. 1 (1973) pp. 16–23.
3. L. G. Rayburn, 'Cost Standards for Bank Advertising', *The Bankers' Magazine*, (USA), vol. 161, no. 4 (July/Aug. 1978) pp. 33–8.
4. Ibid.
5. H. Limberg, *How to Meet Management's information Needs* (New York: The Association for System Management, 1970) p. 39.
6. D. E. Moran, 'Improving Branch Office Performance', *Management Focus* (May/June 1979) pp. 24–7.
7. P. Kotler, *Marketing Management – Analysis, Planning and Control,* 4th edn (Prentice-Hall International, 1980) pp. 628–9.
8. A. Meidan, 'Marketing Applications of Operational Research Techniques', *Management Decision*, vol. 19, no. 4/5 (Dec. 1981) p. 86.
9. Ibid.
10. J. A. Rossier, 'The Coming Crisis in Bank Management', *The Bankers' Magazine* (Aug. 1973) pp. 7–9 and 53–7.
11. Moran, 'Improving Branch Office Performance'.
12. P. Doyle, I. Fenwick and G. P. Savage, 'Management Planning and Control in Multibranch Banking', *Journal of Operational Research Society*, vol. 30, no. 2, pp. 105–11.
13. D. French and H. Saward, *Dictionary of Management* (London: Gower Press, 1975) p. 90.
14. A. Meidan, 'The Appraisal of Managerial Performance' (AMACOM), *American Management Association* (New York, Nov. 1981).
15. J. F. Ligaya, 'A Computer Based Planning Model for the Economic Evaluation of Proposed Investments', *Cost and Management*, vol. 51, pt 1 (1977) pp. 30–1.
16. J. A. Healey, 'ABLES: An Automated Branch Locations System', in L. L. Lundsten (ed.) *Market Share Forecasting for Banking Offices* (UMI Research Press, 1978) pp. 43–4.
17. Ligaya, 'A Computer Based Planning Model for the Economic Evaluation of Proposed Investments'.
18. W. F. Wertz, *Marketing Research* (Harper & Row, 1979) p. 456.

19. Ibid.
20. I. Fenwick and G. P. Savage, 'Management Planning and Control in Multi-Branch Banking', *Journal of Operational Research Society*, vol. 30, no. 2, pp. 105–11.
21. I. Fenwick, 'Forecasting Performance of Financial Outlets', *European Journal of Marketing*, vol. 13, no. 5, pp. 332–40.
22. C. J. Clawson, 'Fitting Bank Locations Performance Standards and Marketing Strategies to Local Conditions', *Journal of Marketing*, vol. 38, no. 1 (1974) pp. 1–10.
23. 'Tyros in the Marketing Planning Game', *Business Week* (15 Sept. 1973) p. 129.
24. Clawson, 'Fitting Bank Locations Performance Standards and Marketing Strategies to Local Conditions'.
25. G. D. Hughes, 'Predicting Bank Deposits and Loans', *Journal of Marketing Research*, vol. 37 (Feb. 1970) pp. 95–100.
26. G. D. Hughes, 'The Boston Five Cent Savings Bank', research paper *Graduate School of Business, Harvard University*, Boston, 1969).

8 BANK MARKETING STRATEGIES

1. D. Hargreaves, 'Corporate Planning – A Chairman's Guide', *Long Range Planning*, vol. 1, no. 3 (Nov./Mar. 1969) pp. 28–37.
2. F. F. Gilmore and R. G. Brandenburg, 'Anatomy of Corporate Planning', *Harvard Business Review*, vol. 40, no. 6 (Nov./Dec. 1962) pp. 61–9.
3. R. A. Kirk, 'Coordinating the Marketing Effort', *Burroughs Clearing House* (June 1969) pp. 64–9.
4. I. Dugdale 'Corporate Planning and Control Systems in Williams and Glyn's Bank', *Long Range Planning*, vol. 11 (Oct. 1978) pp. 38–43.
5. D. Hughes, 'Predicting Bank Deposits and Loans', *Journal of Marketing*, vol. 34, no. 1 (1970) pp. 95–100.
6. P. Kotler, *Marketing Management: Analysis, Planning and Control*, 4th edn (Prentice-Hall, 1980) p. 188.
7. A. Meidan, 'Bank Marketing Strategies', *International Journal of Bank Marketing*, vol. 1, no. 2 (June 1983) pp. 3–17.
8. Kotler, *Marketing Management*, p. 281.
9. 'A Branch? Where? What Kind? The Branch Office Decision Becomes More Scientific', *Savings and Loan News*, vol. 99, no. 7 (July, 1977) pp. 58–68.
10. D. Jones, 'Williams and Glyn's Breaks out of the Heartland', *The Bankers' Magazine* (UK), (Jan. 1981) pp. 12–16.
11. M. Brandenberg, 'The Changing Face of High Street Banking', *Accountancy* (Aug. 1977) pp. 50–2.
12. G. Wasem, 'How to Select a Marketing Strategy', *Bankers' Monthly* (USA), vol. 87 (July 1970) pp. 27–9.
13. J. Pattison and J. Quelch, 'Branch Banking Strategies', *The Bankers' Magazine* (UK), (Jan. 1979) pp. 17–23.
14. J. E. Stafford and R. H. Brien, 'The Myth of Marketing in Banking', *Business Horizons*, vol. 10 (1967) pp. 71–8.
15. M. J. Boleat, 'Competition Between Banks and Building Societies', *National Westminster Bank Quarterly Review* (Nov. 1980) p. 43.

9 MARKETING OF BANK CREDIT CARDS

1. L. Mandell, 'Credit Card Use in the USA', *ISR* (University of Michigan, 1972).
2. P. J. Gray, 'The Case for Credit Cards', *The Bankers' Magazine* (USA), vol. 161, no. 4 (July/Aug. 1978) pp. 26–30.
3. H. S. Nilson, 'The Future of Credit Cards, *The Bankers' Magazine* (USA), vol. 162, no. 2 (Mar./Apr. 1979) pp. 54–60.
4. Mandell, 'Credit Card Use in the USA'.
5. Access Company, *The Credit Card in the UK* (1980). Issued by the Joint Credit Card Company Ltd, Southend, the control service company of Access.
6. D. B. Fitzpatrick, 'An Analysis of Bank Credit Card Profits', *Journal of Bank Research* (Autumn 1976) pp. 199–205.
7. I. Ross, 'The Credit Card's Painful Coming-of-Age', *Fortune,* vol. 34, no. 4 (Oct. 1971) p. 109.
8. Fitzpatrick, 'An Analysis of Bank Credit Card Profits'.
9. H. C. Krummel, 'The Credit Card: From Infant to Institution', *Journal of Consumer Credit Management* (Spring 1973) pp. 17–23.
10. E. J. Malechi and L. A. Brown, 'The Adoption of Credit Card Services by Banks: A Case Study of Innovation Diffusion', *Bulletin of Business Research,* vol. 2, no. 8 (Autumn 1975) pp. 1–4.
11. D. Hanson, *Service Banking* (UMI Press, 1979) pp. 217–62.
12. 'A UK Credit Card Survey', *The Banker,* vol. 125, pt 2 (1975) pp. 1132–8.
13. Mandell, 'Credit Card Use in the USA'.
14. T. Hindle, 'Credit Cards – Time to Come Clean', *The Banker*, vol. 129, pt 1 (1979) pp. 31–6.
15. Opinion Survey, 'Shops and Credit Facilities', *The Banker*, vol. 129, pt. 1 (1979).
16. Ibid.
17. Hanson, *Service Banking.*
18. Mandell, 'Credit Card Use in the USA'.
19. H. L. Mathews and J. W. Slocum, 'Social Class and Commercial Bank Credit Card Usage', *The Journal of Marketing,* vol. 33 (Jan. 1969) pp. 71–8.
20. J. W. Slocum and H. L. Mathews, 'Social Class and Income as Indicators of Consumer Credit Behaviour', *Journal of Marketing,* vol. 34 (Apr. 1970) pp. 68–74.
21. Mathews and Slocum, 'Social Class and Commercial Bank Credit Card Usage'.
22. Mandell, 'Credit Card Use in the USA'.
23. Gray, 'The Case for Credit Cards'.
24. R. Y. Awh and D. Waters, 'A Discriminant Analysis of Economic, Demographic or Attitudinal Characteristics of Bank Charge Card Holders: A Case Study', *Journal of Finance,* vol. 29 (1974) pp. 973–80.
25. Mandell, 'Credit Card Use in the USA'.
26. J. L. Goldstucker and E. C. Hirschman, 'Bank Credit Card Users: New Market Segment for Regional Retailers', *MSU Business Topics* (Summer 1977) pp. 5–11.
27. Ibid.
28. Krummel, 'The Credit Card: From Infant to Institution'.
29. Slocum and Mathews, 'Social Class and Income as Indicators of Consumer Credit Behaviour'; and 'Social Class and Commercial Bank Credit Card Usage'.

30. Ross, 'The Credit Card's Painful Coming-of-Age'.
31. Awh and Waters, 'A Discriminant Analysis of Economic, Demographic or Attitudinal Characteristics of Bank Charge Card Holders: A Case Study'.
32. Nilson, 'The Future of Credit Cards'.
33. Ibid.

10 BANK MARKETING ADMINISTRATION

1. L. L. Berry, W. J. Kehoe and J. H. Lindgren, Jr; 'How Bank Marketeers View Their Jobs', *The Bankers' Magazine* (USA), vol. 163, no. 6 (Nov./Dec. 1980) pp. 35–40.
2. J. P. Carroll, 'How the Changing Environment Impacts the Organisational Structure in Banking', *Management Controls* (Dec. 1975) pp. 188–91.
3. Berry, Kehoe and Lindgren, 'How Bank Marketeers View Their Jobs'.
4. R. H. Preston, F. R. Dwyer and W. Rudelius, 'The Effectiveness of Bank Premiums', *Journal of Marketing*, vol. 42, no. 3 (July 1978) pp. 91–6.
5. Ibid.
6. H. A. Brown and K. J. Cohen, 'Bank Corporate Services are Coming of Age', *The Bankers' Magazine* (USA), vol. 161, no. 4 (July/Aug. 1978) p. 18.
7. R. A. Duke, 'Cash Management Services – A Marketing Approach', *Journal of Commercial Bank Lending*, vol. 58 (Dec. 1975) pp. 16–19.
8. J. I. Bonocore, 'Making Cash Management More Marketable', *The Bankers' Magazine* (USA), vol. 163, no. 6 (Nov./Dec. 1980) pp. 46–52.
9. M. Blanden, 'The Changing Shape of the Future', *The Banker*, (Sept. 1980) pp. 82–7.
10. E. P. Williams, 'Banks Service Multinational Needs', *The Bankers' Magazine* (UK) (Apr. 1976) pp. 41–5.
11. G. R. Thomas, 'How to Serve the MNC Market', *The Banker* (Aug. 1977) pp. 82–90.
12. J. A. Rossier, 'The Coming Crisis in Bank Management', *The Bankers' Magazine* (UK), (Aug. 1973) pp. 7–9 and 53–7.

Index